P9-CLF-848
SHELTON STATE COMMUN
COLLE
JUNIOR DIVISION
LIBRARY
DISCARDED

1
THE DEMOCRATIC MACHINE
1850–1854

FRANKLIN PIERCE

STUDIES IN HISTORY, ECONOMICS AND PUBLIC LAW

EDITED BY THE FACULTY OF POLITICAL SCIENCE
OF COLUMBIA UNIVERSITY

Volume CXI] [Number 1

Whole Number 248

THE DEMOCRATIC MACHINE

1850-1854

BY

ROY FRANKLIN NICHOLS

AMS Press, Inc.

New York

1967

AMS Press, Inc.
New York, N.Y. 10003
1967

Manufactured in the United States of America

To

JEANNETTE PADDOCK NICHOLS

TABLE OF CONTENTS

LIST OF ILLUSTRATIONS

ACKNOWLEDGMENT

The author has received much help and many favors during the period of his research. Officials of many public and semi-public libraries have extended much-needed and much-appreciated cooperation. Especially to Mr. John C. Fitzpatrick of the Division of Manuscripts of the Library of Congress does the author wish to acknowledge his indebtedness. For the space of six months and more the writer spent most of his time in the Manuscript Division and as a result he desires to be one of the many who in growing numbers give testimony of their appreciation of Mr. Fitzpatrick's knowledge of the manuscript sources and his willingness to bear all sorts of importunities from historical students.

Mrs. George H. Dana of Burkehaven, New Hampshire and Mrs. Andrew Marshall of Boston generously placed at the author's dispósal invaluable historical material which has been of great use in the preparation of this study.

Miss Mary A. Reilly has taken great pains to transcribe the rather involved manuscript for submission and printing and has consequently saved the author much worry and labor.

Professor John Hubbard Logan of Rutgers College was largely responsible for the author's interest in personalities and politics and has read this study in manuscript.

There are three men, however, to whom the author feels especially in debt. This study was undertaken under the guidance of the late Professor William Archibald Dunning and during the early stages of the enterprise, sometimes discouraging and often uncertain, Professor Dunning was always sympathetic, always encouraging and always inspiring. The author has many happy recollections of the reports and consultations which resulted in the acceptance of the plan of the study substantially as it is here set forth. Professor Dunning died before any of the manuscript was ready but his death only strengthened the author's realization of the quality and value of his influence, an influence powerful because of the rare combination of human sympathy and natural dignity which made this teacher a great man. When the first draft was completed Professors Dixon Ryan Fox and Nathaniel Wright Stephenson gave the author unsparingly of their time and attention. They carefully read and criticized the manuscript and to them are owed a very large number of helpful and valuable suggestions which have been incorporated into the following pages. The author has been extremely fortunate in his advisers and critics. To the one to whom he is most deeply indebted, the author has dedicated this book.

ROY FRANKLIN NICHOLS.

COLUMBIA UNIVERSITY, MARCH 3, 1923.

FOREWORD

History and the Ways of Politicians

Politicians have their "trade psychology"; they are in the business of carrying elections and running governmental enterprises, "selling" candidates and platforms. Like other entrepreneurs, their chief aim is success—success that means the wielding of power. The gaining and retaining of power and the satisfaction of vanity secured from occupying public place become their outstanding characteristics, and to obtain the satisfaction of these desires they bend their energies. Some are scrupulous, some are not; some are high-minded, many think they are; some strive for principles, some for graft, but the majority for the satisfaction of success. This political psychology has had its effect upon history. The politician's place in our national development can be understood only in the light of a knowledge of these dominant traits. The history of the Democratic party during the interlude between the sectional struggles of 1850 and 1854 presents an excellent field for the study of the *genus* politician. In those days public opinion was generally apathetic and the politicians plied their trade with little interference. As most of the leading Democrats of this period were prominent in the strife which led to secession and civil war, the study which follows is an introduction to the part played by the Democratic party in the years from 1854 to 1860.

ERRATA

Page 69, last line *for* " democrats " read " Democrats "
83, " " " disruptable " read " disreputable "
84, line 3 *for* " subjuct " read " subject "
85, 17 " ocasionallly " read " occasionally "
85, 18 " acquainstances " read " acquaintances "
86, 25 " simplicty " read " simplicity "
89, 19 " varitable " read " veritable "
90, 9 " democrats " read " Democrats "
91, 10 " Case " read " Cass "
93, 10 " belongs " read " belong "
99, 22 " Crosswell " read " Croswell "
100, 23 " Tennesse " read " Tennessee "
101, 8 " write " read " wrote "
109, 8 *insert* comma after " in "
114, 1 *for* " willigness " read " willingness "
114, 23 " simular " read " similar "
120, 8 " ando " read " and "
122, 2 " suporting " read " supporting "
130, 3 " Caroll " read " Carroll "
135, 3 " Meeting again at four," read " They met again at four; "
136, 12 " Deleware " read " Delaware "
136, 24 " Indian " read " Indiana "
137, 23 " Caroll " read " Carroll "
139, 13 " us " read " up "
139, 15 " delgates " read " delegates "
139, 20 " Deleware " read " Delaware "
147, 20 " emplowering " read " empowering "
147, 23 " Committee " read " committee "
159, 6 " wote " read " wrote "
154, 4 " Thes " read " These "
162, 18 " committe " read " committee "
168, 1 " county " read " country "
172, 15 " sems " read " seems "
173, 26 " states' " read " state's "
174, 15 " had " read " hand "
177, 12 *after* " third " insert " and fourth "
181, 22 *for* " Marcly " read " Marcy "
182, 20 " in " read " on "
185, 1 " resolution " read " resolutions "
186, 13 " leaders " read " leader's "
189, 24 " adminstration " read " administration "
193, 24 " undersirable " read " undesirable "
195, 7 " members " read " member "
202, 26 " Cochran " read " Cochrane "
203, 4 " Cochran " read " Cochrane "
203, 12 " Cochran " read " Cochrane "
206, 4 " manoeuvers " read " manoeuvres "
208, 9 " bolter's " read " bolters' "
211, 2 " PePter " read " Peter "
216, 3 " seceder's " read " seceders' "
218, 10 " years " read " year's "
221, 15 " succed " read " succeed "
223, 21 *omit* " a growing "
226, 15 *for* " displeasng " read " displeasing "

CHAPTER I

THE DEMOCRACY IN CHAOS

ANDREW JACKSON had been the personification of the Democratic party; around him it united. He attracted personal admirers, true lovers of the ideal of democracy, and men who felt it expedient, from motives of personal ambition, to be among the associates of a powerful leader. His animosities and his prejudices determined the platforms of the Democratic party; his personal enemies became its opponents. For nearly a decade, under the rallying cry of "Old Hickory," the party won a series of unbroken victories. It weathered the storm of Calhoun's withdrawal and lived to receive him back. And as the Old Hero had planned, in the heyday of his power, to be succeeded by Martin Van Buren for two terms and by Benton for two more, the faithful with but slight objection accepted "Little Van" as their leader's chosen successor.

But thereafter Jackson's party came upon evil days. Economic conditions were bad. Van Buren, shrewd politician that he was, had neither the heroic mold nor the personal appeal of the Old Hero of the Hermitage. As 1840 drew on, after the reverse of 1838, the weakening party had recourse to principles and laid down a platform. It formulated a creed, the articles of which were the lessons learned behind the banner of Old Hickory. According to the platform, the federal government was one of limited powers: it could neither undertake a system of internal improvements nor assume state debts contracted for that purpose:

it could not grant protection to industry by means of high tariffs: it could not operate a bank: its funds must be carefully guarded in the vaults of the national treasury from manipulation by the money power. The platform reaffirmed the democratic doctrines of the Declaration of Independence, yet in regard to slavery it made the following pronouncement:

Resolved, That Congress has no power, under the Constitution, to interfere with or control the domestic institutions of the several States, and that such States are the sole and proper judges of everything appertaining to their own affairs not prohibited by the Constitution; that all efforts of the Abolitionists or others, made to induce Congress to interfere with questions of Slavery, or to take incipient steps in relation thereto, are calculated to lead to the most alarming and dangerous consequences, and that all such efforts have an inevitable tendency to diminish the happiness of the people, and endanger the stability and permanency of the Union, and ought not to be countenanced by any friend to our political institutions.

But the platform proved of no avail. Without the personal appeal of a popular leader the party was powerless against the rollicking Log Cabin and Hard Cider Whigs. Disaster complete was the result.

Defeat taught the necessity for organization; for the next four years the party was being prepared for 1844. Van Buren and his lieutenants were recruiting for his renomination; John C. Calhoun and his friends were building up their machine; and in the southwest and northwest new leaders like Robert J. Walker and Lewis Cass were marshalling their forces to dispute Van Buren's claim to leadership. At the Convention of 1844 it appeared that each section was mobilized; the captains of the hundreds and the captains of the thousands were there. A spectacular combination was made; Walker and Calhoun joined forces to such effect that Van Buren was defeated and James K. Polk was nominated. The Democratic party, now well-disciplined, so cleverly manipulated the issues and the votes, that their comparatively unknown candidate defeated the popular Whig idol, Henry Clay, hampered by his shattered cohorts. Thus was the Democratic party formally organized, but it was no longer the party of Jackson.

The years from 1844 to 1849 showed that the party had developed personal and sectional differences. There were at least three distinct and often discordant factions. Van Buren had come out against the annexation of Texas. In 1844 this pronouncement gave his opponents the opportunity to inject the slavery issue into national politics and to give his candidacy a sectional tinge. At the Convention he was defeated for the presidential nomination by means which led his friends to charge treachery. Polk's distribution of the patronage and his treatment of Van Buren's friend, Silas Wright, embittered the former President's friends the more. When Wright was defeated for governor of New York in 1846 they openly declared it was accomplished by the treachery of Polk's official appointees in that state. Also certain northwestern elements were disaffected. Polk had compromised on Oregon. He had vetoed a rivers and harbors appropriation bill especially desired by the northwestern members of Congress. He had failed to satisfy the demands of that section for patronage. All these disaffected elements joined to support the Wilmot Proviso. The organized projectors of this measure were joined by the disgruntled Van Burenites and by those Democrats opposed on principle to slavery or its further extension. This amalgamation made up the northern radical or " free soil " wing of the party. It lacked a leader.

Another faction appeared in the south. This group were inspired by the political doctrines of John C. Calhoun and had wished to make him President. They were jealous of the interests peculiar to their section and they subscribed to the extreme states rights doctrines which had become prominent in nullification days. They wanted to obtain as much slave territory as possible and resented any attempt to regulate or restrict the institution of slavery. These constituted the radical southern or "states rights" wing of the Democratic party.

The third and largest division of the party was the immobile mass of Democrats in both sections of the nation, especially important in the north. This body of partisans was actuated by two motives, a love for the Union and a desire to see their party always in office. As for slavery, many, like Douglas, cared not whether it was voted up or down. Cass, Buchanan and Marcy were the prominent members of this conservative or "hunker" group. Like the free soil faction, this wing enjoyed no real leadership; for Cass, its most prominent member, lacked the energy and strength necessary to dominate his party. Thus matters stood in 1850.

The discovery of gold in California had caused a great rush of men of all types to that region. In the heterogeneous mass that arrived there were politicians, old and disappointed, young and hopeful. They saw the advantage to themselves of becoming leaders in a possible new state. Therefore they constructed the machinery for political organization. The result was the adoption of a constitution in accordance with the Democratic principle of "squatter sovereignty"; this document was silent on slavery. In the ensuing election a Democratic governor, legislature and Congressmen were chosen and a short while later the legislature elected two Democratic Senators. In due time official word of these actions was brought to a Congress which was of like political complexion. In spite of the complete control of California by the Democratic party there was opposition to her admission to statehood. The more radical of the southern leaders felt they could not retain the support of their constituencies if they voted to permit another free state to enter the Union and destroy the precious balance of fifteen slave and fifteen free states. In order to save the Union from a threatened secession of the southern states a compromise was formed whereby, among other provisions, a strict fugitive slave law was offered as an offset to the south for the admission of California. This in turn the northern radicals felt they could not support and retain their seats. So they rose up in arms. There ensued a formidable legislative battle, wherein party lines broke down entirely. The only possible adjustment was the acceptance of the Compromise of 1850. To bring this about the conservative or hunker wing of the Democracy led by Cass joined the Clay Whigs in support of the Compromise measures and outvoted the radical legislators of both north and south, Whig and Democratic. But why should the strict, partisan, conservative Democrats be so anxious to pass these bills as to join their ancient foes in voting for them?

The Democratic and Whig parties were numerically nearly equal, both in the north and in the south.[1] To win elections, therefore, the party could spare no strength and needed a united front. The question of the status of slavery in newly acquired territory was continually making trouble between the free soil and states rights wings of the party

[1] Roughly two-thirds of the whole number of voters were divided almost equally between the two parties in the fifteen free states and the remaining one-third in like manner in the fifteen slave states. *Whig Almanac*, 1850, p. 2.

and causing defection and defeat at important elections, as in 1848. It naturally occurred to the conservative hunker or national Democrats, who cared little for slavery and much for Democratic ascendancy, that the loyal thing to do would be to settle the disputed question in a manner which would prevent its recurrence. This the Compromise of 1850 seemed to do by accepting their principle of squatter sovereignty. Thus it won their support and was passed. Since it wrote squatter sovereignty into the nation's statute law and added the Democratic state of California to the galaxy of stars in the Democratic banner, they felt that a good deed had been well done for the party and the Union. They then began to prepare for the election of 1852 with the hope that the other wings would join them and that a Democratic president would enter the White House, March 4, 1853. However, the prospects were rather dubious. In spite of the fact that the Democratic party had governors in twenty-five of the thirty-one states, many of the elections had been so close that any serious defection in the Democratic ranks would mean disaster. A survey of the party in the various states showed that dangerous defections were too numerous.

In the north there were bitter divisions in many states. That in New York was the worst. The Democratic party of the Empire State was suffering from factions which had their origin in the politics of the past few decades. Differences of an economic, psychological and personal nature were responsible for the appearance of three groups, more or less unfriendly. In the late twenties popular unrest burst forth, kindled by the agitation of theorists, the rise in the cost of living, the development of the new manufacturing enterprise, and the backfire of the western spirit. A demand was awakened for labor organization, hard money, destruction of the currency-issuing monopoly of the state banks, and economy in state expenditures especially as regards the proposed system of canals. The sponsors of these demands were known as " radicals " or " loco-focos " and numbered in their ranks Martin Van Buren, Silas Wright, John A. Dix, and Azariah C. Flagg. In natural opposition to these preachers of dangerous doctrines were the "conservatives " who represented the merchant capitalists, bankers and contractors. These had as prominent figures—Senator Tallmadge, Daniel S. Dickinson, Horatio Seymour, Edwin C. Croswell and sometimes William L. Marcy. The split between these factions was made wider by the personal antagonism of the two United States Senators, Silas Wright, radical, and Nathaniel P. Tallmadge, conservative. These rivals continued their struggle for mastery of the party with alternating successes and defeats for a decade.

As has been said, Van Buren's humiliation in 1844 and Wright's loss of the governorship in 1846 brought on a fresh crisis. The radicals blamed the administration for these catastrophes and began to retaliate. They in common with the free soilers and opponents of the Polk régime championed the Wilmot proviso. When they demanded that the state convention of 1847 endorse this measure they were outvoted by the hunkers under Marcy and Dickinson. They immediately withdrew and held a separate convention; after this secession they were generally known as " barnburners ". Each group claimed to be the true Democracy and each nominated delegations to the Convention of 1848. That body recognized them both but demanded a pledge of support of the platform to be adopted before admitting either. The barnburners felt that this creed would be southern in tone; therefore, deeply disappointed at the joint recognition policy, they refused the pledge and withdrew. They put forward Van Buren as an independent nominee.

To his standard flocked the Free Soil party and numerous disaffected Democrats from other states, thus defeating Cass, and throwing the national victory to the Whigs. In New York the barnburners had carried their heretical tendencies further by nominating a full state ticket; the Whigs easily defeated both tickets but the combined vote of the two sections of the Democratic party, however, was in excess of that of the victors.

The long-headed members of both factions saw the folly of the resulting loss of all the patronage. Seymour of the hunkers, therefore, made advances to John Van Buren and it did not take the two long to see the wisdom of union for the spoils. The year 1849 brought reunion and partial success. However, there was an element of ultra-hunkers, or hard-shells, who felt that the Van-Burenites had been welcomed back without sufficient punishment. Their worst fears were confirmed by the Whig triumph of 1850, when the enemy captured the legislature and displaced the hard-shell leader, United States Senator Daniel S. Dickinson. Thus the three factions stood: ultra-hunkers or hards, led by Dickinson, conciliatory hunkers or softs, led by Marcy and Seymour, and the barnburners, led by John Van Buren, John A. Dix and Azariah C. Flagg. In such a condition was the Democracy of the Empire State as the presidential campaign approached.[1]

[1] Trimble, William, "New York Democracy and the Loco-Focos," *Am. Hist. Rev.*, vol. xxiv, p. 415; Alexander, D. S., *Political History of New York*, vol. ii, pp. 56-144; Jenkins, J. S., *Lives of the Governors of the State of New York*, pp. 518-9, 597, 705; Jenkins, J. S., *Life of Silas Wright*, p. 226; Hammond, Jabez D., *Life and Times of Silas Wright*, pp. 693-5; Gillet, R. H., *Life and Times of Silas Wright*, vol. ii, pp. 1789-1791; Shepard, E. M., *Martin Van Buren*, pp. 354-363; Quaife, M. M. (ed.), *Polk's Diary*, vol. ii, p. 218; Fox, D. R., *The Decline of Aristocracy in the Politics of New York*, pp. 381-408; Hammond, J. D., *History of Political Parties in New York*, vol. ii, pp. 487-503.

In Massachusetts, too, things were not as they should have been. The leaders of the party there, David Henshaw, Charles G. Greene, editor of the *Boston Post,* and Benjamin F. Hallett, had been dispensing federal patronage under Jackson, Van Buren and Polk. For this reason they had caused state platforms to be adopted, pleasing to Washington but unpopular in Massachusetts. This had made the Democratic machine, so far as state and local elections were concerned, generally unsuccessful. The final blow had been the election of Taylor. This the leaders attributed to Democratic defection in the south and they were not disposed to discourage retaliation. Hallett, therefore, as chairman of the resolutions committee in the state convention of 1849 reported a platform which declared that, "We are opposed to slavery throughout all God's heritage". The adoption of this plank attracted the Free Soilers who had seceded from both major parties in 1848. They formed local coalitions with the Democrats which brought about a general state coalition in 1850. They secured a coalition legislature in 1851 and the election of Charles Sumner, free soil Whig, to the United States Senate despite the bolting of twenty-eight hunkers under Greene, Hallett and Cushing. This result made coalition unpopular with all hunkers.[1]

In New Hampshire party lines had broken down so that in 1847 the prominent free soil Democrat, John P. Hale, was elected to the Senate by a combination of Whigs and free soil Democrats in spite of the strong opposition of the future President Pierce and the hunkers.[2] Following this the free soil element gained control of the state convention of the Democratic party in 1851 and nominated a candidate.

[1] Boutwell, *Reminiscences,* vol. i, pp. 114-116; Wilson, *Rise and Fall of the Slave Power,* vol. ii, p. 339.

[2] *Ibid.,* pp. 626-8.

Pierce sponsored a movement of the hunkers which led to the nomination of a bolting candidate who was elected over the Whig and regularly nominated Democratic candidates.[1] In Maine, Hannibal Hamlin had been reelected United States Senator in 1850 by a combination of Democrats and free soil Whigs[2] and the year previous in Ohio Salmon P. Chase had been elected to the same body by a coalition of Democrats and Free Soilers who preferred him to the Whig "butcher" Tom Ewing.[3] In fact the situation was such that Toombs could write that the free soil members controlled the Democratic organizations in all free states except New Jersey, Pennsylvania, Illinois, Indiana and Iowa.[4] It was evident to the Washington leaders that the northern Democracy was in danger of being ruined as an efficient party machine.

In the slave-holding states the situation was of a different character. The adjourned Nashville Convention had met November 11-18, 1850, and though non-representative and abortive, had provided a stage for many southern rights sectional speeches.[5]

In Alabama there was a large section of the Democratic party opposed to the Compromise measures. The leader of this group was the ultra-radical William L. Yancey. He began to be prominent in an effort to organize the "Southern Rights Associations" composed of Democrats and others who believed that the rights of the south had been sur-

[1] *N. H. Patriot*, Feb. 13 and 20, 1851; Pierce to Burke, May 4, 1851, Burke MSS.

[2] Hamlin, *Hannibal Hamlin*, p. 250.

[3] Hart, *Chase*, p. 111; *Cong. Globe*, 32nd Cong., 1st Sess., p. 327.

[4] "Correspondence of Robert Toombs, Alexander H. Stephens, Howell Cobb" (Phillips, ed.), *Annual Report of the American Historical Association*, 1911, vol. ii, p. 229, hereafter cited as *Toombs Corr.*

[5] White, *Secession Movement in the U. S.*, 1847-52, pp. 80-83.

rendered by the Compromise. These associations put up candidates for Congress in the Congressional elections of 1851. In opposition to them, those favoring the Compromise nominated union tickets and succeeded in defeating the southern rights candidates in five of the seven districts; they also gained control of the legislature. This campaign had temporarily obliterated party lines and Democrats were prominent on both sides. The unity of the party was shattered.[1]

In Georgia, Speaker Howell Cobb combined ambitions for higher national office with the conviction that the Compromise measures alone had saved the Union. He and his following of Democrats joined the Whigs led by Alexander H. Stephens and Robert Toombs. This group formed a Compromise union party, December, 1850, and drew up the famous Georgia platform. They declared acquiescence in the Compromise but stated that the south would yield no more. In June, 1851, they nominated Cobb for governor. The majority of the Democrats would not follow the Speaker, and joining with some like-minded Whigs, nominated Charles J. MacDonald on a states rights platform of rebellion against the Compromise. The result was Cobb's election as governor and Toombs' elevation to the Senate. This produced two factions, the Cobb faction and the states rights group, each claiming to be the true Georgia Democracy.[2]

In Mississippi, Senator Henry S. Foote and his colleague, Jefferson Davis, were personal enemies. During the debates on the Compromise, Foote resented the dictatorial pronouncements of Davis on the attitude of Mississippi. He became the ardent champion of these measures and

[1] White, *loc. cit.*; Hodgson, J., *Cradle of the Confederacy*, pp. 264-7, 321.

[2] *Toombs Corr.*, pp. 215-293, *passim*. Phillips, U. B., "Georgia and States Rights," *Amer. Hist. Assoc. Rept. for 1901*, vol. ii, pp. 163-4.

when the Democrats of his state nominated the states rights Democrat, Quitman, for governor in 1851, Whigs and the few union Democrats united on Foote as their candidate. He stumped the state with such success that Quitman withdrew and at the election Foote defeated Senator Davis who had been substituted. Foote rose mightily in his own estimation but the union legislature which was elected did not send him back to the Senate, choosing a Whig instead. Here as in Georgia this situation brought on a dispute as to who were the true Democrats.[1]

In Missouri, Benton and the states rights wing of the Democracy led by Senator D. R. Atchison had waged a war which broke the party in two and elected a Whig Senator.[2] Also the Whigs had captured a Senator in Louisiana and a Senator and the governor of Tennessee. The Democratic organ in Washington, the *Union,* charged that these losses were due to coalitions of union men against secessionists. The net results of the union parties was to bring defeat upon the Democrats in Mississippi, Georgia, Louisiana and Tennessee, with the loss of five United States Senators.[3] With state organizations crumbling north and south there is no wonder that many thoughtful Democrats were anxious for the future safety of the party. But it was not only state disintegration that threatened.

The national organization seemed in danger. Many New York merchants and bankers were fearful for the Union; if southern states seceded there would be the disruption of a profitable trade and they would lose much. Also trouble might disrupt international business relations; as a contem-

[1] Dodd, *Jefferson Davis*, pp. 124-8; *Washington Union*, Jan. 20, 1852; *Congressional Globe*, 32nd Cong., 1st Sess., pp. 735-6.

[2] Jas. B. Bowlin to Donelson, May 5, 1851, Donelson MSS.

[3] *Washington Union*, March 5, 1852.

porary capitalist wrote, "Unless something be done before long the Englishmen will begin to send home our stocks again."[1] So in order to promote good feeling between the sections on the basis of the finality of the Compromise, a mass meeting was held at Castle Garden in New York City, October 30, 1850. Here was appointed a "Union Safety Committee" of fifty New York business men.[2]

This movement spread and similar meetings were held in Philadelphia[3] and Boston.[4] Politicians, too, took up the strain and when Congress met in December, 1850, Clay fathered an attempt to unite all Compromise men of either faith into a union party based on the Compromise measures. Between the conservative wings of both parties negotiations were on foot in which Clay, Webster, Cass and Dickinson were prominent. The high point was reached in January, 1851, when there was published an agreement pledging its signers to support for President and Vice-President only such men as upheld the Compromise measures as a finality. Of the forty-four members of Congress who signed this but five were Democrats, Senators Rusk of Texas, Clemens of Alabama, Gwin of California and Foote of Mississippi and Howell Cobb, Speaker of the House.[5] As the small proportion indicates, this movement appealed but little to the Democrats who suspected it to be a means for making Clay or Webster President. Neither free soil nor states rights men in either party nor the Fillmore administration would countenance any plans for a union party

[1] P. M. Wetmore to W. L. Marcy, March 19, 1850, Marcy MSS.

[2] *Proceedings of a Union Meeting held at Castle Garden, October 30, 1850.*

[3] C. J. Ingersoll to Buchanan, November 12, 1850, Buchanan MSS.

[4] W. L. Marcy to Buchanan, December 19, 1850, *ibid.*

[5] *Congressional Globe,* 31st Cong., 2nd Sess., Jan. 22, 1851; Du Bose, *Yancey,* p. 253.

and the national convention which some hoped might be held at Philadelphia on February 22, 1851 never materialized.[1]

The movement for a union party with the Compromise as its platform was not dead but sleeping and the approach of the fall elections in 1851 awakened it. Again it started in New York City; the Union Safety Committee, known also as the "Union Cotton Committee" and as an advertisement of Wall Street for the southern trade, revived, and on October 20 issued an address which called upon the people to vote only for union men. In the furtherance of this endeavor they picked out a state ticket from those nominated by the two parties and endorsed three Democrats and four Whigs. Though this endorsement had no discernible effect they persisted and got up a scheme for a presidential ticket to be composed of a Democrat and Whig, both union men. They presented the project to Senator Foote and he agreed to cooperate. The men selected for such honor were Cass and Clay, and this committee sent formal letters to each, through Foote, asking public approval of the plan. Clay, Foote declared later, agreed to accept if Cass would, but Cass upon consultation with Dickinson and Douglas declined.[2] Thus the scheme came to nought although talk of a third party persisted until the National Convention.

Abortive as these attempts were, the leaders at Washington were filled with fear. Coalition was their nightmare. The campaign of 1852 was at hand and where was the Democratic organization? In the north and in the south the party seemed disintegrating and even national movements

[1] F. P. Blair, Sr. to Martin Van Buren, Dec. 30, 1850 and Feb. 6, 1851, Burwell to John Van Buren, Jan. 4, 1851, Van Buren MSS.; *Toombs Corr.*, p. 220.

[2] *N. Y. Herald*, Oct. 20, 25, 29, 1851; Linn, *Greeley*, pp. 161-2; Foote, *Casket*, p. 83; Sargent, *Public Men and Events*, vol. ii, pp. 386-7.

were on foot to form new alignments. Loyal Democrats staunchly true to the Republican doctrines of '98, sound money, revenue tariff and all, were forgetting their antipathy for a bank, national improvements and protection, and were joining hands with their Whig enemies. Why? Because the vexatious question of slavery was poisoning the minds of the masses. Unless an antidote was found the Democrats would not as victors possess the spoils of 1852, the official patronage which amounted annually to $50,000,000.[1]

[1] *Register of Officers*, 1853.

CHAPTER II

ATTEMPTS TO EVOLVE COSMOS FROM CHAOS

How was order to be brought out of this chaos? There was the party machinery. The head of this organization was the National Democratic Executive Committee. This body consisted of one member from each state appointed for four years by the National Convention on the nomination of the state delegates. This committee was in general charge of the party's national welfare while state affairs were watched over by the state committees and their subordinate county, town and ward managers. This far-reaching organization worked well in the individual states, but not in the nation at large. The national committee, because of its scattered membership and the states rights doctrines of the party, did little or nothing. Indeed, it held but one meeting after the campaign of 1848 and then, December 29, 1851—January 1, 1852, contented itself with designating June 1, 1852, and Baltimore as the date and place of the National Convention.[1] Plainly this machinery was not sufficient to order the party. Leadership in bringing the Democracy into line must come from some other source—this source was at hand.

In the Senate of the Thirty-first and Thirty-second Congresses the thirty-five Democrats composed a slim majority of the sixty-two Senators. This majority was divided into two groups, the hunkers and the states rights sympathizers. The prominent Senators among the hunkers were Cass of Michigan, Douglas of Illinois, Bright of Indiana, Bradbury

[1] *Washington Union*, January 3, 1852.

of Maine, King of Alabama and Rusk of Texas. Their states rights colleagues were fewer in number and had as a central clique, Mason and Hunter of Virginia, Butler of South Carolina and Atchison of Missouri; these four formed a "mess" and boarded and lodged together while in Washington. Fully cognizant of the condition of the party the hunker leaders mentioned above set out to unite the party on their principle of "The Compromise—a final settlement". Union on such a fundamental they felt would drive the distracting question from politics, remove an easy issue from the reach of any who might wish to revolt, make unnecessary a third or Compromise party and bring victory —and spoils in 1852.

The focal point for all effort, of course, was the nomination of a candidate who could unite the party and carry the election. This nomination would be made at a convention meeting in June, 1852, composed of delegations from each of the thirty-one states, each state casting as many votes as it had presidential electors. These delegations were chosen by the party in each state in such manner as each might decide. Their choice would begin in June, 1851,[1] when the New Hampshire state convention was to choose a delegate at large for that state, and would extend to May, 1852, just before the National Convention. The work then before the controlling senatorial coterie was to convince the

[1] Delegates were divided into two classes; two votes from each state were cast by delegates-at-large while the remainder were controlled by delegates representing the various Congressional districts. Most states chose the district delegates at district conventions although some elected them at state conventions. The delegates-at-large were chosen by a state convention, by the district delegates or by legislative party caucus. The same state sometimes used different methods in different presidential years. The number of delegates sent to the convention was not always governed by the number of votes to which the state was entitled, Virginia in 1852 sent nearly 100 men to cast fifteen votes.

other party leaders that only a Compromise man would have any chance of carrying the election and that the nomination of a states rights or free soil Democrat would mean defection in the opposing section and sure defeat. They felt that if this were thoroughly understood state and district conventions would select delegates determined to choose only a "National" man. In order to get this fundamental fact before the Democratic party it was necessary to gain control of agencies to distribute this propaganda. The first move was to obtain control of the former Polk organ at the capital, the *Washington Union,* which since 1845 had been the national spokesman of the party. To do this required some political management, for there was an obstacle in the way. The paper was owned, controlled and edited by old "Father" Ritchie; he must be separated from his paper if it was to be of any value to those anxious to use it. There were several reasons for this: he was seventy-three years of age and in failing health; he was untractable and had decided opinions; he had been working hand in hand with Clay to put through the Compromise and his relations with the Whigs were too close to suit the states rights men. On the other hand, he was charged by Douglas and other northern Democrats with being too much in sympathy with the states rights wing. Besides these objections to his personality and views there were more serious drawbacks. Blair and Rives whom he had supplanted as owner of the organ hated him and had charged that he had bought the *Union* with money supplied by the United States Treasury through R. J. Walker and Simon Cameron. Also in order to get the government printing he had bid through an agent and had obtained it at a figure so low that he lost money. As was the custom, he applied to Congress for relief to the amount of $100,000. The debates on his behalf gave his enemies the chance they desired. All sorts of charges of corruption were given wide publicity and his relief was several times defeated. Altogether Mr. Ritchie needed to defend himself too much and explain too many things to be an ideal popular editor who could soothe wounded feelings, conquer personal prejudices and unite factions. Consequently the senatorial group was looking around for a new man. There was some talk of Edmund Burke, a former assistant of Ritchie, and also of John W. Forney, editor of the *Pennsylvanian* and a warm supporter of Buchanan. Just at this juncture, in February, 1851, there arrived in Washington the very man needed. Andrew Jackson Donelson, late minister to Prussia and the Federal Government of Germany, was at the State Department settling his accounts. His qualifications were of the first order. He was the adopted son of Andrew Jackson, the patron saint of the party whom the rank and file yet worshipped. He was of sufficient southern soundness to have been approached by Polk for editor in 1845, but on the other hand, he had shown that he was no radical fire-eater by his denunciation of the Nashville Convention. Who could be better qualified? He, then, was approached by the senatorial group. But he had his objections. Only a year since he had returned from a foreign mission in debt; he needed to devote his time to his plantations in order to free himself from his obligations. The *Union,* besides, was an unprofitable venture without the government printing, and under the contract system instituted in 1846 this printing had been awarded to a lower bidder. However, the friends of this move showed Donelson that the returns of the census of 1850 had not yet been printed and they made him believe that if he would take over the *Union,* they would influence Congress to pass a census contract for him. Thus he would make one or two hundred thousand dollars. With a suitable profit provided for there was still the question of cash capital with which to purchase the plant and good will. John C. Rives was approached but refused, and finally another Tennessean, Robert J. Armstrong, a favorite of Andrew Jackson, was brought to Washington to supply the capital ($10,000) and manage the business. The next step was to get Ritchie to sell. That was not difficult.

His friends in the Senate, principally Foote, advised him that his relief would not be accomplished when he hoped it would, namely during the extra session of the Senate then meeting, March 4-13, 1851. He was in great need of money; consequently, when he was convinced that his claim for relief would have no chance before Congress unless he withdrew from the paper, he placed his affairs in the hands of his friend the banker Corcoran to get the best bargain possible. On March 11, 1851, the *Union* was sold to Armstrong and Donelson for $20,000. On April 15 following, Donelson entered into the editorial management with the understanding that " the Compromise was to be treated as a law which was not to be disturbed ", and with the intention of being absolutely neutral as to preference for any candidate before the Baltimore Convention.[1] To this task he set himself, calling for a union of all sections of the Democracy upon the Compromise. He published from time to time items showing how compact the party was; he deprecated all third party moves. The old Jacksonian Democracy was to be revived. " Everything for principles, nothing for

[1] The account of the change of ownership of the *Union* is drawn from the following:

Donelson to his wife, Feb. 24 and March 7, 1851, Donelson to his son, May 12 and June 22, 1852, Donelson MSS.; Ritchie to Corcoran, March 8 and March 11, 1851, Donelson to Corcoran, March 11, 1851, Corcoran MSS.; Blair to Van Buren, 22 Jan., 10 and 15 March, 30 April, 1851, Van Buren MSS.; Buchanan to Cave Johnson, March 22 and April 27, 1851, Donelson to Buchanan, October 18, 1851, Alfred Balch to Buchanan, Nov. 18, 1851, Buchanan MSS.; *Toombs Corr.*, pp. 262, 264, 293, 294, 303, 317.

men." [1] Donelson, in spite of his good intentions and his backing, was not a success. The group headed by Mason, Hunter, Butler and Atchison, and the states rights men generally, did not like him because of his denunciation of the Nashville Convention, his ardent support of the Compromise and his choice by the hunkers. Also the fact that Arnold Harris, Armstrong's son-in-law, was connected with the steamboat companies and was continually lobbying for claims before Congress, led some to believe that the organ was to be used to push corrupt enterprises. Further, Donelson's predilections for Cass could be seen continually in his paper in spite of his efforts to be neutral. Consequently it was going to prove difficult for the hunkers to carry out the understanding in regard to the printing subsidy.

When Congress met in December, 1851, Bright immediately set to work to settle the matter by introducing a resolution giving the printing of the census to Donelson and Armstrong. Immediately there were objections. There was already a government printer who was under contract to do all the work, A. Boyd Hamilton, a Pennsylvanian. He must be removed. This, as will be readily seen, gave the states rights Democrats and the Whigs an excellent chance for political capital, and they denounced the scheme. In vain the regulars declared that the Whigs had done the same thing in Harrison's administration, in vain they proved Hamilton's work to be inferior and below contract stipula-

[1] Donelson and Armstrong felt the need of a wider circulation for their gospel and attempted to set up a paper in New York. Negotiations were made through Arnold Harris, Armstrong's son-in-law, with John P. Heiss, a former business manager of the *Union*. The aid of Marcy and some New York merchants was enlisted. However, Heiss purchased the *New Orleans Delta* and the project did not materialize. A. Campbell to Marcy, April 26, 1851, J. A. Thomas to Marcy, May 6, June 26, 1851, Marcy MSS. Marcy to Donelson, May 7, 1851, Donelson MSS.

tions. The breach between states rights and Compromise men was only emphasized. Donelson had too many southern enemies. Consequently on January 27 the project was buried in the House in Committee of the Whole by vote of 134 to 51, and on February 6, in spite of Cass' efforts, the Senate defeated it on a test vote, 16 to 28 by a combination of states rights men, freesoilers and Whigs. Thus the scheme of government subsidization of the *Union* failed[1] because of southern opposition and Donelson's unpopularity. Under the circumstances the leaders felt it inopportune to attempt to put through the claim that had been promised Ritchie. Donelson was deeply in debt. Without the printing the *Union* did not pay, so there was but one thing for Donelson to do. On May 12, 1852, he published a card stating he would withdraw "perceiving that there are obstacles to the harmony of the democratic party growing in some degree out of alleged differences of opinion respecting the political views which have been maintained by the *Washington Union*". Thus he retired from the active editorial management although retaining silent connection with it. This disturbing element, which had ruined many of the fond hopes of the Compromise men, was eliminated but two weeks before the Convention met.[2]

Others in Congress besides this senatorial group felt that the Compromise should be a finality and sought to have it formally adopted as such by both the Democratic party and Congress itself. All Democrats who had risked membership in southern union parties felt that their political futures depended upon the adoption by the national party of their

[1] Donelson received a small sop doled out by the Committee on Printing in April, *viz.* that part of the House printing which Hamilton could not do. *Cong. Globe*, 32 Cong., 1 Sess., p. 1342, 1794.

[2] *Cong. Globe*, 32 Cong., 1 Sess., p. 407, 471 *et seq.*; A. W. Venable to Buchanan, May 19, 1852, Buchanan MSS.; see also references under note, p. 34.

Compromise as the official slavery plank. This would show their stand to have been the regular one, and make them the orthodox Democracy. They made their first move when the Democratic members of the House met in caucus on November 29th, 1851, to choose officers for the new body. Here they attempted to have the party endorse the Compromise. George W. Jones of Tennessee drew up, after consultation with Cobb, the following resolution, which was introduced by William H. Polk of Tennessee:

Resolved, that the series of acts . . . . known as the Compromise are regarded as a final adjustment and a permanent settlement of the questions therein embraced and should be maintained and executed as such.

The caucus was poorly attended; only eighty-nine of the one hundred and forty-three Democrats were present. Most of the southern rights Democrats, knowing that this resolution was coming up, stayed away. They wanted it defeated without voting against it. R. W. Johnson of Arkansas moved as a substitute for the Polk resolution a longer one embodying the substance of it but making a pledge against further encroachments upon slavery. Whereupon F. P. Stanton, another Tennessee member, moved to refer the matter to the National Convention. No sooner had he done this than Cartter of Ohio, a free soil member, moved to lay the whole question on the table. This motion carried, 59-30; those supporting the affirmative were mainly free soil and states rights Democrats. The reasons for this vote lay in the small attendance, the near approach of the National Convention, southern opposition and the fear of losing some free-soil support. Disappointed, a number of Compromise supporters left the caucus.[1]

[1] *Cong. Globe*, 32-1, p. 8, and Appendix, p. 420; *N. Y. Herald*, Dec. 2, 1851; *Toombs Corr.*, pp. 218, 267-270.

After this defeat, Senator Henry S. Foote felt called upon to try another means of endorsement, namely, to have the Senate place the stamp of its approval on the Compromise as a finality. He was fresh from victory in Mississippi, extremely narrow though it was, and was filled with pride. Moreover, he was busy trying to manœuvre himself into a strategic position so that he would receive a vice-presidential nomination from some party, whether union or Democratic, he did not seem to care. Immediately on the convening of the Senate, December 2, he gave notice that he would introduce a resolution declaring the Compromise to be "a definite settlement of the distracting question growing out of the system of Domestic slavery . . . . to be acquiesced in and respected by all good citizens." [1] This resolution, introduced on December 8, caused desultory debate until February 28, 1852. During this period most of the prominent Senators took occasion to speak, and each side made repeated attempts to foist upon the other the odium of opposition to the Compromise. The friends of the resolution justified themselves for reopening the question. As Cass put it, "Reports have gone forth that [the Compromise measures] would be assailed in Congress and some of them repealed, or so modified as to destroy their efficiency or acceptability. Agitation is thus kept alive by the expectation of change, and prepared to renew its fearful work, and in this state of things I find myself face to face with a resolution which asserts as I believe the true character and just inviolability of these measures, and seeks thereby to remove from the public mind all apprehension that the perilous contest . . . . will again be renewed." [2] However, no vote was taken. The scene of action was shifted to the House.

The efforts of the southern unionists were unremittent.

[1] *Cong. Globe*, 32-1, p. 12.

[2] *Cong. Globe*, 32-1, p. 146.

Cobb came up from Georgia about the first of March and the Compromise men who had been waiting for an opportunity since their defeat in the Congressional caucus, now laid a plan to gain the endorsement of the House. On March 1, 1852, Fitch of Indiana, hunker Democrat, moved for a suspension of the rules, so that he might introduce the following resolution without unanimous consent:

Resolved: That we recognize the binding efficacy of the compromises of the Constitution, and believe it to be the intention of the people generally, as we hereby declare it to be ours individually, to abide such compromises, and to sustain the laws necessary to carry them out—the provision for the delivery of fugitive slaves included: and that we deprecate all further agitation of questions growing out of that provision, of the questions embraced in the acts of the last Congress known as the Compromise, and of questions generally connected with the institution of slavery, as unnecessary, useless, and dangerous.

This resolution failed to get the necessary two-thirds vote; eighty-two Democrats voted for it and thirty-six against it, the latter including the prominent states rights and free soil men.

On March 22nd Fitch's resolution was again introduced, this time by Jackson of Georgia, a union Democrat, with the words "and the act of the last Congress for that purpose" inserted after "fugitive slaves", a change made on consultation at the suggestion of the Georgians. This did not come up to vote until April 5. On this date there were a multitude of roll-calls and much wrangling. During the turmoil, Hillyer of Georgia, a union Democrat, amended the resolution by adding Polk's caucus resolution as a second part. Finally the Fitch-Jackson resolution was passed 101-64 and the Hillyer resolution 100-65. This vote showed that while a strong majority of the southern men favored the Compromise only a bare majority favored its finality, and that considerably less than a majority in the north favored either. Nearly thirty per cent of the Representatives of this section were for some reason or other absent. Unlike the Senate, the House could make a ready disposition of the finality of the Compromise.[1] The significant fact of this episode was the formation of a non-partisan coalition. Had not the Compromise Whigs voted with the Compromise Democrats, the disorganization of the Democratic party on the Compromise was so great that unaided it could not have carried the endorsement. A non-partisan coalition had passed it, a coalition of free soilers and states rights men had opposed it.[2]

The extended and fruitless debate in the Senate and the votes in the House showed that the supposedly harmonious Democrats were so divided that some friends of the Compromise feared an inability to get the Convention to adopt it and others even apprehended a disruption of the party. Talk of a union party of Compromise Whigs and Democrats again became open. Neither in choice of an organ nor in attempts at endorsement had the Congressional leaders unified the party on the Compromise. Could the Convention do it? Was there a candidate who could harmonize the factions? There were plenty who were willing to try.

[1] *Cong. Globe*, 32-1, pp. 659, 825, 976-985 and Appendix, p. 317; *Washington Union*, Apr. 6, 1852; *ibid.*, Apr. 30, declared that of the 82 northern Democrats 49 were for the Compromise, and of the 60 southern Democrats 47 were in favor of that measure—thus 67% of the total number of Democrats and a majority in each section were favorable. Jenkins to Marcy, Mar. 31, 1852, Marcy MSS.

[2] This was not the only sign of the strength of this coalition. Boyd who had been elected Speaker as a Compromise man had appointed many prominent southern rights and free soil men to important committee chairmanships. *Toombs Corr.*, pp. 271-274.

CHAPTER III

THE LAST OF THE HEROES

THE disturbed condition of the party seemed to place no damper upon its presidential aspirants. In more auspicious times, when a Democrat dwelt in the White House, controlling the patronage, candidates found it rather difficult to get much support from the office-holding local leaders. The tenure of the latter depended upon the executive pleasure and, if the President had second-term plans of his own, or wished to name his successor, they were chary of supporting anyone displeasing to him. Thus candidates other than those with executive approval were often discouraged, because it was difficult to proceed very far without machine support. But as 1852 drew near a Whig administration was in power and there was no network of Democratic office-holders throughout the states working under orders from the departments at Washington. Thus it was to be a free-for-all with no fears of offending the executive. The result was a multiplicity of candidates.

Lewis Cass was the best known of all those mentioned for the nomination. He had been the Democratic candidate in 1848 and before that had seen many years of public service. As soldier, governor of Michigan, Secretary of War under Jackson, Minister to France, and Senator, he had long been in the public eye. His main characteristics were his hatred for all things English, acquired while dealing with the British on the Michigan and northwestern frontier; his propensity for straddling an issue as long as possible, as evidenced by his Nicholson letter;[1] and his intense love of the Union, as demonstrated by his recent hearty support of the Compromise of 1850. For these reasons he was, to the rank and file, the foremost Democrat, the last of the heroes. Also his defeat in 1848 was felt by many to have been caused by treachery in the ranks, and had given some the impression that he was entitled to another chance. These elements of popular favor did not carry with them commensurate advantages. For, since public opinion in the Democratic party was apathetic, the choice of the nominee actually rested with the leaders. Even with them Cass's position was not unfavorable.

Cass had been the nominee in 1848. During that campaign it had been understood that many rewards in the shape of federal office would be distributed among local leaders. The Democrats who had pinned their hopes to those promises had been disappointed by the Whig victory. Now, however, if Cass were renominated, the claims of 1848 would still hold good. Therefore, looking toward the fulfillment of deferred hopes, various of the captains were preparing to support him again. A second class was for him just so long as he seemed to be the leading candidate. Finally, there were groups who used his name as a rallying center for the defeat of opposing factions. Here was a nucleus around which Cass might have recruited a campaign organization. But Cass was not a good drill sergeant—indifference and sluggishness made him his own worst enemy.

He was nearly seventy, obese and inactive. His rather grotesque figure, topped by an ill-fitting wig, and his poor delivery as a speaker, made him a bad campaigner.[2] He

[1] For the Nicholson letter *v.* p. 48.

[2] Grinnell, J. B., *Men and Events of Forty Years*, p. 64; McLanahan to Buchanan, Jan. 8, 1850, Buchanan MSS.; McLaughlin, A. C., *Lewis Cass*, *passim*.

seemed unable to work to his own political advantage. Besides, the bitterness of the previous contest and his defeat had left him rather loath to reenter the lists; and in addition he had written in 1848 that he would never again become a candidate: a declaration cited with avidity by his enemies in 1852.[1] Furthermore, he preferred not to antagonize old associates.[2] He was even tolerant of Douglas' campaign in his own section, although, toward the end of it, his patience seems to have been exhausted.[3] In tardy fashion, he bestirred himself to get his colleague, Senator Felch, to send out a few copies of the *Washington Union* containing his views.[4] But in general, his attitude was one of waiting on fate. In October, 1851, he wrote, "The matter may go to its consummation, but I should pass four years at the decline of life far more happily without the Presidency than with it." [5] However, the events of the spring of 1852 must have aroused some hope, for in April he wrote, "I do not mean to suffer my equanimity to be disturbed by setting my mind too much on the result." [6] Such were the facts for the consideration of the leaders.

Politically speaking, the Democratic party was a confederation of the leaders of the east, south and west. Among them the support tendered Cass varied widely. In the east his most active followers were to be found in New York among the hunkers. In this movement the most prominent leader was ex-Senator Daniel S. Dickinson. To him party loyalty was a religion. The barnburners had left the party

[1] John H. Wheeler to Buchanan, May 30, 1852, Buchanan MSS.

[2] William R. King to Buchanan, March 6, 1852, *ibid.*

[3] *Ibid.*, W. W. Snow to Marcy, Dec. 27, 1851, Mar. 13, 1852, Marcy MSS.

[4] *Toombs Corr.*, p. 291.

[5] Cass to A. J. Donelson, Oct. 31, 1851, Donelson MSS.

[6] Cass to Lewis S. Coryell, Apr. 24, 1852, Coryell MSS.

and had caused the defeat of Cass for President. Without punishment they had been received back into the fold, but, according to Dickinson's belief, they had been treacherous and had caused his defeat for the Senate. Consequently he was determined that the state organization should not be controlled by them and that New York's delegation to the National Convention must be made up of hunkers. He also felt that as New York had defeated Cass in 1848 her undivided support must now go to him in 1852. Thus would the sin of party treason be in a manner atoned for, the barnburners would be placed in a subordinate position, and the hunkers would control the policy of the state organization. The nomination of Cass thus became a personal matter with him and events were to make it more so.

Other hunker leaders were to support Cass for different reasons. The New York City Democracy was in a turmoil. The various factions were engaged in a death struggle for control. Elijah F. Purdy, Isaac V. Fowler, and other barnburners were in alliance with the political trimmer, Fernando Wood, and had triumphed over the hards led by Daniel E. Sickles, Mike Walsh, and James T. Brady. These latter were determined to dominate and give no quarter to the barnburners. As one mode of accomplishing this they set out to control the New York City delegation to Baltimore. For this purpose they sought to rally around the standard of Cass.[1] However, he was not found to be very popular in New York City, and when the name of William L. Marcy, Polk's Secretary of War, began to be prominently mentioned for the Presidency, they sought to make use of it. Some of their number, including Sickles and Augustus M. Schell, worked up a plan. They decided to show Marcy that Senator Stephen A. Douglas of Illinois

[1] Myers, G., *History of Tammany Hall*, pp. 142-160, *passim*.

was developing a campaign in New York which was in danger of electing a lot of rowdies as delegates to the National Convention, and to suggest that as Cass was not popular enough to offset this movement they would like to use Marcy's prestige to defeat the Illinois Senator's friends. They conferred with Marcy at the Irving House in New York in November, 1851; he made no objections to the plan.[1] Then on November 27, Cass arrived in New York on his way to Washington,[2] and thereafter Douglas men began to support Cass.[3] What may have been Sickles' real plan then began to appear, namely, Marcy's name was being used in New York City to elect Cass delegates and to defeat anti-Cass barnburners.[4] The scheme was a success, most of the city delegates were chosen for Cass, and on April 1 both Old and Young Tammany gave him their official endorsement.[5]

While these manoeuvrings were going on, Dickinson was not idle. He expected that all hunkers would be solidly at his back. But Marcy, mainly backed by barnburners, was becoming an active candidate and Cass men were in many cases supporting him. In Dickinson's eyes this made Marcy a traitor. He was sure that barnburning treachery had defeated him for reelection in 1851, and now, when Marcy was receiving his chief support from barnburners, he began to entertain the suspicion that Marcy had countenanced and perhaps aided the loss of his seat.[6] Conse-

[1] Marcy to Samuel Beardsley, Dec. 10, 1851, Marcy MSS.

[2] *N. Y. Herald*, Nov. 28, 1851.

[3] John Addison Thomas to Marcy, Dec. 29, 1851; Marcy to James G. Berrett, Jan. 2, 1852; Marcy to Archibald Campbell, Jan. 16, 1852, Marcy MSS.

[4] *Ibid.*

[5] *N. Y. Herald*, Apr. 2, 1852; this surprised the *Herald* which had thought the Young Democracy of Tammany were for Douglas.

[6] Marcy to A. Campbell, March 25, 1852, Marcy MSS.

quently all the efforts of the friends of Dickinson [1] were turned toward the defeat of Marcy, and the feud became increasingly bitter. Birdsall and Beardsley went to Washington to injure Marcy by claiming that he was a barnburner and that he could not carry New York. Birdsall was exceedingly intemperate in speech and went to great lengths.[2] This violence on the part of his lieutenants led many to believe that Dickinson was out for himself and was using Cass's name for his own benefit.[3] Others declared that he wished to be Vice-President on the Cass ticket which, considering that statesman's three score years and ten, might prove a place of opportunity.[4] Sporadic support was given him in the south, especially in Virginia.[5] Marcy's friends took pains to inform Cass as to what they considered Dickinson's real motives.[6] Cass, however, gave no credence to these charges; a few days after the appearance of Dickinson's answer to the Scott letter,[7] in which he denied that he

[1] His principal aids were Ausburn M. Birdsall, husband of his niece, Judge Samuel Beardsley and David Wager of Utica. Less active was Edwin Croswell, the "Thurlow Weed" of the Democratic party.

[2] Horatio Seymour to Marcy, Apr. 26, May 2, 1852; W. W. Snow to Marcy, April 29, 1852; A. Vanderpool to Marcy, May 12, 1852; Marcy to Berret May 15, 1852, Marcy MSS.

[3] Marcy to Berret, Feb. 4, 1852; Snow to Marcy, April 20, 1852; Eames to Marcy, May 16, 1852, *ibid.*

[4] L. B. Shepard, Dec. 5, 1851, *ibid.*

[5] Campbell to Marcy, March 23, 1852; W. W. Snow to Marcy, April 10, 1852, *ibid.*

[6] S. B. Jewett, May 29, 1852, *ibid.*

[7] A Virginia editor, Robert G. Scott, on May 17, 1852, addressed to the fifteen men whom he thought were presidential possibilities, Cass, Douglas, Houston, W. R. King, Dickinson, Thomas J. Rusk, Buchanan, Joseph Lane, Robert J. Stockton, Linn Boyd, George M. Dallas, General John E. Wool, Marcy, Pierce, and Butler, asking three questions: 1. Would you do everything in your power to sustain the Compromise and the Fugitive Slave Law? 2. Would you do all you could to prevent

was a candidate, Cass wrote him, May 27, 1852, "I know you are as true a man as ever walked the earth."[1] However, of the thirty-five New York delegates, Cass had but eleven and the campaign strife had built up an insuperable barrier of unfriendliness to him on the part of the remaining twenty-four. Cass had been served "not wisely, but too well."

In Pennsylvania Cass' support was of a different type. There Simon Cameron and others felt that the "Buchaneers", as those who followed Buchanan were called, had too complete control of the party organization. They sought the management by uniting Buchanan's opponents in an attempt to win delegates for Cass. Their plans failed and they concentrated their efforts on spreading abroad the report that Buchanan was popular with only a faction and could neither unite the state nor win its electoral vote.[2]

In New England Cass seemed strong. Here the hopes of 1848 and the desire to support the leading man were the strongest motives. His main backers in this section were Benjamin F. Hallett of Boston, chairman of the national committee, and Charles G. Greene, editor of the *Boston Post*.[3]

In the south Cass was weakest. He was unpopular with the southern rights group for several reasons. The first of these was his active support of the Compromise of 1850.

change in the Fugitive Slave Law to make it less effective? 3. Would you veto a law impairing the Fugitive Slave Law? All replied except Pierce, and the replies were published broadcast. *N. Y. Herald*, May 25, 1852.

[1] Dickinson, *D. S. Dickinson*, vol. ii, p. 469.

[2] Alfred Gilmore to Buchanan, Sept. 9, 1850, Dec. 24, 1850, Jan. 25, 1852, Buchanan MSS. George Plitt to Buchanan, May 25, 1852, Buchanan-Johnston MSS.

[3] Alfred Gilmore to Buchanan, Apr. 15, 1852, Buchanan MSS.; Isaac O. Barnes to J. C. Breckinridge, Jan. 19, and Feb. 22, 1852, Breckinridge MSS.; *N. Y. Herald*, Oct. 14, 1851.

Not only had he warmly advocated these measures, which this faction felt detrimental to their section, but what was worse, he had failed to vote for the Fugitive Slave Act, the only part of the settlement which the south considered to its advantage. This was brought into the campaign when the Cass organ, the *Detroit Free Press,* attacked Buchanan as not favoring the Compromise. Buchanan's editor, Forney, countered by showing that Cass had not voted for this measure and by demanding the reason.[1] As Cass thought that any explanation he might give in answer to this attack would be too apparently a bid for support, he refused to reply. His friends knew that his failure to vote was due to the attitude of southern leaders. They had refused to allow the act to contain a clause granting to a fugitive slave, who protested that he was free, a jury trial in the county from which he was alleged to have escaped.[2] In addition he had reiterated his approval of the Compromise in its entirety in a speech to the Senate, December 23, 1851, in which he denounced Rhett and disunion and gave emphatic endorsement to the Foote resolution.[3] His opinion he made more decisive in his reply to the Scott letter, in which he answered all the questions in the affirmative.[4]

A second reason for his unpopularity in the south was the Nicholson letter. This document, written in December, 1847, was not altogether pleasing. The general interpretation was that Cass conceded to the voters of each territory the right to decide whether they would tolerate the institution of slavery. This was anathema to the many southern-

[1] *Pennsylvanian,* Sept. 4, 1851. Charles Eames to Marcy, Sept. 14, 1851, Marcy MSS.

[2] This he himself declared after the convention in a speech before the Senate, Aug. 26, 1852, *Cong. Globe,* 32C-1S, Appendix, pp. 1124-1125.

[3] *Ibid.*, p. 146.

[4] *N. Y. Herald*, May 26, 1852.

ers who maintained that territorial voters had no control over forms of property recognized by any of the states. Some enemies said the letter was intended to deceive the south by hiding a denial of protection to slave property in the territories.[1] To answer this, the *Washington Union* published a letter from Jefferson Davis, late Senator from Mississippi, refuting the charge but disagreeing with Cass as to the power of territories to regulate slavery. Thereupon Cass, in a speech in the Senate, March 19, 1852, specifically stated in explanation of the Nicholson letter that he believed Congress could impose no restriction upon the power to regulate the relations of master and servant in the territories. Territorial legislatures alone had full power to do this. He furthermore stated that while he did not believe that the Constitution gave anyone the right to take slaves into the territories regardless of the wishes of the territorial legislatures, he was nevertheless willing to submit the question to the Supreme Court.[2] The denial of Congressional power to protect slavery and the bestowal of sovereignty upon territories did not help Cass in the south.

A third reason for unpopularity in the south was Cass' action in regard to the Kossuth affair. The Hungarian, Louis Kossuth, after an unsuccessful attempt to establish a republic in his native land, had been expelled from that country by the intervention of Russia. The United States government invited him to America, and upon his arrival, in December 1851, he was the recipient of much attention. While visiting Washington, he was given two dinners, on January 7 and 8, at which Cass and many notables spoke. Cass declared himself sympathetic with Kossuth and his mis-

[1] Quaife, M. M., *Doctrine of Non-intervention with Slavery in the Territories, passim.*

[2] *Washington Union*, Mar. 17, 1852; *Cong. Globe*, 32C-1S, p. 784.

sion, in glowing periods stated his opposition to any form of tyrannical intervention in the affairs of a nation struggling toward freedom, and expressed himself as ready to vote for a resolution denouncing Russia's action as a patent violation of international law. As this whole movement of indorsing Kossuth was accompanied by panegyrics on the subject of liberty, the supersensitive southern slaveholders were suspicious of it as a covert attack upon their institution. As a result of this complex Cass fell further in the estimation of southern leaders.[1]

What little strength Cass had below the Potomac came from the southern unionists. The most active of these were the Georgia union Democrats, although Cobb had leanings toward Buchanan, and those Democrats in Mississippi following the lead of the redoubtable Henry S. Foote.[2] Such support availed him little, in fact it harmed him. These men were felt by the orthodox to be heretics because of their fraternizing with the Whigs, and when rumors were rife of a union ticket of Clay and Cass, the purists began to suspect Cass and he was spoken of as a "cats-paw of Clay and the Union Whigs".[3] The *New York Herald* declared several times that Clay was going to support Cass for

[1] These views Cass elaborated in a speech before the Senate, Feb. 10, in which he practically declared for what is now called self-determination, and roundly condemned Austria and Russia for interference in Hungary. The United States, however, could only protest, for he believed a foreign war to aid Hungary to be impossible. *Cong. Globe*, 32C-1S, pp. 158-165. Rhodes, J. F., *History of the United States*, vol. i, pp. 231 and 242; Bancroft, F., *Life of Seward*, vol. i, p. 317; McMaster, J. B., *History of the People of the United States*, vol. viii, pp. 154-155; N. O. Weekly *Delta*, Feb. 15, 1852.

[2] *Toombs Corr.*, p. 299; John A. Thomas to Marcy, Mar. 17, 1852, Marcy MSS.; *Washington Union*, Feb. 10, 1852.

[3] Ambler, C. H. (ed.), "R. M. T. Hunter Corr.," *Am. Hist. Assocn. Rept.*, 1916, vol. ii, p. 137, hereafter cited as *Hunter Corr.*

President and had a letter written in his behalf.[1] Indeed Cass was approached to join a Whig on a union ticket,[2] but he saw fit to refuse all such advances. Thus the chief result of these negotiations was to cause the southern rights men to look upon him with more disfavor than ever.

Some southern endorsement, however, came to Cass from different motives. In Louisiana there was bad blood between the romantic and sensational Soulé and the heavy, practical Slidell. This culminated in the state convention of March 9, 1852; at that gathering in order to defeat the Soulé faction who were for Douglas, Slidell and the Buchanan men joined the Cass supporters and sent a delegation instructed for the Senator from Michigan.[3]

In Missouri, the state convention of April 8, 1852, was the scene of a bitter struggle between the Benton men, who were for William O. Butler, and the anti-Benton forces, who rallied around Cass. A Butler delegation was chosen, but at a late hour when but "a few delegates were present and when it was so dark in the room that it was impossible to see whether the persons called were those who voted", instructions for Cass were pushed through by anti-Benton managers voting counties not represented and counties whose members were out of the hall.[4]

The west was his stronghold, but even there Douglas was questioning his sovereignty. Michigan was steadfast. Most of Ohio could be counted on; but Douglas had injured

[1] *N. Y. Herald*, Jan. 15, 1852. Clay had written a N. Y. supporter the previous year stating his belief that a Democrat was likely to be elected in 1852 and that he preferred Cass. Colton (ed.), *Clay Corr.*, p. 619.

[2] *v. supra*, p. 28.

[3] Slidell to A. G. Penn, Mar. 11, 1852; William R. King to Buchanan, Mar. 24, 1852, Buchanan MSS.

[4] F. P. Blair, Sr. to Martin Van Buren, Apr. 30, 1852, Van Buren MSS.; H. A. Clover to Buchanan, Apr. 13, 1852, Buchanan MSS.

him there. Illinois would go to her favorite son, and the pivotal state of Indiana was successfully masking any preferences her politicians may have had under their instructions for the Hoosier, General Joseph Lane.[1]

Thus, in spite of everything, Cass approached the Convention as apparently the most formidable candidate, but his support was scattered and illusory. He had a majority of the New England delegates, for a while at least, and a bitter minority in New York; in the south only Louisiana and Missouri were openly for him; in the west, loyal Michigan and most of Ohio.[2] This was to be the nucleus which was to attract various odds and ends of support in the Convention. Widespread and varied was Cass' following, more important as to numbers than morale, much of it willing to drop him and take up anyone with a better chance of success. As the first of June approached, the idea "he can't get elected" became increasingly prevalent.[3] Taken altogether, it seemed probable that Cass would get more votes to start with than any other candidate, but their number was by no means a majority, much less the necessary two-thirds. His great weakness was the fact that no pivotal state had declared for him—there seemed no possibility of his obtaining the votes of Virginia, New York, or Pennsylvania, and the south would have none of him.

[1] *Washington Union*, March 3, 1852.

[2] The legislature of Maryland had endorsed him and the New Jersey convention had passed a resolution in his favor, but the delegates from both states were technically uninstructed. *Washington Union*, April 8, 1852; *Newark Morning Eagle*, May 8, 1852.

[3] Blair to Van Buren, May 12, 1852, Van Buren MSS.

CHAPTER IV

The Sage of Wheatland

Buchanan was as anxious to be nominated as Cass was indifferent. He had served his apprenticeship long and faithfully as Senator from Pennsylvania, Minister to Russia and Secretary of State under Polk. To him it was an apprenticeship—an apprenticeship to the Presidency. For a decade he had nourished ambitions, and in 1848 had been Cass' principal competitor before the convention. Immediately after the election of that year he began planning for 1852. He was over six feet in height, white-haired, and benevolent-looking. One of his eyes was near-sighted and the other far-sighted, so that he carried his head slightly askew and appeared peculiarly one-sided. A close observer noted that one of his eyes was blue and the other hazel. A rich but honest old bachelor of benign aspect and precise habits, he had been careful and conscientious, but never brilliant in the fulfillment of his duties. He was not sufficiently adaptable to understand changing conditions; his caution bordered on timidity. His chief characteristics were his conservatism and his desire that everything should proceed decently and in order.[1]

He had lived all his life in a political atmosphere and had his methodical mind strongly set in politicians' grooves.

[1] Curtis, G. T., *Life of James Buchanan*, vol. ii, p. 672; Wise, J. S., *Recollections of Thirteen Presidents*, p. 67; McClure, A. K., *Old Time Notes of Pennsylvania*, vol. i, p. 275; H. D. Gilpin to Van Buren, Jan. 27, 1850, Van Buren MSS.

Therefore there seemed to him to be but one way to be nominated. He believed implicitly in the Divine Right of Parties. You served your party early and late, in seedtime and in harvest, and in due season if you fainted not you received the crown of your ambition's choice at the hands of party leaders with a "Well done, good and faithful servant". Buchanan had served seven years and yet another seven, and now he felt that he had fulfilled his time. His reward he sought from those who could give it—the politicians. But was it not the people's gift? No—leaders who had borne the burden and heat of the day were alone capable of judging the merit of the faithful partisan — theirs was the sole concern. This was Buchanan's creed and he accepted it without question. Accordingly he set about to place himself before his brother politicians.

To aid him in this project Buchanan had active friends who were busy in various parts of the country emphasizing his eminent qualifications. His principal ally in the Senate was William R. King, its presiding officer, a prim, amiable mediocrity, whose large figure lent dignity to the Vice-Presidential chair in spite of his wig.[1] More active was John Slidell of New Orleans and New York, a crafty, worldly-wise, cold-hearted schemer, whose only warmth seemed his friendship with Buchanan; their intimacy began when Slidell was sent to Mexico in the forties and closed when Slidell became a secessionist.[2] Closely connected with Slidell was his relative, August Belmont of New York, wealthy representative of the Rothschilds, whose interest in politics was not entirely unselfish; his influence in New York's financial district was important when it came to collecting

[1] The only correspondent who addressed him "Dear Buchanan". Buchanan was evidently not a man to inspire familiarities.

[2] Sears, "Slidell and Buchanan", *Amer. Hist. Rev.*, vol. xxvii, pp. 709-729.

the sinews of war. Less influential were Cave Johnson of Tennessee and Isaac Toucey of Connecticut, Postmaster-General and Attorney-General in Polk's cabinet. In Virginia was a rather inconspicuous but very industrious man, Colonel John A. Parker, who was to be one of the instruments in committing a greater than he to the cause, Henry A. Wise, once a Tyler Whig and now an avowed Democrat. In Pennsylvania Buchanan had the ardent backing of John W. Forney and Robert Tyler, newspaper men of influence, Congressmen Alfred Gilmore and J. Glancy Jones, and lesser lights such as James C. Van Dyke, David Lynch, and George W. Plitt; these relieved Buchanan of all the *practical* side of politics. In addition Buchanan had many correspondents. He was a tireless letter writer and kept in touch with a large number of men, some of whom were very insignificant. Last but not least must be chronicled the ladies. Buchanan, confirmed bachelor as he was, was a great ladies' man, and numbered many politically minded of the fair sex among his ardent followers. In his niece Harriet Lane he had an attractive companion.

Besides this widespread network of influences Buchanan had another decided advantage; this was his position in the south. The radical southerners who did not approve the doctrines of Cass' Nicholson letter found solace in Buchanan's famous letter of August 25, 1847.[1] Herein he declared against the Wilmot proviso and for the extension of the Missouri Compromise line to the Pacific. This he felt was only giving the south its fair share of the common territory. When the various southern leaders were seeking a candidate, it seemed to be the general feeling that only a northern man would be considered; they could carry the south but they needed a man with some influence in the north to secure enough states there and prevent the northern

[1] *Works*, vol. vii, p. 385.

opposition from crying sectionalism. The three prominent candidates were Cass, Buchanan, and Woodbury. The first and the last were objectionable, the former for his support of the Compromise, and the latter for his friendship with Benton, Blair and questionable free soilers. Buchanan's standing on the doctrine of the extension of the Missouri Compromise was irreproachable. Then, too, he was of national reputation and powerful in Pennsylvania, the second largest state in the Union. Many who refused to support him in 1848 now thought he was the most available candidate.

This advantage Buchanan was following up by methods outlined above, and was also making attempts to build up his strength in the north. He opened correspondence with his colleague in the Polk cabinet, Toucey of Connecticut.[1] Also he attempted to revive friendship with F. P. Blair, Sr., ex-editor of the *Globe*. Because of Polk's action in suppressing the *Globe,* Blair had little use for him or any of his administration; especially had he become unfriendly with Buchanan as he believed that he had been active in defeating Benton for the Lieutenant-Generalship in the Mexican War. Buchanan knew that Blair still had the ear of Van Buren and Benton who, though they had lost ground, were still not quite impotent politically. Desire to conciliate this faction, perhaps, was the motive for opening this correspondence. Blair in reply stated his grievance and Buchanan answered, defending himself though admitting that he had not thought it wise to put Benton at the head of the army. This effort accomplished nothing. Blair did not trust Buchanan.[2] Meanwhile Buchanan remained quietly

[1] Buchanan to Toucey, 1 June, 1849, *Works*, vol. viii, p. 362.

[2] Blair to Buchanan, 22 Nov., 1849, *ibid.*, p. 365; Blair to Van Buren, 3 Dec., 1849, 24 Mar., 1850, Van Buren MSS.; Buchanan to Blair, 27 November, 1849, *Works*, vol. viii, p. 367.

at "Wheatland near Lancaster", Pennsylvania, reading, writing letters and meditating.

Then without much warning a portentous cloud arose on the horizon. In January, 1850, began the bitter conflict over the measures known as the Compromise of that year. Up to that time Buchanan had been following Slidell's advice on the slavery question. He had kept silent publicly for, as his mentor wisely wrote, the southern leaders were aware of his views and satisfied with them. Expressing them further would only stir up the free soilers in the north, who otherwise would bear him no grudge if he did not come immediately into conflict with them.[1] But now Cass was coming out openly with views favoring the Compromise and other prominent Democrats were getting notoriety because they expressed opinions on these measures. Buchanan felt a desire to maintain his ground by issuing a letter favoring, as usual, the extension of the Missouri Compromise line to the Pacific. He prepared such a letter advocating this doctrine, declaring against the Wilmot Proviso and the abolition of slavery in the District of Columbia and advocating a strict fugitive slave law. Before publishing it, however, he sought counsel with his friends. He received conflicting advice. Marcy, his erstwhile colleague in Polk's cabinet, wrote that there was not strong enough demand for it as yet, while Senator King thought it might aid his popularity.[2] However, as the Compromise controversy advanced it appeared that the south was not going to make a stand upon the Missouri line, but was going to demand only non-intervention. Consequently, why should Buchanan ask for more than the south? Also as the south

[1] Slidell to Buchanan, 25 July, 1849, 7 Dec., 1849, Buchanan MSS.

[2] Buchanan to W. R. King, 6 Mar., 1850, *Works*, vol. viii, p. 369. Marcy to Buchanan, 10 Mar., 1850, Buchanan MSS., King to Buchanan, 11 Mar., *ibid.*

didn't demand it and it was contrary to the Baltimore program, the Nicholson letter, Cass' speeches and the proceedings of the Pennsylvania Democracy, such a statement would only tend to promote useless controversy; and that was never Buchanan's desire. He would wait until the present plans (the Compromise) failed and then issue his solution.[1] Adhering to this determination he refused Foote's request to write on behalf of the Compromise. He did not approve it; California was too large for a single state, squatter sovereignty would open the way for a race of pro and anti-slavery settlers and consequent civil war; as Buchanan considered the Mexican law abolishing slavery still in force in the new territories, non-intervention was, in effect, the same as the Wilmot Proviso.[2] This policy of silence until the storm was over aided Buchanan in the south because the dominant states rights group felt that in a measure they had been cheated, and they were determined to support no one who had actively engaged in or pronounced on the subject.[3] However, this silence could not last long.

The passage of the Compromise and the wave of union sentiment which immediately swept over the country could not be ignored. All politicians were hastening aboard the band wagon and Buchanan took the occasion of an invitation to a union meeting in Philadelphia, November 21, 1850, to write a letter expressing guarded sentiments. He made a strong plea for the union and urged that all agitation in the north on the subject of slavery be put down. He gave it as his positive belief that had not this agitation grown up in the thirties, laws would have been passed in Maryland,

[1] Buchanan to Jefferson Davis, 16 Mar., 1850, *Works*, vol. viii, p. 372. Buchanan to King, 20 Mar., 1850, *ibid.*, p. 374.

[2] Buchanan to King, May 13, 1850, *ibid.*, p. 383; Buchanan to Henry S. Foote, May 31, 1850, *ibid.*, p. 385.

[3] Marcy to Berret, Dec. 14, 1851, Marcy MSS.; Marcy to Buchanan, Nov. 24, 1851, Buchanan MSS.

Virginia, Kentucky, and Missouri for gradual emancipation. Finally he demanded that the Fugitive Slave Law be executed in its letter and spirit as it was the only portion of the Compromise favorable to the south.[1] His friendship for the south and his lack of endorsement of any part of the Compromise except the Fugitive Slave Law were apparent.

Upon the doctrines of his letters of August 25, 1847, and November 21, 1850 Buchanan was to make his stand for preferment in 1852. These constituted his political philosophy: slavery should be kept out of politics entirely; but if it was not, the south must have fair play and a guarantee of her property rights in her own states and in all territories.

In spite of Buchanan's advantage of position due to his views, he had the serious disadvantage of a bitter feud in his own state. Simon Cameron, capitalist and iron master, demanded protection for the iron industry, and as the southern leaders opposed high tariffs, he was an anti-slavery man. Buchanan was a low tariff man and friendly with southern leaders. Consequently these men were opponents. Cameron sought to control the party in the state, to regain his seat in the Senate where he might work for various ends best known to himself. Buchanan sought to prevent this. In the conflicts that inevitably grew out of the struggle in the various conventions, state and local, of the Democracy of Pennsylvania, a bitter personal enmity developed.[2]

[1] *Works*, vol. viii, pp. 390 *et seq.*

[2] Buchanan alluded to Cameron as a "scamp," Buchanan to Davis, Mar. 16, 1850, vol. viii, p. 372, while Cameron denounced Buchanan as an old political hack so fallen that he couldn't carry a county, Cameron to Frazer, Mar. 19, 1851, *Pa. Mag. of Hist.*, vol. xxxix, p. 495. McClure, *Old Time Notes of Pa.*, vol. i, p. 92, Buchanan to L. Kidder, May 16, 1851, *Works*, vol. viii, p. 417. The author confesses his inability to find any material giving Cameron's side of the case except this letter here quoted. Any manuscript material in regard to Cameron, which may exist is well concealed from the investigator. This condition may have produced an unconscious bias in the account of his activities.

Cameron was unscrupulous; he and his associates managed to control the canal board and in this way had a great deal of the public plunder at their disposal. Using this, they carried on a constant guerilla warfare within the party for delegates and legislators. In a tight place their men often allied with the Whigs and got a measure through or a candidate elected. Buchanan's, however, was the dominant faction.

Very early in the Taylor administration Cameron set out to disappoint Buchanan's presidential aspirations. Part of his tactics was a device that had hurt Buchanan very much in the Convention of 1848, namely spreading abroad the report that Buchanan was weak in Pennsylvania with only a remnant behind him.[1] To make this hypothesis seem true and to poison the minds of some of Buchanan's southern friends Cameron spent some time in Washington during February and March, 1850. He told Jefferson Davis that Buchanan was opposed to the Missouri Compromise line, showing him a copy of some anti-slavery resolutions which had been passed at a public meeting in 1820 by the citizens of Lancaster, Pa., and which bore Buchanan's signature. Simultaneously, whether at Cameron's instance or not is undisclosed, there were circulated at Washington reports that Buchanan was opposed to the extension of the Missouri Compromise line if slavery were to be permitted south of that line. This was unfavorably compared with Cass' reputed statement that he would go that far. Also John P. Hale charged Buchanan with saying that the northern Democracy was a natural ally of the slaveholders of the south. In these attacks Buchanan detected a "concerted scheme". He wrote long letters to King and Davis defending himself in which he stated: "I am committed for the Missouri Compromise *and that committal shall stand.*" He admitted

[1] Albert C. Ramsey to Buchanan, Jan. 23, 1850, Buchanan MSS.

the resolutions but pleaded his youth and the fact that they were drawn up by his law preceptor for whom he had great affection.[1] Cameron's scheme in Washington failed since Buchanan's rebuttal strengthened him in the regard of southern senators.

Cameron then transferred the scene of his activities to Pennsylvania. Here he had the aid of Colonel Reah Frazer of Buchanan's town, Lancaster, Barrett, editor of the Harrisburg *Keystone,* and others of lesser note. To these were added Senator-elect Richard Brodhead, a bitter hater, who felt that Buchanan and his friends had opposed his election to the Senate. Buchanan attempted to conciliate him by explaining that, while he had at first preferred another, when he discovered Brodhead and others were desirous of the place he became neutral; not till later did he learn that his friends had opposed Brodhead. This did not help matters. Buchanan, therefore, had the only Democratic Senator from his state opposed to him and continually working against him.[2] This combination undertook a campaign to control the forthcoming state and local conventions. To this end they joined Cass' friends in working for the choice of delegates for that old war-horse.

These attacks and machinations led Buchanan and his friends to look to their fences. Buchanan's organization in Philadelphia was not strong. Robert Tyler, son of the ex-President and an editor in the Quaker City, together with Forney and others, sought to arrange an alliance with James Campbell, a prominent Philadelphia city politician, whose religion gave him the backing of the masses of the Catholic faith. The terms of this alliance seem to have been support for Buchanan from the Philadelphia delegates in return

[1] *Works*, vol. viii, pp. 370-6.

[2] Brodhead to Forney, Jan. 20, 1851. Buchanan to Brodhead, Feb. 3, 1851, H. A. Wise to Buchanan, Mar. 3, 1852, Buchanan MSS.

for Campbell's nomination to one of the state supreme court justiceships to be filled that fall (1851).[1] As an additional precautionary measure Buchanan went up to Harrisburg and arranged a reconciliation and alliance with ex-governor David R. Porter, who had worked with Cameron in 1848.[2] Besides he suggested to Harriet Lane that while on a visit to Pittsburg she try to show attention to one David Lynch and his wife. Lynch was a powerful and clever political worker who stood low in the social scale because of poverty.[3] Everything was being done to fortify the lines for the first conflict.

The first trials of strength were to be at Reading, June 4, when the state convention met to choose candidates for governor and most of the state officers, and at Harrisburg, June 11, where a similar meeting was held to nominate the state judicial ticket. Cameron, who had had a conference with Cass in New York City in December, 1851, was waging an active campaign in the local conventions where delegates were to be chosen for Reading and Harrisburg. His tactics were to introduce unexpectedly into strong Buchanan conventions resolutions endorsing Cass. Buchanan's friends were unprepared for this, and besides did not want to come into open conflict with Cass so early in the game. Consequently the resolutions often passed and spread abroad the conviction that Buchanan was weak.[4] In spite of all, Bu-

[1] Robert Tyler to Buchanan, Jan. 7, 1851, J. B. Baker to Buchanan, Jan. 29, 1851, Buchanan MSS.; W. B. Pettit to Welles, Nov. 3, 1851, Gideon Welles MSS.; *N. Y. Herald*, Nov. 8, 1851.

[2] Cameron to Reah Frazer, Mar. 19, 1851, *Pa. Mag. of Hist.*, vol. xxxix, p. 495; Mueller, H. R., *Whig Party in Pa.*, p. 143.

[3] Buchanan to Harriet Lane, Nov. 4, 1851, *Works*, vol. viii, p. 422. James May to Buchanan, Mar. 5, 1851, Buchanan MSS.

[4] A. Gilmore to Buchanan, Sept. 9, 1850 and Dec. 24, 1850. Robert Tyler to Buchanan, Sept. 13, 1850, Buchanan to C. Johnson, Mar. 22, 1851, Buchanan to C. B. Colter, May 1, 1851, Buchanan MSS.

chanan's friends controlled both conventions and nominated William Bigler for governor and Campbell for one of the places on the supreme bench. The latter nomination called forth a great deal of protest. Campbell was denounced as a common ward politician with absolutely no qualifications for the judicial office other than his ability to swing the Irish vote of Philadelphia. Buchanan was denounced for entering into a bargain.[1] Campbell, however, was a man of respectable if not spectacular attainment, and later served acceptably as Postmaster General; Buchanan knew little of the matter; Forney and Tyler, as usual, were the principals in the arrangement. So far difficulties had been overcome.

The situation was now complicated by a third participant in the lists. Some politicians desiring a Pennsylvanian for President, but one more flexible than Buchanan, brought out former Vice-President Dallas. They circulated a letter of his stating that the Compromise measures were a failure and that the Constitution should be amended to settle the difficulty. Opponents of Buchanan seem to have used Cass and Dallas interchangeably, as one waned in popularity the other was taken up.[2] This, however, added to the impression that Buchanan had not the united support of Pennsylvania, especially as Senator Brodhead was franking broadcast in the south copies of the *Keystone* containing accounts of all anti-Buchanan activities.[3]

Furthermore Colonel Reah Frazer, Buchanan's fellow townsman, stirred up a revolt, as the Buchanan men said, of free soilers and barnburners, for the disruption of the De-

[1] Mueller, *op. cit.*, pp. 180-1. W. V. Pettit to Welles, Nov. 3, 1851, Welles MSS.

[2] McClure, *op. cit.*, p. 104; *Newark Daily Advertiser*, Oct. 17, 1851 (Letter of July 25. 1851); *Life of Horace Mann* by his wife, p. 354.

[3] *Daily Pennsylvanian*, Aug. 30, 1851.

mocratic party. In August and September these held mass meetings at Lancaster, Buchanan's home town, and declared for Cass. This got abroad and the press reported that Buchanan's own county had instructed its delegates to the Baltimore Convention for Cass. The report was not true, as the delegates were not to be chosen until the next spring; but Cass' organ, the *Detroit Free Press,* took it up and accused Buchanan of being opposed to the Compromise because he had endorsed only the Fugitive Slave Act. This Forney in the *Pennsylvanian* countered by declaring that Buchanan was for the Compromise but that neither Cass, Douglas, or Dickinson had voted for the Fugitive Slave Law. This controversy widened the breach between the supporters of Cass and Buchanan.[1]

Pennsylvania political activity closed for the year with the success on October 14, of the entire Democratic state ticket with the exception of Campbell; he was defeated by anti-Catholic reaction, the popularity of his opponent, and the "decent element".[2] As matters stood Buchanan's supporters were in comfortable control, but he had bitter enemies at home and at Washington who lost no opportunities to represent him as much weaker than he really was. Consequently Buchanan was willing to take no chances and kept up his letter-writing. His conception of political methods is well illustrated by one of the many letters he wrote at this time:

[1] *Daily Pennsylvanian,* Aug. 18, Sept. 4, 1851; Morristown (N. J.), *True Democratic Banner,* Sept. 3, 1851; *Newark Morning Eagle,* Sept. 11, 1851; *N. Y. Herald,* Sept. 11, 1851; Eames to Marcy, Sept. 14, 1851, Marcy MSS.

[2] Mueller, *op cit.,* pp. 190-2; *Works,* vol. viii, p. 430, Buchanan to Cave Johnson, Dec. 22, 1851.

Private and Confidential

WHEATLAND, NEAR LANCASTER, 12 DEC., 1851.

My dear Sir: A friend from Cumberland County, who has recently been in Perry, expresses much doubt about your county and says that unless strong efforts shall be made, it will go for Cass. I understand you elect by county meeting; and this mode is not a fair method of ascertaining public opinion throughout a larger county. What can be done? My enemies perceiving that my prospects are daily becoming brighter and brighter throughout the Union are now intent upon producing such an appearance of division at home as they imagine may deter other States from voting for my nomination. In this point of view it is important I should carry Perry, if this can be done by fair and honorable means. Cass, their apparent but not their real candidate, can now make no show; but they will go for any candidate against myself. Pennsylvania has now for the first time in her history an opportunity of furnishing the candidate, should she think proper to exert her power with a reasonable degree of unanimity. I intend to write to my friends Black and Steward; but my main reliance is on yourself. General Fetter and Judge Junkin were formerly my warm friends—whether they are so now or not I do not know. Are A. B. Anderson and young McIntire my friends? I think you once told me they were. I am informed that young Miller is my bitter foe.

Could you make a trip over the county and ascertain the state of public opinion? I should esteem it a very great favor if you would; and in that event, I should insist that you shall not spend your own money in supporting me. This would be both unreasonable and unjust. If you could pass a few days in this manner, you would confer a favor upon me which I trust I may some day be able to repay. But you must not go at all unless at my expense. Your services will place me under obligation which I shall never forget without expending your own money for my benefit.

If you should ascertain that the county is against me and

cannot be carried, as the Perry *Democrat* indicates, then it would be useless to make the effort. If it can be carried, then we must go to work and have the proper concert of action to bring my friends to the county meeting.

Will you let me hear from you soon on this subject, and believe me ever to be sincerely and gratefully your friend.

JAMES BUCHANAN.

Hon. George Blattenberger.

P. S. Jos. Bailey, who is a strange, capricious man, is now against me, though in 1843 he was one of my warmest friends and supporters, as you will perceive by the address which I send you. What have I done since? [1]

Besides his own state, Buchanan felt reasonably certain of the important cotton states. Slidell and Cave Johnson sent favorable reports, and various newspapers, including the Savannah *Georgian* and Yancey's organ, the Montgomery *Advertiser,* hoisted his name. [2] But this was not enough. With the west and middle west pretty sure to go to either Cass or Douglas, Buchanan must gain support in Virginia, the border, middle and New England states. Slidell recognized this necessity early and through his business connections in New York City and his relative, August Belmont, he set about campaigning to push Buchanan.

Slidell was accustomed to spend his summers at Saratoga Springs, N. Y. Here in 1850 he met many politicians. In discussing candidates he found that Buchanan was objectionable to no one in spite of the numbers of Cass supporters. [3] He later met the Pennsylvanian in New York City during October and plans were discussed for establishing a paper friendly to their interest in the metropolis. The

[1] McClure, *Our Presidents and How We Make Them*, p. 151.

[2] G. P. Hamilton to Buchanan, May 13, 1851, Buchanan MSS.

[3] Slidell to Buchanan, August 6 and Oct. 9, 1850, Buchanan MSS.

venture was to be placed in charge of John W. Forney.[1] Nothing was then accomplished. The next summer (1851) Slidell was again in New York and soon urged Buchanan to leave Wheatland and travel about, especially in the west. He was very earnest in his request that he come to that summer center of politicians, Saratoga. Here he could meet Marcy and perhaps gain his interest. Buchanan remained at Wheatland. Nothing daunted, Slidell worked with Marcy himself and became convinced that he had accomplished something. Then he again took up the project of a New York paper and enlisted Belmont's aid. The banker solicited funds from the merchants of the city and himself contributed $10,000, while Slidell concerned himself with the editorial management of the paper. He considered first Caleb Cushing of Massachusetts, and then settled on Theodore Sedgwick. He again urged Buchanan to come to New York at which place Buchanan arranged to meet Marcy on October 21. On that occasion he found Marcy jovial and non-committal, but could get no satisfaction out of him. Shortly thereafter Sedgwick had an interview with Marcy and declined the editorship. Arrangements were then concluded with Forney to undertake it, but after a visit of Marcy to New York in November and a series of conferences held there the wind changed. Francis B. Cutting and Charles O'Conor declined to support the project unless it

[1] Buchanan to Harriet Lane, *Works*, vol. viii, p. 389. Forney was a product of the Pennsylvania machine, an energetic and resourceful though none too scrupulous political manipulator and editor, who formed warm attachments and exhibited hearty loyalty (generally to some one who could advance him) but when slighted became most wickedly vindictive. He was at this time an ardent and important supporter of Buchanan. The latter had used his influence in vain to get him elected clerk of the House for the Thirty-first Congress but failed. He was now going to undertake it for the Thirty-second. Buchanan to Corcoran, Nov. 26, 1849, Corcoran MSS.

was entirely neutral on the presidency. This, of course, was contrary to the promoters' plans, and again the matter was dropped. Buchanan and Slidell put the blame on Marcy's presidential ambitions, but the truth of the matter was that as no prominent New Yorkers except Belmont favored Buchanan they would not aid a paper supporting him.[1] On December 27 Slidell wrote: "I fear that the favorable moment for action in New York has been irretrievably lost." Marcy was now definitely a candidate and his struggle with the Dickinson and Cass men left no room for Buchanan in New York.[2]

In Virginia, too, Buchanan's interest was early pursued. His most active supporter in the "old Dominion" was John A. Parker, an editorial writer for the Ritchies who had a wide acquaintance among Virginians. He set about to influence Henry A. Wise, then favorable to Stockton, toward Buchanan. Wise and Parker were opposed to "Father" Ritchie and his efforts on behalf of Cass and also opposed to the extreme states-rights group or the "Chivalry" led by James A. Seddon, Lewis E. Harvie, T. S. Bocock and John B. Floyd. In the past Wise had been a Tyler Whig and more or less of a free lance. In order to keep down the opposing factions and strengthen his own pretensions of

[1] Slidell to Buchanan, 8 Aug., 5 Sept., 29 Sept., 10 Oct., 17 Nov., 27 Dec., 1851. Marcy to Buchanan, 6 Oct., 16 Nov., 24 Nov., Belmont to Buchanan, 6 Dec., Buchanan MSS.; Buchanan to Cave Johnson, 22 Dec., 1851, *Works*, vol. viii, p. 428; Buchanan to Marcy, 30 Sept., 8 Oct., 10 Oct., 1851, Marcy to Campbell, 10 Nov., 1851, Thomas to Marcy, 27 Oct., 1851, Marcy MSS.; Sears, L. M., "Buchanan and Slidell", *Amer. Hist. Rev., loc. cit.*

[2] Belmont was not discouraged. He kept at work and succeeded in forming a "General Buchanan New York Committee", and also he got control of a "small but widely circulated morning paper", the *Morning Star*. This began to quietly boom Buchanan, April 12, 1852. These efforts had little effect other than to put Buchanan under obligations to Belmont. Belmont to Buchanan, April 5, 1852, Buchanan MSS.

leadership, a meeting was called to answer a union meeting in Pennsylvania and to take from the Whigs their claim of being the real union party. This meeting of Richmond delegates held two sessions, February 13 and 19. Here Wise attempted to secure the passage of resolutions inviting other states, especially Pennsylvania to join Virginia and suggesting plans for the reorganization of the Democratic party on the basis of the union and the rights of the states. These were passed, but reference to Pennsylvania was stricken out. This effort was the result of Wise's conviction that there should be an alliance between Virginia and Pennsylvania—that without a northern state Virginia could accomplish no national project. New York was Whig, therefore Pennsylvania was the logical ally. In reporting this meeting to Buchanan Wise declared himself willing to back Buchanan, Dallas, or Stockton for the Democratic nomination, whichever could obtain the united support of Pennsylvania. Thereupon he began to write often to Buchanan and advise him. He repeatedly urged him to come to Virginia, and was joined in his solicitation by William R. King. The candidate, however, disliked locomotion and went no nearer Richmond than Washington. He did, however, write a public letter to the Central Southern Rights Association of Virginia in response to an invitation to visit them. In this message he gave a careful endorsement to the Virginia Resolutions of '98, which is reported as having been "highly elating" to southern rights editors.

The June conventions were the turning points with Wise; they demonstrated Buchanan's control of his state and the Virginian was now openly for him. He set about to organize Virginia sentiment for Pennsylvania's favorite son. Perhaps more important for Buchanan's purposes was the favor with which his name was received by the older conservative democrats (except "Father" Ritchie) who looked upon John Y. Mason and men of his type as leaders. Buchanan opened a cordial correspondence with his erstwhile colleague in that famous Polk cabinet and learned with pleasure of the good will of the old conservatives. Because of their friendship he was bitterly opposed by the secessionists and younger Democrats and the contest for the control of Virginia's delegation promised to be warm.[1]

Efforts were not lacking in New England. Here Woodbury's death seemed to make a favorable opening and Congressman Gilmore of Pennsylvania got in touch with New England politicians such as Hubbard and Bradbury of Maine and Hibbard and Peaslee of New Hampshire. He followed this up by a trip down east in the spring. Then Buchanan had the active aid of Isaac Toucey of Connecticut, a former cabinet colleague, while still another of the Polk cabinet, Clifford, was favorable to him in Maine. A few delegates might be picked up there.[2]

The meeting of Congress at the close of the year brought consolation; for Forney was elected clerk of the House, and another supporter, Adam J. Glossbrenner Sergeant-at-arms. Also the refusal of the Democratic Congress to endorse the Compromise was taken as favorable to Buchanan, and had been accomplished partly by the effort of his friends. Soon the conventions for the choice of delegates would give more accurate indications of his prospects.[3]

January 8, the anniversary of the Battle of New Orleans,

[1] *Hunter Corr.*, pp. 124-142; Parker to Buchanan, Jan. 16, Mar. 28, Apr. 18, July 20, 30, Aug. 29, 1851; Wise to Buchanan, Feb. 20, Mar. 11, Apr. 20, June 8, July 8, 1851; King to Buchanan, March 13, 1851, Buchanan MSS.

[2] Gilmore to Buchanan, Sept. 22, 1851, Toucey to Buchanan, Nov. 13, 1851, Buchanan MSS.; Clifford, *Nathan Clifford-Democrat*, pp. 254-261.

[3] Buchanan to Marcy, Nov. 10, Dec. 3, 1851, Marcy MSS.; R. Tyler to Buchanan, Nov. 30, 1851, Buchanan MSS.

was a popular date for Democratic State Conventions. On this day in 1852 Tennessee, Mississippi, Ohio, and Kentucky were to hold meetings of the Democracy for the choice of delegates to the National Convention. In the last two Buchanan had no chance, but from the others he expected delegates.

In Tennessee he had the help of Cave Johnson, while he encountered the active opposition of a group of Douglas men largely stimulated by the desire of Gideon J. Pillow to become Vice-President. To head off this movement Johnson and his friends brought out Governor Trousdale for a Vice-Presidential endorsement, hoping thus by the governor's popularity to defeat Pillow and choose a delegation for Buchanan. After a struggle, however, a compromise had to be arranged, no instructions were given, Trousdale and Pillow were both recommended as worthy of the Vice-Presidency. Of the delegates chosen six were for Buchanan, six against him.[1]

In Mississippi, as noted above,[2] the Democracy had suffered a split in its ranks over the Compromise question. Now each of the factions claimed to be the true party. The minority or Union Democrats, followers of Foote, held a convention January 5, and chose a delegation anticipating the action of the Southern Rights or majority party, who were going to meet on the 8th.[3] To this latter group Buchanan pinned his hopes. On the advice of a friend, the editor of the *Mississippian,* he had written a letter which was circulated among the delegates; therein he set forth his belief in the Virginia and Kentucky Resolutions, in strict construction, and in the absolute authority of each state to

[1] *Washington Union,* Jan. 11, 1852; Balch to Donelson, Dec. 28, 1851, Donelson MSS.

[2] *v. supra,* p. 25.

[3] *Washington Union,* Jan. 20, 1852.

govern its own affairs including slavery; and he declared strongly against centralization of power in the federal government [1]—an announcement which was very satisfactory to the latter group. A delegation was chosen which, though uninstructed, was favorable to Buchanan.[2]

Alabama was next in line, and here there were more groupings than in Mississippi. The dominant faction had as opponents an ultra-states-rights wing under Yancey, which claimed to yield allegiance to no party, and a unionist group led by Senator Jeremiah L. Clemens. The unionists declined to participate in either Whig or Democratic Conventions and called a union gathering to meet in Washington on the second Monday in June. The states rights group which met on March 4 also declined to participate in a national convention, but decided to put off final action till after the two conventions met. The large majority of the Democrats, however, were believers in southern rights, and the abstract right of secession, but, although convinced the Compromise of 1850 was wrong, acquiesced in it. These looked up to Senator King as their leader, and in their convention nominated him for the Presidency—because of King's friendship for him this course meant votes for Buchanan.[3]

During this period Buchanan had had a group working for him in Maryland. They accomplished little but they gave Buchanan an opportunity to write a letter. In response to an invitation "to partake of a public dinner" he declared at last that the Compromise was a "finality".

[1] *Works*, vol. viii, p. 431.

[2] These conflicting delegations made an agreement among themselves prior to the convention and supported Buchanan. *V. Proceedings of the Baltimore Convention of 1852* (Hincks), p. 32.

[3] *N. Y. Herald*, Dec. 16, 1851, Jan. 19, 1852; *Washington Union*, Jan. 31, 1852.

This pleased union Democrats and was to have some good effect in the national convention.[1] Now the Pennsylvania and Virginia conventions loomed up.

Cameron, Frazer, Barrett, Senator Brodhead, the *Keystone* and the *Lancasterian,* friends of Cass and friends of Dallas had been moving heaven and earth to bring about Buchanan's defeat at home. Their efforts, however, were not proving fruitful. Buchanan's friends had staged a large rally in Lancaster in January to show the spurious character of the much heralded Cass meeting of September. The proceedings of this meeting were spread abroad to counteract the impression made by the former. Old and stale charges which had been brought up against him were answered. At Washington friends were at work repelling the insinuations of Broadhead and Congressman Dawson. When the convention met, March 4, Buchanan was endorsed and his delegation chosen. His enemies, however, would not be downed, and thirty-three of the one hundred and thirty-two delegates signed a protest against Buchanan's nomination. Nevertheless the convention was heralded as a Buchanan triumph and was expected to aid him in the coming Virginia meeting.[2]

But before this took place misfortune befell. News came that California had gone against Buchanan;[3] Maryland failed in spite of Gilmore's efforts,[4] but worse still Louisiana endorsed Cass. With the backing of Slidell Buchanan had felt confident of this state. The unforseen had happened.

[1] *Works,* vol. viii, p. 434; L. K. Bowen to Buchanan, Dec. 18, 1851, Buchanan MSS.

[2] McClure, *op. cit.,* vol. i, p. 104. *Washington Union,* Mar. 9, 1852; *New York Herald,* Mar. 7, 1852; King to Buchanan, Mar. 6, 1852, Buchanan MSS.; Angel to Marcy, Mar. 11, 1852, Marcy MSS.; *Works,* vol. viii, pp. 442-446.

[3] James Blair to F. P. Blair, Jr., Mar. 1, 1852, Van Buren MSS.

[4] Alfred Gilmore to Buchanan, Mar. 13, 1852, Buchanan MSS.

To defeat Soulé, Slidell had been compelled to join with the Cass forces, feeling that while Cass men might turn to Buchanan, Soulé's Douglas men never would.[1] He had made the best of a bad bargain.

Virginia yet remained. Buchanan felt that his chances hinged on her. "With Virginia in my favor I shall be nominated, if against me the result is extremely doubtful." [2] Here the work had been going on steadily. The chief obstacle encountered was the hostility of the younger extremists who laid claim to Senator Hunter, then thought to have longing eyes turned toward the Vice-Presidency on a ticket with Douglas. To attract that gaze in another direction the Wise group threw their support to Hunter and insured his re-election to the Senate. This was alleged to have satisfied Hunter and quieted the activity of his friends for Douglas. Just at this time Buchanan was finally induced to come to Richmond. John Y. Mason had invited him to make a visit, Senator King had urged him to come to Washington for conference, and finally Gilmore had reported that certain Virginians, such as Bocock, were afraid that Pennsylvania was not unitedly behind Buchanan. All these considerations moved him, and he arrived in Richmond on February 11. Here, and a few days later in Washington, he devoted his time to political conference. Later, as the time for the Virginia convention was drawing on, it appeared that ex-Governor Porter of Pennsylvania happened to be going to Virginia, so Buchanan wrote Wise apprising him of this fact and hinting that Porter might be useful in giving "accurate and reliable information on the subject of [his] strength at home and the reckless and

[1] King to Buchanan, Mar. 24, 1852, Slidell to Penn, Mar. 11, 1852, Buchanan MSS.; *Washington Union*, Mar. 11, 1852.

[2] *Works*, vol. viii, p. 441.

disorganizing character of the opposition". In addition he provided Wise with material to refute charges.[1]

The impulsive, hot-headed, bombastic, ill-balanced Wise went on with his work with headlong energy, emphatically demanding that Virginia openly endorse Buchanan. Here, however, precedent was against him. Virginia never instructed her delegates. Wise only hindered his own cause by his overabundant enthusiasm. No instructions were given though the Buchanan supporters were in the majority. Nevertheless J. Y. Mason could write, "I think the vote of the state in the Baltimore Convention may be relied on for your man." Also papers such as the *Baltimore Sun, Washington Union,* and the *National Democrat* declared the same. John A. Parker, David R. Porter, and David Lynch, all trusted lieutenants, gave Buchanan similar assurances on the authority of John S. Barbour, president of the Convention, though King regretted that Wise had pushed the matter against precedent fearing that it had reacted to Buchanan's disadvantage. This wide publishing of the opinion that Virginia was for Buchanan alarmed his opponents, and in a few days Barbour publicly denied in the columns of the *Union* that he had said the Virginia Convention was for Buchanan.[2]

[1] Wise to Parker, Oct. 24, 1851, Parker to Buchanan, Dec. 26, 1851, Jan. 22, 1852, Gilmore to Buchanan, Jan. 25, 1852, Wise to Buchanan, Mar. 3, 1852, Penn to Buchanan, Mar. 20, 1852, King to Buchanan, Jan. 16 and Mar. 24, 1852, D. H. Loudon to Buchanan, Mar. 26, 1852, John Y. Mason to Buchanan, Mar. 30, 1852, Buchanan MSS., *Works*, vol. viii, pp. 436-446.

[2] Parker to Buchanan, Mar. 31 and Apr. 1, 1852, Porter to Buchanan, Mar. 31, 1852, Lynch to Porter, Mar. 26, 1852, King to Buchanan, Mar. 31, 1852, Buchanan MSS. Parker suggested that as Barbour was seeking the support of Douglas for a bill involving $100,000 or $200,000, this might have influenced his change. It was also reported that Barbour had been approached when drunk and induced to sign this denial.

The assurances from Virginia and the favorable report of Gilmore from New England [1] were counterweighted by New Jersey's action.

In New Jersey Commodore Stockton was largely interested in the joint monopoly of the Delaware and Raritan Canal and the Camden and Amboy Railroad, which largely dominated the state—he was for Buchanan although desirous of the nomination in the event of none of the prominent candidates being successful. Consequently his men desired to nominate a delegation of friends of Stockton who were also friendly to Buchanan. These plans aroused Cass' supporters and those opposed to the power of the monopoly, and the result was that they gained control of the convention and sent an uninstructed delegation to Baltimore to support Cass. This was a blow that almost made the faithful despair.[2]

Meanwhile Parker and Lynch acted as a self-appointed committee at Washington and dug out of the files of the *Union* a sheaf of references to prove that Buchanan was the first northern Democrat to make war on the Wilmot Proviso.[3] Last-minute advice came, the tenor of which was that everything should be done to conciliate rivals. No personal animosity must prevent possible transfers of votes in case any of the candidates might become hopeless.[4] Also he was complimented on his female support and even advised

[1] Gilmore to Buchanan, April 15, 1852, Buchanan MSS.

[2] *Works*, vol. viii, p. 451; Rutan to J. C. Breckinridge, May 26, 1852, Breckinridge MSS.; *Washington Union*, May 7 and 12, 1852; *New York Herald*, May 9, 1852; *Newark Morning Eagle*, May 8, 1852; *Morristown True Democratic Banner*, May 5, 12, 1852; John R. Thomson to Buchanan, May 1, 1852, Buchanan MSS.

[3] Parker to Buchanan, May 5, 1852, Buchanan MSS.

[4] John H. Houston to Buchanan, May 4, 1852; King to Buchanan, May 13, 1852, *ibid.*

to marry Mrs. Polk as she was familiar with the White House.[1]

As May wore on delegates began to arrive in Washington and a group of better-known men became a nucleus for Buchanan work—Cave Johnson, Isaac Toucey, William R. King, Congressman Penn (Slidell's lieutenant), Appleton of Maine, and others. After deliberation they advised Buchanan not to come to Washington, declaring it was no place for a high-minded man. To them Buchanan submitted the question as to whether he should answer the Scott letter,[2] following their advice to do so. While thus engaged Gilmore wrote that the whole affair was a fraud. To make sure, Buchanan communicated with Mason, who telegraphed a reply that the letter was bona fide. Thus assured, Buchanan sent two replies to his Washington friends — one more explicit than the other. Acting upon their advice once more he sent the more explicit, answering yes to all the questions.

This group was also busy with last-minute activities. Unpledged delegates were arriving in Washington who might be won. Douglas was plead with, as he was urging his claims, to wait four years when Pennsylvania would aid him. Also there were hints of defection in the Pennsylvania delegation itself. Some wanted to bring out Dallas —Van Dyke reported he was offered any office if he would go for Dallas after Buchanan was through. Congressman Dawson was attacking Buchanan. He was accused of not being right on the tariff. Cameron's aids offered to wager $10,000 that Buchanan could not carry Pennsylvania. Buchanan's friends hastened to cover the bet but Cameron money was not forthcoming. In spite of this, the story circulated soon after from Cameron sources that Buchanan

[1] Johnson to Buchanan, May 6, 1852, *ibid.*

[2] *v.* p. 46, n. 7.

men had refused to take the wager. Thus there was this continual sniping and wire-pulling until the delegates left Washington for Baltimore, and then the scene only shifted.[1]

Thus the Buchanan forces went to the convention with the open endorsement of Pennsylvania and the implied support of the "Old Dominion", Alabama, Mississippi, North Carolina, and Arkansas. In other words, Virginia with an important nucleus of states rights delegations was in alliance with Pennsylvania. Would this combination be strong enough?

Meanwhile at Wheatland near Lancaster Buchanan expectantly waited. He had done what he thought befitting his dignity to gain the prize, his lieutenants had worked hard. What was to be the result?

[1] Toucey to Buchanan, May 16, 1852; King to Buchanan, May 17, 1852; Penn to Buchanan, May 22, 1852; Gilmore to Buchanan, May 23, 1852; King to Buchanan, May 24, 1852; Porter to Buchanan, May 24, 1852; Van Dyke to Buchanan, May 24, 1852; Mason to Buchanan, May 26, 1852; Cave Johnson to Buchanan, May 29, 1852; Gilmore to Buchanan, May 29, 1852; Van Dyke to Buchanan, May 30, 1852; Buchanan MSS.

CHAPTER V

Jackson's Heir

When Jackson died his mantle descended upon Martin Van Buren, Thomas Hart Benton, his chosen successors, and Francis P. Blair, Sr., his editor. But new leaders had arisen and Robert J. Walker and John C. Calhoun had dragged that mantle in the dust. To the old leaders, Van Buren, Benton and Blair, there still remained loyal a remnant who sighed for other days and other times and remembered the years of power. They styled themselves the "True Jacksonian Democracy"; the others, to adopt Benton's vivid phraseology were the "rottens". The hope of regaining control had never died out and while 1852 was yet afar off Jackson's heirs were making plans.[1]

In January, 1851, prospects were not bright. Benton was defeated for reelection to the Senate and the old Jackson influence had almost disappeared from Congress. But one way seemed open. The national party convention had proved disastrous to this group; it had defeated Van Buren in 1844. Consequently to the little Jacksonian coterie in Washington, Francis P. Blair, Sr. and Congressmen Preston King of New York and David Wilmot of Pennsylvania, it seemed that Benton should announce his independent candidacy immediately without endorsement by a party convention, going back to the old days when candidates were nominated "whenever two or three . . . . could be gathered together in Legislative Halls, in towns or at crossroads or

[1] I. O. Barnes to B. F. Butler, 12 Mar., 1851, Butler MSS.

wherever the spirit moved." He was to announce himself as the champion of the old order of "retrenchment, reform, judicial pacification, unsparing denunciation of the doctrine of secession and all doubters about the union." The point of this action would be to make "the politicians see that those who were sick of the corrupt intriguing selfish sort of government set up over the people by rogues (whose trade is buying and selling all that belonged to the people) were in earnest in the purpose of choosing some man for President who would put down with a strong hand and begin a new Jackson Era." This they thought would give Benton such prestige before the people that the Democratic leaders would be compelled to take him or be defeated by his bolt.

Blair got the consent of Martin Van Buren, but the active and practical politician of the family in those years, John Van Buren, saw immediately that Benton because of his personality and his neutral views in regard to slavery would not be eligible for the support of the New York barnburners. Blair, however, acted upon Martin Van Buren's approval, and about February 1, 1851, approached Benton on the subject. Benton immediately declined. He had his memoirs to write and also was going to get back into Congress; besides he had another candidate.

The Democracy in New England had not, for many years, been in a flourishing condition. Of the six states in that section Massachusetts and Vermont had never cast an electoral vote for a Democrat, and in the last three campaigns Rhode Island and Connecticut had been carried by the Whigs. Maine had redeemed herself from her Whig enthusiasm of 1840 by votes for Polk and Cass in 1844 and 1848, but only New Hampshire had remained steadily faithful. This faithfulness had given the Granite State much weight in the national councils. Her leading son was Justice Levi Woodbury of the United States Supreme Court, ex-United States Senator, ex-Secretary of the Treasury under Jackson and Van Buren, firm Jackson supporter with no bias for or against slavery. He represented the presidential hopes of a group of New England politicians desirous of increasing the influence of the section in the party. The nucleus of this group was found in New Hampshire, Massachusetts and Maine. In New Hampshire the so-called " Concord Cabal ", a group of railway lawyers, Charles G. Atherton, Charles H. Peaslee and Franklin Pierce were Woodbury's backers. In Massachusetts he was supported by his brother-in-law, Isaac O. Barnes, ex-marshal, and his nephew, Charles Levi Woodbury; these were allied with certain politicians such as Caleb Cushing and Benjamin F. Butler of Massachusetts, who were at war with Cass' supporters, Hallett and Greene. Hannibal Hamlin, United States Senator from Maine, had the following of a large proportion of the Democrats of that state in his conflict with hunkers or " wildcats "; the Hamlin men, often called free-soilers, were desirous of nominating Woodbury.

At the time when Benton needed a name to use in his fight against his enemies in Missouri, the Woodbury movement was becoming apparent. Benton did not have the highest regard for Woodbury but after communication with Senator Hamlin he decided to support the judge. Benton's friends, the Van Burens and Blairs, were not very favorable to his choice. John Van Buren openly balked at aiding Woodbury and Blair neither liked nor trusted him. But in spite of their dislike Benton and Blair accepted him because he was the candidate most obnoxious to Cass, Buchanan and Marcy, and because he was " available ". He had been on the bench for the last six years, consequently he had been out of political controversy. He had never antagonized the south, in fact he had received a majority of the votes of

Georgia and Alabama in the convention of 1848. Above all, he had been one of the Jackson régime.[1]

At Benton's solicitation, Woodbury gave him his consent to manage his campaign in the south and west. "Old Bullion" began writing editorials in favor of the judge and contemplated establishing a paper in Washington. The New England manoeuvers were started by the New Hampshire Democracy. They formally placed him in nomination at their convention June 11, 1851. During the summer the project gained some momentum and then September 4, Judge Woodbury died.[2]

His supporters were at sea. Who would take his place? Talk of Benton was again revived[3] but another figure was coming to the fore. Samuel Houston had long enjoyed the glamour of a picturesque career. He had occasionally been mentioned as a presidential possibility and now his friends began to hope that he might receive the Woodbury support. He was popular in New England; Hamlin favored him and his organ, the *Augusta Age,* began to puff him. In Connecticut Gideon Welles was favorable to him. Those who were inclined toward free soil doctrines felt that they could depend on him more than upon any other southerner. For lovers of the Union he was conspicuous as being the only Senator to vote for all of the Compromise measures. John A. Dix wrote almost immediately after Woodbury's death to Blair, suggesting that he talk with Benton about pushing

[1] F. P. Blair, Sr. to Martin Van Buren, Dec. 30, 1850 and Jan. 26, 1851; Preston King to John Van Buren, Feb. 6 and 25, 1851; John Van Buren to Martin Van Buren, Mar. 4, 1851; F. P. Blair, Sr. to John Van Buren, Mar. 24, 1851; Van Buren MSS. Bigelow, *Retrospections of an Active Life*, vol. i, p. 112.

[2] Blair to Van Buren, June 17, 1851, Van Buren MSS.; Hamlin, *Life of Hamlin*, pp. 250-6; *New Hampshire Patriot*, June 19, September 10, 1851.

[3] Welles to John M. Niles, Sept. 9, 1851, Welles MSS.

Houston. Blair really had favored Houston more than Woodbury and was nothing loath. But Benton vetoed the scheme. Houston's past was against him; he had deserted his wife and fled to Texas. His residence in that slave locality would enable the Whigs to draw away northern Democrats.[1] Besides these, other difficulties were in the way.

On August 22, 1851, there had appeared in the *New York Herald* a group of letters known as the Greer correspondence. A writer purporting to be C. H. Donaldson, a member of the National Committee from Texas, and N. C. Greer of Iowa sent letters to various prominent Democrats of all branches including Giddings, Chase, Cobb, B. F. Hallett (Chairman of the National Committee) and many others asking for advice as to when to hold the national convention. Donaldson appeared to be in favor of Houston, and in a letter of his to Greer, which was in the lot, linked up Houston's name with prominent free soilers. The reason for this letter writing has never been found. Donaldson does not seem to have existed at all.[2] But mysterious as it was the affair injured Houston in so far as it made it appear that his friends were courting free soil support,[3] in spite of his denial of any connection with it. Houston's friends claimed a plot had been hatched to make it appear that Houston was trying to become President by means of a secret and disruptable bargain with the free soilers.

[1] Blair to Van Buren, Sept. 14, 1851, Van Buren MSS.

[2] While it is not known who was the author of the Donaldson letters, they actually were sent and replied to. One of them still exists and may be found in the *Toombs Corr.*, p. 244, where it is wrongly attributed to Andrew J. Donelson. The *Augusta Age* on Oct. 16, 1851, suggested the author might be ex-Senator Westcott of Florida, then an editor of the *Herald*.

[3] *N. Y. Herald*, Aug. 22, Aug. 30, Sept. 25, 28, Oct. 11, 13, 1851, Jan. 11, 1852, *Augusta* (Me.) *Age*, Sept. 18, Oct. 16, Nov. 6, 1851.

Not only was Houston tainted with free soil, but he was a temperance advocate. His various lectures on that subjuct delivered in different sections brought down the displeasure of those who felt that the Maine Law was not to be tolerated.[1] His prominent support gradually dwindled down to that of his colleague, Senator Thomas J. Rusk, who had published a letter in his behalf, and who further declared for him in answer to the Scott letters.[2] In spite of all, many, especially in New England, preferred Houston, but the superior availability of other candidates prevailed. Houston remained hopeful and occasionally even up to the time of the convention he was spoken of as a possibility, but for all intents and purposes he was out of it.

After Benton refused to take up Houston, Blair immediately suggested William O. Butler of Kentucky. This tall rugged old soldier, who resembled Jackson in appearance, had been a protegé of "Old Hickory". He had fought with distinction in the Mexican War and had been placed upon the Cass ticket in 1848 as its southern representative. Benton readily consented to support him. The dull, trusting and honest Kentuckian fitted the needs of these men. He lived in a slave state and owned a few slaves; this would suffice for the south. On the other hand, he came from a Pennsylvania family, many of whom had been soldiers; in regard to slavery he was known to be against its extension and in favor of gradual legal emancipation; these circumstances and opinions would make him acceptable in the north. For Blair and Benton, too, he had the added qualification of his hatred of the Polk-Walker régime which had treated him badly as a general, and had preferred Cass to him as a candidate in 1848. His great friendship

[1] *N. Y. Herald*, Feb. 2, 18 and 19, 1852.

[2] *Augusta Age*, June 5, 1852.

for "Old Hickory" also had its effect and, last but not least, Benton felt he could influence him. Obviously he was the man.[1] Thus within two weeks after Woodbury's death a candidate was in his place. Then began the drive to get support for him.

And never was there such a pair of managers. Thomas Hart Benton, as opinionated a man as ever lived, had an overwhelming sense of his own importance. He seemed to feel that the only necessary step was the announcement of the fact that Benton had chosen Butler for President and a worshipping populace would reverently approach the polls to say Amen. His co-worker, Francis Preston Blair, suffered from enthusiasms and violently loved and hated; since Jackson's death Van Buren was his patron saint and Thomas Ritchie his chief enemy. Possessed of a moderate fortune he peacefully farmed his broad acres at Silver Spring, occasionallly riding into Washington from Maryland to see his old partner Rives or to chat with old acquainstances at the Capitol. Politically he had been dead since 1845. He now was certain that all that was necessary was to bring forward Butler as the heir of Jackson and immediately all the enthusiasm of 1828 and 1832 would be unleashed and would sweep Butler into the White House as the apostle of a purified Democracy. But as practical John Van Buren said, "Benton and Blair are so inattentive to details and mix so little with men that I doubt if they can give [a candidate] ten votes in a national convention whereas they will certainly drive more than that from him." [2] Into the hands of the self-blinded Benton and the visionary Blair, Gen. Butler, honest, confiding—one is almost tempted to say

[1] Blair to Van Buren, Sept. 14, 1851; Van Buren MSS.; Bigelow to Chas. Sumner, Sept. 22, 1851, Sumner MSS.; Welles to John M. Niles, Oct. 12, 1851, Welles MSS.

[2] John Van Buren to Martin Van Buren, Mar. 4, 1851, Van Buren MSS.

simpleminded—commended his candidacy, rather awe-struck and conscience-stricken that his name should even be thought of before that of his former running mate, Cass. How far were the blind to lead the blind?

First of all, Blair, who knew Butler's simplicity and openness, got him to promise not to commit himself to anything or write any letters. Then Blair and Benton got in touch with Dix, hoping to rally the barnburners' strength. Here, however, they found that Marcy was dividing the friends of Van Buren. Most important of all was the endorsement of Butler's own state and Blair's efforts were put forth in that direction.

He conferred with the members of the Kentucky delegation in Congress among whom was his kinsman, John C. Breckinridge, and suggested that they write back to their friends in Kentucky to get Butler nominated at the coming state convention. This idea did not at first appeal to them, but after Blair had shown them a letter he was sending to Governor Powell they decided to work for Butler, and Breckinridge, at least, entered into correspondence with Kentucky lieutenants.[1]

Elsewhere Butler's candidacy began to grow in popularity. His character suited the needs of many who were, to say the least, derisive when Benton, Blair, or Van Buren were mentioned. His honesty and simplicty, his military fame and his freedom from the taint of politics made a popular appeal. Blair had encouraging reports from the west. Jesse D. Bright of Indiana assured him that Butler would have the vote of that state in the Convention. The support by the barnburners of Marcy, it was rumored, was only a blind to get delegates for Butler. In New England Benton and Hamlin were corresponding. The Bostonians who had

[1] Benton to Dix, Nov. 4, 1851; Blair to Van Buren, Nov. 24, 1851 and Jan. 2, 1852; Van Buren MSS.

planned to push Woodbury had had several meetings to consider whom they should put in his place, and had informally decided to take up Butler with Pierce for Vice-President to represent New England on the ticket. Plans were on foot to have him formally nominated by the New Hampshire state convention and by the Maine and Massachusetts legislative caucuses. New England seemed to be rallying to the standard.[1]

Butler's candidacy was becoming formidable and his stock was rising when on January 8, the Kentucky Democracy assembled in convention. Their favorite son had been the object of attacks and his opponents had been persistently calling him the free soil candidate and pointing to the Benton-Blair-Van Buren support as proof. His boom, it was charged, was the result of a plot hatched by Blair and Van Buren on a fishing trip on the St. Lawrence and consummated at a meeting between Blair and Butler on an Ohio steamboat.[2] These attacks annoyed the General, who was by no means an ardent candidate, and who did not feel quite right about seeking the place which Cass was being groomed for. Consequently when the Kentuckians friendly to Cass, who were in control of the party in the state, felt called upon by the popular clamor to endorse Butler they decided to tack Cass' principles to the endorsement. In this platform was a plank declaring that Congress had no power to prohibit a slave-holder from carrying his slaves into any territory of the United States. Butler felt it was but honorable to make known his deep convictions and thus rid

[1] Barnes to Breckinridge, Jan. 19, 1852, J. C. Breckinridge MSS.; Hamlin, *op. cit.*, pp. 250-6; Blair to Van Buren, Jan. 18, 1852, Van Buren MSS.

[2] There was just enough truth in these charges to make them plausible. Blair had visited Van Buren and had met Butler quite by accident on a trip west; these events had in reality little political significance. Blair to Van Buren, Nov. 24, 1851 and Feb. 18, 1852, Van Buren MSS.

himself of the odium of the free soil name. Therefore when the resolutions were submitted to him, before their adoption by the convention, he approved them—in spite of his promise to Blair to make no commitments. The publication of these resolutions struck consternation in the hearts of some of his northern friends; Bigelow of the *New York Evening Post* feared he had killed himself politically. His closer friends like Blair and Preston King were inclined to excuse it as a necessary concession to the south, feeling confident that the General would not do anything to permit slavery to spread. Some were sure that the resolutions had been passed without Butler's knowledge.[1] But the matter did not end here.

The Thirty-Second Congress became the scene of much political jockeying. The Democratic caucus had voted down a resolution endorsing the Compromise while the Whigs had adopted one. Consequently the latter party claimed, and on all possible occasions attempted to prove, that they were the only true Compromise party, and that the Democrats were controlled by an alliance of southern and northern radicals. The opening gun was fired on February 3, 1852, when Representative E. C. Cabell of Florida, a Whig, rose in the House while it was in committee of the whole on a bill for the "Assignability of Bounty Land Warrants". He took for his text a newspaper appeal to the Constitutional Union men of Georgia to send delegates to the National Democratic Convention. This appeal he ridiculed on the ground that the Democrats were the last ones who would satisfy the Georgians by endorsing the Com-

[1] Blair to Van Buren, Jan. 24, Feb. 18, Feb. 22 and Mar. 2, 1852, Van Buren MSS.; Bigelow to Sumner, Feb. 1, 1852, Sumner MSS.; Wm. Tanner, Dec. 11 and 27, 1851, Feb. 3, 1852, W. W. Stapp, Jan. 2, 1852, D. Meriweather, Jan. 24, 1852, W. O. Butler, Feb. 3, 1852, all to John Breckinridge, J. C. Breckinridge MSS.

promise; the Whig Convention surely would. He predicted that the Democratic Convention, like the House caucus, would vote down the Compromise, and, what was worse, would nominate "some such man as William O. Butler of Kentucky, a man whose opinions are not known, except that he has happened to own some slaves, and who will be sustained by Van Buren and Company as a southern man with northern sentiments, and by the Southern Rights men as one of themselves", in other words he would be a "mum candidate". Cabell also made some disparaging remarks as to Kentucky's fondness for this kind of a candidate, pointing to Butler's endorsement by the state convention.[1]

The situation made by this Whig attack, unpleasant as it was to Kentucky and her son, Butler, was made more unbearable by one even more bitter. Butler by refusing to support a fellow Kentuckian, Lewis Sanders, in a local election had made an enemy of him and his sons. One of these was George N. Sanders, a hot-headed, ill-balanced, vindictive man, a varitable stormy petrel in politics. He was determined to do all he could to injure Butler. Consequently in his capacity as editor of the *Democratic Review* he launched forth into a fiery denunciation of the candidate. For his February issue he wrote a vitriolic attack on Butler as a candidate of unknown principles who must be taken on trust; in this article he carried his venom to downright scurrilous insult.[2]

These attacks incensed patriotic Kentuckians, and John C. Breckinridge, who had received much urging from his friends, decided to reply. On March 3, 1852, when the House had resolved itself into a committee of the whole on the Homestead Bill he rose and answered the attack. In

[1] *Cong. Globe*, 32nd Cong., 1 Sess., p. 454.

[2] *Democratic Review*, vol. xxx, p. 182. James G. Leach to J. C. Breckinridge, Jan. 27, 1852, Breckinridge MSS.

the course of his reply he showed conclusively that Butler's opinions were known—pointed to his career in Congress during which he had voted for the "gag" resolution and against its repeal. He also read a letter to Blair from Butler in which the latter openly avowed that he had been consulted about the Kentucky resolutions beforehand, and that he firmly agreed with them. This open avowal of the General's concurrence in the Kentucky resolutions finished him in the eyes of free soil democrats and left no room for any lingering doubts as to his responsibility for these heresies.[1]

All the support which had been gathering melted away like snow in spring-time. The leaders, or rather the panicky followers of what they thought was public opinion, immediately took fright. True the Butler whom they were now deserting was the same Butler that they had been supporting, his late utterances gave voice to opinions which they had been well aware that he possessed. The unpardonable sin was that they had been published in black and white so that they could be quoted. For when these southern opinions were quoted those who because of principle or necessity were so placed that they could not oppose "free soil" doctrines, could not defend their candidate. Butler had violated one of the fundamental rules of 1852 and had expressed an honest opinion which might be used against him before a considerable body of voters, consequently he was now unavailable.

In this manner Butler was killed in the north and his supporters were without a standard-bearer. The Speaker of the House, Boyd of Kentucky, thought himself a fit successor, and one morning in March each member of Con-

[1] *Cong. Globe*, 32 Cong., 1 Sess., *Appendix*, pp. 299-302; F. P. Blair to J. C. Breckinridge, Feb. 6, 1852, P. R. George to J. C. Breckinridge, Mar. 23, 1852, J. C. Breckinridge MSS.

gress found Boyd's biography laid on his desk and his candidacy formally announced. However, this boom "died a-borning" and Boyd relapsed into his dull routine of presiding ponderously and stupidly over the House.[1] Blair yearned half-heartedly for Houston, but confessed himself through with president-making.[2] The New York support turned to Marcy and New England had plans of its own. Nevertheless the idea of Butler remained in the background and in spite of a letter of his withdrawing in favor of Case [3] the assembling of the Convention found him a potentiality still.

Meanwhile this lack of coherence among the northern leaders, the general feeling that the more prominent candidates could not succeed, the local conditions peculiar to New York State, these had all combined to bring forward another Democratic warhorse.

[1] Geo. N. Sanders to Breckinridge, undated, J. C. Breckinridge MSS.; *Washington Union*, Mar. 6, 1852.

[2] Blair to Van Buren, Feb. 24, 1852, Van Buren MSS.

[3] *New Orleans Weekly Delta*, June 13, 1852.

CHAPTER VI

THE STATESMAN OF THE DEMOCRACY

AGAIN must we speak of barnburners and hunkers, soft-shells and hard-shells, again must we delve into the intricacies of New York politics. It is repetition to say that the barnburners and hunkers were in a continual struggle for control of the New York Democracy. It has already been stated that the struggle had split the hunkers and that the soft-shell portion had formed an alliance with the barnburners against the hard-shells. But these facts must again be our text or no adequate understanding can be had of the events that so nearly made William L. Marcy President of the United States.

Soon after the reunion of 1849 the lines began to form for 1852. The hard-shells were determined that the barnburners must do penance for 1848 by swearing fealty to Cass. The barnburners were just as determined that they would have none of Cass. The soft-shells were his friends, how could they be wooed from his standard to support a leader favored by their allies. To Flagg and his barnburner associates occurred a scheme.[1] They would support a prominent soft-shell and appeal to the people of the state to back a New York candidate—this would win the softs, prove popular with the masses and relieve them of the dilemma of opposing Cass, for the favorite son by unwritten law had first claim to all local support. Who was to be this one? In Albany in retirement lived a man whose biography

[1] Flagg to Van Buren, Jan. 26, 1852, Van Buren MSS.

filled many pages, Governor, Senator, Judge, Comptroller, Secretary of War—in public life for thirty years, William L. Marcy was a man known to all. Shrewd, clear-headed, with a dry humor, philosophical temperament and well-developed political sense he was the most statesmanlike of the Democratic politicians. Untroubled by moral scruples as to the question of slavery he was ever ready to give the south her legal rights. A man whose first law was expediency, he had been willing to receive back the barnburners and forget the past. He was for party harmony at all times, for was he not the author of the phrase ' To the victor belongs the spoils ". To the eager barnburners he was the man.

Early in 1851 his name began to be mentioned and Marcy, who was in Washington, began to receive rumors of barnburner support. He was none too well pleased. He was growing old, the fires of politicial ambition were burning low. His books, his whist, an occasional journey to Washington were enough. He felt that his life had been lived. Besides he was a friend of Cass and he trusted none too well the Greeks bearing gifts. He saw through their motives and had no wish to be their tool.[1] The support of barnburners like John Van Buren he felt would damn him to begin with and he sensed that he was being tricked to use his influence and that of his friends to secure " a set of delegates who though ostensibly for [him could] be used in the national convention for ulterior purposes " by the barnburners.[2] To aid such a cause he would take no active steps. But forces were gathering momentum.

Innuendo was at work. Cass was shown to be hopeless; the party in the state needed the cementing force of a com-

[1] Marcy to Wetmore, Sept. 8, 1851, Marcy MSS.

[2] "... his [J. Van Buren's] advocacy would blast the prospects of any man and defeat almost any measure." Marcy to J. Stryker, Sept. 30, 1851, *ibid.*

mon aim, the success of one of its sons. Gradually Marcy came to see that in spite of the motives and quality of some of his supporters he was needed for the Empire State. He was to be the state's candidate.[1] This seems to have been driven home by the New York Convention of 1851.

From September 10 to 12, 1851, this body met at Syracuse. Here the softs and Van Burenites worked together and the results were a national platform endorsing the Compromise, a state committee on which nine hunkers out of sixteen were appointed so that the barnburners and softs could control; and a state ticket with several barnburners on it.[2] This was considered a triumph for Marcy and after a conference with Peter Cagger, the leading barnburner of Albany, Marcy presided over the Democratic meeting of September 25 held to ratify the work of the convention.[3] This triumph of Marcy's views and his reappearance in public after a long absence from politics formally launched his candidacy. It proved attractive. The *New York Herald* commented on him as a possibility;[4] he began to receive letters from former Cass men declaring for him.[5] Under these circumstances Buchanan and Slidell in their negotiation met with no response and the Buchanan-Marcy conference in New York on October 21 came to naught.[6] Other support came from a strange source.

[1] Marcy to Isaac Davis, Feb. 2, 1852, Isaac Davis MSS.; Marcy to Wetmore, Nov. 29, 1851, Marcy MSS.

[2] *New York Herald*, Sept. 13 and 18, 1851; Welles to Niles, Sept. 25, 1851, Welles MSS.

[3] *New York Herald*, Sept. 26 and Oct. 2, 1851; Marcy to Wetmore, Sept. 15, 1851, Marcy MSS.

[4] *New York Herald*, Oct. 4, 1851.

[5] Ogden to Marcy, Oct. 4, 1851, Guinness to Marcy, Oct. 5, 1851, Marcy MSS.

[6] Campbell to Marcy, Nov. 5, 1851, Marcy to Campbell, Nov. 10, 1851, *ibid.*

Thurlow Weed, the Whig boss, was confident that a Democrat would be elected President. Consequently, he was anxious that the Democrat in question should be one with whom he was acquainted. He labored to smooth away the path for Marcy. During the fall he interested prominent barnburners such as Addison Gardner, Simeon B. Jewett, and Dean Richmond, and arranged meetings between them and Marcy. Also he cleared away a misunderstanding between John McKeon and Marcy. As his final piece of work before he sailed for Europe late in November, 1851, he attempted to bring about an entente cordiale between Marcy and Dickinson. His plan was to have the solid vote of the state go to whichever one was stronger. Marcy approved, and Francis B. Cutting and Elijah F. Purdy undertook to approach Dickinson. However, they delayed.[1]

As in 1848 the barnburners were determined to have none of Cass. The hunker faction was strongly for him so the only way to defeat him was to draw away some of the hunker support. As has been noted in a preceding chapter hards and softs were but badly united, consequently the more practical of the barnburners had begun to seek a soft alliance. Marcy was a man of much influence, so Azariah C. Flagg and other barnburners felt that by supporting him as against Cass they could gain enough soft support to reduce Cass' delegates to the national convention.

Two problems confronted the Marcy workers: the Douglas candidacy and the method of choice of the state delegates. In his October visit, Marcy had found Douglas adherents growing in numbers in New York City. When he made a second trip to the city early in November, he met Charles Eames, an assistant editor of the *Union*. Eames was exer-

[1] Barnes, T. W., *Memoir of Thurlow Weed*, pp. 197-8; Perley Poore, B., *Perley's Reminiscences*, vol. i, p. 412; Weed to Marcy, Feb. 1, 1852, Marcy MSS.

cised about Douglas' popularity, and Marcy commissioned him to convey a message of friendship and good will to Douglas, with the additional hint that New York was concentrating on Marcy. Eames saw Douglas and gave the message, to which Douglas replied in a manner which convinced Eames of his sincerity. Douglas expressed gratitude for Marcy's friendship and declared that he had made up his mind not to move in New York now, holding it unfit for him to take any action in Marcy's own state, just as he would regard it unfit for Marcy to make an attempt to win support in Illinois. Unlike Eames, Marcy did not seem to put much faith in this avowal. He felt that the Cassites were in league with Douglas men to aid the Illinois senator.[1] He had reasons for feeling this way. These reasons sprang from the second problem.

The manner in which the New York delegates to the national convention were to be chosen had to be decided upon. There was no set rule and this year the state convention had left it in the hands of the state committee, which was to decide it late in November. Two methods were under consideration. One was to have another state convention at which the delegation would be chosen all at once on a general ticket. The other was to have the delegates from each congressional district chosen by a district convention, and the delegates at large, or senatorial delegates, chosen by the district delegates. Marcy and his barnburner friends originally favored the first plan. They felt that their soft-barnburner alliance could easily control this convention, as it had the one in September, and thus a unanimous Marcy delegation would be chosen. In New York City Douglas' hold was so strong that he was sure of the choice of his delegates under the district system. Hence

[1] Marcy to Archibald Campbell, Nov. 10 and Dec. 6, C. Eames to Marcy, Nov. 11; Marcy to James G. Berret, Nov. 30, 1851, Marcy MSS.

the city delegation would be opposed to Marcy and would give outsiders the impression that he could not count on the undivided support of his own state. This united front was essential if his candidacy was to impress other sections of the country. Consequently, when Marcy came down to New York City after the November election, he let it be known that he wished the state convention method. His plan was of course obnoxious to Cass and Douglas men, who saw in it the destruction of all hope of delegates for them. The New York City hunkers feared that in a state convention barnburner delegates would be elected from New York City and would increase the latter's strength in the city machine. Therefore, Daniel E. Sickles and Augustus Schell sought to dissuade Marcy. They had a conference with him in the city in November. At that time they argued that if a state convention was held and a Marcy delegation chosen, John Van Buren or some other notorious barnburner would demand a prominent place on it. This would give Marcy's candidacy a free-soil tinge which would injure it in the south. On the other hand, if the district plan were used, Sickles explained, in answer to Marcy's apprehension of a divided delegation, Cass men would support Marcy delegates in the New York City districts where Cass was not strong enough to defeat Douglas. This would ensure a practically unanimous delegation. As Marcy and his friends had been worried by the free soil charge, and this seemed a way to get the troublesome New York City delegation, they agreed to the district plan. When the state committee met, Marcy's soft friends joined with the Cass hunkers and by a vote of 9 to 7 defeated the barnburners and chose the district plan. This elated the Cass men who were confident that they had won an advantage. Later events justified their delight. When Cass passed through New York City immediately thereafter, a mutual and rather inebriated friend, Henry K. Smith of Buffalo, attempted to bring about a rapprochement between the two without success. Presently Cass men and Douglas men were found uniting against the barnburners.[1]

A debacle of conflicting desires was now let loose among Marcy's friends. Many Cass men, though realizing that he could not be nominated, and desiring to support Marcy, insisted on choosing delegates willing to vote for Cass for a few ballots by way of compliment. Some were opposed to having any barnburners chosen as Marcy delegates. Others wanted Marcy to run only in districts where Cass was impossible, and there play the rôle of cat's-paw. On the other hand, barnburners wanted as many of their own number chosen as possible in order to show their strength in the party. Barnburners were charged with using Marcy for a blind. Marcy was charged with being a traitor to Cass and a free soiler. Marcy felt that he was being tricked and deceived, and that his broth was being spoiled by too many cooks.[2] The culmination of this mixup came at the district conventions of January 8th, when Cass men captured eleven delegates mostly from New York City, and Marcy obtained twenty-two.[3]

[1] Thomas to Marcy, Oct. 31, Nov. 6, Dec. 29, 1851; Smith to Marcy, Nov. 11, 1851; Warren Bryant to Marcy, Nov. 11, 1851; L. B. Shepherd to Marcy, Nov. 26, 1851; Jewett to Marcy, Nov. 26, 1851; Wetmore to Marcy, Nov. 28, 1851; Marcy to Berret, Nov. 30, 1851; Seymour to Marcy, Dec. 1, 1851; Marcy to Campbell, Dec. 6, 1851; Newell to Marcy, Nov. 27, 1851; Croswell to Marcy, Dec. 10, 1851; Marcy to S. Beardsley, Dec. 10, 1851; Beardsley to Marcy, Dec. 16, 1851; Wager to Marcy, Dec. 17 and 22, 1851; Marcy to Wager, Dec. 26, 1851; Wager to Marcy, Dec. 29, 1851; Marcy to Wetmore, Dec. 29, 1851, Marcy MSS.; Byrdsall to Buchanan, Dec. 1, 1851, Buchanan MSS.

[2] Marcy to Wetmore, Nov. 29, 1851; to Berrett, Nov. 30, Dec. 14, 1851, and Feb. 4, 1852; to Campbell, Dec. 6, 1851; Croswell to Marcy, Dec. 10, 1851; Thomas to Marcy, Jan. 20, 1852; Marcy to C. T. Chamberlain, Feb. 2, 1852, Marcy MSS.

[3] Attempts were made at reconciliation between Cass and Marcy men.

By this outcome Marcy was forced to appear before the party as unable to command the entire delegation of his own state. This was especially galling to him because he believed that he was the choice of a large majority of the New York Democracy. Still he hoped that because of his superior position in the Empire State and his freedom from any utterance during the Compromise controversy that he might be considered available and become the second choice of many delegates. This would bring him into conflict with none of the other candidates, and when the leading men were killed off he would step in and carry away the prize.[1]

To direct the execution of these tactics Marcy carried on a voluminous correspondence and maintained close touch with a small but efficient force of political aides and observers. His closest friends in New York were General John Addison Thomas, Prosper M. Wetmore, Horatio Seymour, John Stryker and Henry K. Smith. Thomas had been a soldier and teacher of international law in a military school until 1846 when he had begun to practise law in New York City and had gone into politics. Wetmore was a speculator who was at that time interested in steamship lines in partnership with Edwin Crosswell and George Law. He had been Marcy's friend for years, and although not active in politics was a keen observer of the game. Stryker and Seymour were active politicians, the latter had been one of the soft-hunker leaders in the legislature and had been narrowly defeated for governor in 1850. Smith was an impetuous, not especially modest, rather convivial local

Cutting and Purdy bestirred themselves to make an arrangement originally suggested by Weed, whereby the united vote of the state would go to either the hunker candidate or Marcy—whichever could get the most outside support. The Cass men declined, saying they were committed to a second choice, which was presumably Douglas; *v.* note, p. 95.

[1] Eames to Marcy, Jan. 4, 1852; Jenkins to Stryker, Jan. 12, 1852; Marcy MSS.

leader in Buffalo. In Washington Marcy's agents and information bureau included Charles Eames, " a mighty, continuous, grandiloquent talker ", whom Donelson had brought up from Tennessee to help edit the *Union*, and Archibald Campbell, a clerk in the War Department, who had been Marcy's chief clerk when he was Secretary of War. With these he corresponded regularly, and they kept him informed of the little that went on in Washington during the absence of Congress. However, as the first Monday in December approached, he felt the need of more partisans; so he wrote to an old acquaintance, James G. Berret, a claims agent of local political prominence in the capital city. He informed him of the situation in New York and of his prospects, and asked him his advice; [1] this letter started a regular series of reports and replies. Furthermore, Marcy chose William W. Snow, a New York congressman, as his personal representative in Congress, and gave him a letter to Berret. Thus the Washington force was officered. Snow was able to report: " Berret is a true friend ", and Berret wrote that " Snow is doing all he can ".[2]

In the south Marcy was not without publicity agents. Thomas had interested his brother James, an editor in Columbia, Tennesse, and he went over to Mississippi to work for Marcy at the state convention in January. Here he hobnobbed with Davis and Quitman, and convinced them of Marcy's soundness on the slavery issue. These leaders declared themselves willing to support Marcy if some demonstration could be made of his ability to carry New York.[3] Before the Virginia convention Berret reported that a friend of Marcy's, Dr. Young, was going to Richmond to

[1] Marcy to Berret, Nov. 21, 1851, Marcy MSS.

[2] Snow to Marcy, Berret to Marcy, Dec. 5, 1851, *ibid.*

[3] Thomas to Marcy, Jan. 12 and Feb. 9, 1852, *ibid.*

take care of his interests.[1] Thomas also decided to go south to Washington, Tennessee and Georgia. His efforts in New York had been continuous. When Cushing and P. R. George had visited New York late in March, he with Stryker had gone to see them, and while the wily politician from Massachusetts would not commit himself definitely, he declared his tendencies were in Marcy's direction,[2] and George write enthusiastically that " Marcy is the man ".[3] Now as the Georgia convention was approaching Thomas decided to go down. For ammunition he took with him an account, furnished by Flagg, of a meeting in Albany in 1835 over which Marcy had presided while governor. This contained evidence of Marcy's loyalty to the south more satisfactory than any letter written on the eve of an election. He arrived in Georgia about April 1, and there met his brother. The two worked hard and could report that they had succeeded in changing the feeling of many from doubt of Marcy's ability to carry New York to a certainty. Marcy was urged to send down a copy of his gubernatorial message of 1836 in which he had taken strong ground against abolitionists and in favor of southern rights.[4]

When Thomas arrived in Tennessee on his way north he heard that Seymour and St. John B. Skinner, Marcy men, had been elected delegates at large from New York on April 8. This good news he took to the Nashville *American* incorporated in an article about Marcy. The editor agreed to print it, and decided to support Marcy. This paper Thomas sent to all delegates from Georgia as well as to many persons in Alabama and Mississippi. Thence Thomas gravi-

[1] Berret to Marcy, Feb. 7, 1852, *ibid.*

[2] Thomas to Marcy, Mar. 25, 1852, *ibid.*

[3] P. R. George to J. C. Breckinridge, Mar. 23, Apr. 2, 1852, J. C. Breckinridge MSS.

[4] *Messages of the Governors of N. Y.*, vol. iii, pp. 572-82.

tated to Washington, arriving about the middle of April. Here he found conditions less to his liking.[1]

At the capital Marcy's friends had been working steadily convincing others and playing for points of vantage. Snow considered the organization of the House under Boyd and Forney as favorable [2] and he bent his energies to undermining Buchanan in Pennsylvania by collaborating with Senator Richard Broadhead in that state.[3] Berret circulated among the powers and reported conferences with Senators Atchison, Rusk, Downs and Mason.[4] Marcy had received his full share of Sanders' abuse, being called a "spavined, wind-blown, strained, ring-boned nag" whom the editor advised to go home to rural pasture to preserve his equine attributes, and not make an ass of himself. This vivid phraseology had a personal animus behind it as Marcy had had occasion to discipline Sanders during the Polk administration for one of his fraudulent activities. So overdrawn an attack acted as usual like a boomerang and was reported to have aided Marcy in the charmed circle of the capital.[5] In the congressional presidential debates during March he received no particular notice. Then Ausburn M. Birdsall, a relative of Dickinson's by marriage, arrived in Washington.

Birdsall had a definite purpose. He denounced Marcy as a barnburner and declared that Marcy could never carry New York. In the midst of his campaign Thomas arrived at Washington. He immediately reported the state of affairs to New York. Meanwhile Seymour had gone to Washington April 23 to do what was possible to offset this

[1] Thomas to Marcy, Mar. 27, April 1, April 23, 1852, Marcy MSS.

[2] Snow to Marcy, Dec. 5, 1851, *ibid.*

[3] Berret to Marcy, Dec. 20, 1851, *ibid.*

[4] Berret to Marcy, Mar. 22, 1852, *ibid.*

[5] *Democratic Review*, Mar., 1852; Campbell to Marcy, Mar. 12, 1852, Snow to Marcy, Apr. 10, 1852, Marcy MSS.

propaganda by conference with prominent southerners. He found Birdsall still at work. Indeed Seymour reported that so intemperate was Birdsall's language that he was engaged in daily altercation with those who did not agree with him. Seymour tried a different method; he was very guarded and conciliatory, and treated these attacks as the natural results of disappointment, avoiding any appearance of annoyance. He believed that "among strangers, cheerfulness and composure imply strength". He reported that Thomas, Berret and Snow were busy and had given Marcy as much prominence as was discreet.[1]

To answer publicly these attacks Congressman Dean of New York made a speech on the floor of the House on April 25. This effort had been carefully revised by Seymour and Snow and was phrased to imply that Marcy was the choice of the united Democracy of the Empire State.[2] Then Seymour and Berret interviewed Mason and Atchison and other leading senators. They were received with great kindness and no promises. Indeed Seymour saw and heard much to worry him. Birdsall had been joined by Samuel Beardsley and they kept up their propaganda. Their abuse of Marcy was so bitter that some began to suspect an ulterior motive; Dawson of Pennsylvania, a Cass man, asked point blank what Beardsley and Birdsall were up to. Suspicions were growing rife that Dickinson was perhaps more faithful to Dickinson than to Cass.[3] Marcy's friends were almost persuaded to abandon their position of attacking no

[1] Marcy to Berret, Apr. 17, 1852; Snow to Marcy, Apr. 17, 20, 1852; Marcy MSS.

[2] *Cong. Globe*, 32nd Cong., 1 Sess., *Appendix*, p. 451; Snow to Marcy, Apr. 29, 1852, Campbell to Marcy, May 1, 1852, Marcy MSS.

[3] Snow to Marcy, Apr. 17, 20, 1852; Berret to Marcy, Apr. 30, 1852; Campbell to Marcy, May 1, 1852; Seymour to Marcy, May 2, 1852; Jenkins to Marcy, May 2, 1852; Campbell to Marcy, May 14, 1852; C. Eames to Marcy, May 16, 1852, *ibid.*

one and spread the story of the attempt of Beardsley and certain of Dickinson's friends to traffic with the barnburners; how in order to procure the choice of Beardsley as one delegate at large they had been willing to make the free soiler, John Van Buren, the other. For some reason they refrained.[1]

So the last month went by, Seymour, Stryker and other friends of Marcy came and went, back and forth between Washington and New York; Birdsall, Beardsley and Mckeon did likewise. The aim of the latter was to convince all that Marcy could not carry New York. The former, on the other hand, sought to prove the contrary, make no enemies, conciliate Cass' friends outside of New York and prove to the Michigan man that Dickinson was really using Cass' name as a cloak for his own ambition. Henry A. Wise, Cave Johnson and other friends of Buchanan when approached expressed good will, but were committed already.[2] Marcy wrote to John Y. Mason, his former colleague, to find out if Dickinson had been operating in Virginia and to warn him against believing all "Scrip Dick" said.[3] Mason consulted Wise about the matter and then replied that he had not heard of any Dickinsonian activities. This interchange of notes was succeeded by another on the appearance of the Scott letter. Marcy sought Mason's advice and upon receipt of it wrote a reply squarely in the affirmative.[4] This letter drew praise from the *New York Herald*, which because of the hostility of the editor J. G. Bennett for Marcy, the outcome of a misunderstanding of

[1] Snow to Marcy, Apr. 10, 17, 1852; Marcy to Berret, Apr. 11, 1852, *ibid*.

[2] Campbell to Marcy, May 3, 1852, *ibid*.

[3] Mason to Marcy, Apr. 23, 1852, Marcy to Berret, May 15, 1852, *ibid*. Dickinson gained this soubriquet because of his fondness for quoting the Scriptures.

[4] Marcy to Mason, May 21, 25, 1852, *ibid*.

the thirties,[1] had been continuously ridiculing "poor old Marcy"; its editorial column proclaimed Marcy's effort as the best letter of all.[2] This was the second statement Marcy had made on the Compromise; a prior one had been called for because the New York delegation had failed to vote for the Compromise Resolutions in the House. To make well known the fact that he was right on the Compromise he sent a letter to be circulated in Washington. In this epistle he said he was satisfied with the Compromise but was not in favor of asking the convention to declare it final. He gave as his reasons for this the fact that some, such as northern Democrats, were opposed to the Fugitive Slave Law and would not declare for it openly. This letter was shown to Hunter, Wise, Meade, Venable and others,[3] and with the Scott letter showed that Marcy was sound on the Compromise. These views were not the unanimous views of the New York Democrats, however. Last-minute speeches were made in Congress by Floyd and King of New York, each attacking the Compromise, the former on the ground that it begged the real question which was: "Does the Constitution give the south the right to extend slavery into free territory and impose upon the north the corresponding obligation to submit to further slave representation upon this floor?" This defiant question was by no means relished by the south and emphasized the lack of harmony in Marcy's own state.[4]

The last days before the Convention were busy ones. Marcy's claims must be put before the delegates now fast

[1] Information from Prof. C. C. Tansill of American Univ., Marcy's biographer.

[2] *New York Herald*, May 27, 1852.

[3] Draft in Marcy MSS.; Campbell to Marcy, Apr. 24, May 3, 1852, *ibid.*

[4] *Cong. Globe*, 32nd Cong., 1 Sess., *Appendix*, p. 588 (May 19, 1852), Snow to Marcy, May 22, 1852, Marcy MSS.

arriving in Washington. Efforts never ceased. All seemed to be going well. In spite of the fact that Marcy's strength was confined almost entirely to New York, he had been able to keep from antagonizing the principals in the contest, and was a very available second choice. But—there was a delegate from New York whose ill-will and distrust he had incurred; Daniel S. Dickinson was determined that Marcy should not be nominated. Hope was high and many of the faithful were fervently praying "May the Lord have Marcy upon us".

CHAPTER VII

THE LOCHINVAR OF THE YOUNG DEMOCRACY

CASS aged 69, Buchanan aged 60, Woodbury aged 62, Butler aged 58, Houston aged 58, Marcy aged 65, had all grown grey in the service of the party; they were veterans of many a campaign and legislative battle and had received many offices as gifts from the hands of a grateful republic. But a new generation was growing up who felt not the quickened heartbeat at the mention of these patriots, and who began to murmur at their continual domination. They had enjoyed too long the spoils of victory; it was time that they were retiring and giving place to younger men. There seemed to be no signs of abdication as 1852 approached, but the seeds of revolt were sown. A new leader appeared out of the west, one who appealed to Young America no longer to yield allegiance to the "Old Fogies". Stephen A. Douglas had established his supremacy in Illinois and had won nation-wide reputation in the halls of Congress and —he was but thirty-eight.

Just when Douglas began to consider himself seriously as a presidential aspirant is not revealed, but in the spring of 1851 his name seems first to have been mentioned, and in that period his first steps were taken as a candidate. There were enormous difficulties in the way. The west had another candidate, Lewis Cass, veteran of presidential campaigns; many felt that Douglas should wait until that Nestor had retired. His youth and the short time during which he had been in politics had prevented his gaining any considerable following. Consequently he had no machine to aid him and what was more, outside of his own state he had the various organizations against him. Yet he was not without supporters.

Others beside himself were tired of serving the elders of the party. A new generation had arisen who were dazzled by the republicanism which was struggling for liberty in Europe during 1848. This generation, with the impetuosity of youth, desired that the United States, a country young but glorious in traditions of freedom, should depart from the conservative policy of the fathers and aid the struggling idealists across the water. In short, they would have the United States bid defiance to the world's autocrats and lead a crusade for the liberation of Europe. At home they would cast aside the cautious elder statesmen and place in the White House a young man with their viewpoint. They took for themselves the title of the "Young Democracy" and spoke of the elders as the "Old Fogies". To such men as George N. Sanders, W. W. Cory, T. DeWitt Reilly, John L. O'Sullivan, Edward DeLeon, the impetuosity, youth and bluster of Stephen A. Douglas strongly appealed. He was the "Little Giant" to drive the ancients from the seats of power.

The Constitution provides that all money paid out by the United States treasury must be appropriated by Congress. The United States had been engaged in three wars; by various treaties the government had assumed claims of foreigners against the United States and of citizens against foreign states; the number of employees of the government had of necessity been large; work done for the government had been generally let out by contract; all these items involved appropriations of money for pensions, claims, salaries and contracts. As it was necessary for Congress to pass upon them all, as Congress was in session only part of the time, as Congress had a multitude of matters other than appropriations before it, and as Congress was composed of men of human limitations, many of them politicians, and unmoral ones at that, it was evident that vast numbers of the items in the voluminous appropriation bills must receive little or no careful attention.[1] Consequently it often occurred that an interested or willing Congressman could slip in along with a lot of similar items, little appropriations of a few hundred or a few thousand dollars, insignificant when compared with the total but when considered in bulk costing the government much. Of course individuals with these claims were often not in a position either to go to Washington, or if arriving there, to bring influence to bear on any Senator or Representative potent enough to gain interest in putting through this appropriation. To remedy this defect a group of claim agents sprang up in Washington who, through reputation, friendship or baser means, had influence with members who could push these claims through. Thus individuals with claims would place them in the hands of these agents who would see the proper members of Congress and when the claim was passed and signed by the President would receive a fee averaging fifty per cent af the claim and often more.[2] This class with contractors and promoters of all sorts formed a lobby to influence Congress to grant them funds. Douglas was in need of supporters and in order to attract a following was lavish in his promises; to his standard flocked men of this type. He himself was a speculator in land and railroads and heartily in favor of western development. Under his régime there would be a new deal and many wished to take advan-

[1] So many were these claims, indeed, that each house set aside one day per week for the consideration and passage of these "private bills". This was the occasion for much log-rolling.

[2] *Senate Report no. 1*, 33rd Cong., special session (Ser. no. 688).

tage of it. Douglas was not particular and welcomed all comers. But this motley throng by its disreputable rags and tatters made the honest and cautious look askance at the young Lochinvar out of the west.

Marshalling these forces, Douglas' course was to be ceaseless attack and tireless activity. The key point in the south was Virginia; Douglas saw its importance and some of his first moves were in that direction. In March, 1851, he made a trip to Richmond where in a public speech he advocated a ticket composed of a compromise northerner and an anti-compromise southerner.[1] This was a bid for the Calhoun faction in Virginia to join him [2] and soon thereafter, perhaps through the instrumentality of George N. Sanders, Senator R. M. T. Hunter, himself but forty-two, began to step forth as a candidate for Vice-President with Douglas.[3]

The key point in the north was New York. During the previous Congress Douglas had been interested in obtaining a charter for a railroad from Chicago to Mobile. In furtherance of this project one of Douglas' lieutenants had entered into negotiations with certain steamship interests which maintained a lobby in Washington, whereby they would aid his scheme if he would not oppose theirs. How these negotiations turned out is not revealed, but when Douglas became a candidate he had the backing of George Law, once a hod carrier, now a wealthy contractor who was much interested in steamship lines. To him, Douglas' advocacy of the acquisition of Cuba would naturally appeal because if

[1] Parker to Buchanan, Mar. 28, 1851, Buchanan MSS.; Blair to John Van Buren, Mar. 24, 1851, Van Buren MSS., *Hunter Corr.*, pp. 126-8.

[2] Welles to Niles, Sept. 25, 1851, Welles MSS.

[3] Hunter's reëlection to the senate, Jan., 1852, with the aid of Douglas opponents satisfied him and he let it be known that he was going to remain a senator. *v. supra*, p. 74.

the United States controlled that island, trade between them would make steamship lines even more profitable.[1] As Law and Sanders had had business connections it may be suspected at least that the latter was active in this relationship also.[2] Douglas went up to New York during May, 1851, and soon thereafter a public dinner was planned to which Douglas and Hunter were invited. At the same time an organization was built up for him which gained the support of the Empire Club. This notorious band was said by its enemies to be a gang of Bowery bums and Tammany toughs whose specialty was the control of ward primary meetings in New York City. On September 1, Douglas received a second dinner in his honor at the metropolis and was initiated into the Tammany Society. Later in the month he addressed an agricultural fair up state where he met Marcy; they did not discuss politics. In the first week in October he was in the city and on October 15 New York saw him again.[3] He was here, there, and everywhere. In November in conversation with Eames he declared that he had decided not to move further in New York but leave the field for Marcy. Shortly thereafter many Douglas men were reported on good authority as supporting Cass.[4] Whatever the secret history of these various moves, in New York as in other states which had favorite sons Douglas ceased to figure as a principal in the contest.

[1] Johnson, *Life of Douglas*, pp. 166-176, Wetmore to Marcy, Nov. 28, 1851, Marcy MSS.; Slidell to Buchanan, Sept. 29, 1851, Buchanan MSS.

[2] *N. Y. Herald*, Feb. 12, 1852; Flagg to Martin Van Buren, Jan. 26, 1852, Van Buren MSS.

[3] Marcy to Campbell, May 28, 1851, Simeon B. Jewett, Nov. 26, 1851, Marcy to Berrett, Nov. 30, 1851, Campbell to Marcy, Dec. 6, 1851, Marcy MSS.; Marcy to Buchanan, Oct. 6, 1851, Buchanan MSS.; *Chicago Democrat*, Sept. 8, 1851; *N. Y. Herald*, Oct. 5, 16, 1851.

[4] J. A. Thomas to Marcy, Dec. 29, 1851, Marcy to Berret, Jan. 2, 1852, Marcy MSS.

New England was worth trying for. Douglas had been born in Vermont. His growing reputation caused the Trustees of Middlebury College in that state to confer upon him the degree of LL.D. on August 20, 1851. Upon this occasion Douglas publicly subscribed five hundred dollars to the college and made a speech. In this town of Middlebury he had learned the trade of cabinet maker and in his speech he so alluded to his early calling that a parallel became immediately apparent. As an aspirant for the presidency he might still labor at *making cabinets.* In less than a fortnight Judge Woodbury died and New England was minus a candidate. Here was Douglas who had just made a clever speech and had very publicly parted with a sum of money—to aid the cause of education—what could be more fortuitous! Douglas immediately began to be taken up and it was variously reported that he was being supported by the more prominent hunker Democrats of New England.[1]

His candidacy boomed decidedly. Politicians who had kept their ears to the ground began to hurry to his standard and even Cass' *Washington Union* was reported as favoring him.[2] His activities were tireless everywhere. He spoke at various fall agricultural fairs in New York, Maryland and Ohio where, though he avoided politics and lauded the arts of husbandry,[3] he nevertheless met the people and his magnetism was irresistible. Born politician, boon companion, hail fellow well met, all who saw him were charmed by his manner, and those undazzled by the glamour of his personality were thrilled by pledges of future office and

[1] *Newark Morning Eagle,* Sept. 4, 1851; *Morristown True Democratic Banner,* Oct. 8, 1851; *Illinois State Register,* Sept. 11, 1851; Gilmore to Buchanan, Sept. 22, 1851, Buchanan MSS.

[2] Balch to Buchanan, Nov. 18, 1851, Buchanan MSS.

[3] *Illinois State Register,* Oct. 9, Nov. 6, 1851; *Chicago Democrat,* Oct. 1, 1851; *N. Y. Herald,* Sept. 20, 1851.

spoil. Promises were lavish. Douglas declared openly that he was in favor of rotation in office and kept on declaring it.

His friends were not idle, for Young America was keen on the scent. George N. Sanders was inspired with renewed zest, for Butler whom he believed a traitor to his father was being groomed. Down to Kentucky he went and began intriguing for the general's defeat.[1] After the fateful 8th of January on which the Kentucky Resolutions were passed, it was claimed that the Douglas influence had been at the bottom of them.[2]

In Tennessee J. Knox Walker, prince of lobbyists, was at work. Douglas' chariot was hitched to the renowned General Gideon J. Pillow and the Cass and Buchanan men felt constrained to look well to their fences.[3]

Soon after Congress met Douglas spoke on the Foote Resolutions. He explained how illness had prevented his voting for the Fugitive Slave Law and pledged his loyalty anew to the Compromise measures which he had helped to frame. He closed this speech with the words:

> I desire to see both the great parties acquiesce in the Compromise as a final settlement, but I do not wish to have a new party organized on the basis of that measure. The Democratic party is as good a union party as I want, and I wish to preserve its principles and its organization and to triumph upon its old issues. I desire no new tests—no interpolations into the old creed.[4]

Also in the Senate and at the Kossuth dinner he made spread-eagle speeches. In these he defied the crowned heads of Europe and declared for self-determination for

[1] Marcy to Buchanan, Nov. 18, 1851, Marcy MSS.

[2] J. P. Beekman to Van Buren, Mar. 9, 1852, Van Buren MSS.

[3] Marcy to Buchanan, Nov. 18, 1851, Buchanan MSS.

[4] *Cong. Globe*, 32nd Cong., 1 Sess., *Appendix*, p. 65.

countries such as Hungary and Ireland. He admitted willigness, under certain rather indefinite circumstances, to have the United States invade Europe by force of arms to aid Kossuth's cause; incidentally he called upon the government to annex Cuba.[1] These speeches were his platform. It was a foundation pleasing to the Compromise men, to Young America and to the southern imperialists. It was a formidable asset but his friends overreached themselves.

Somehow George N. Sanders acquired control of the staid old *Democratic Review* and converted it into the organ of Young America. The new management displayed its purpose in the number for January, 1852. In this appeared a slashing attack on American foreign policy which voiced a demand that the Democracy nominate a bold candidate and one who would " maintain in the teeth of the despots of Europe the democratic doctrines upon which his popularity and success are based ".[2] It contained scurrilous and ill-disguised references to " the ancients ", alluding to Butler as a " judicious bottleholder " whose sole claim to eminence was the fact that he once been a follower of a better man, possibly Cass, a " beaten horse ".[3] A second article on " Intervention " praised extravagantly a foreign policy whic was simular to that advocated by Douglas,[4] and a third contained severe criticism of the Compromise measures as political manœuvres.[5]

Because of the veiled character of their allusions these utterances would not have created much political distur-

[1] *Cong. Globe*, 32nd Cong., 1 Sess., p. 70; *N. Y. Herald*, Jan. 10, 1852; J. Catron to Buchanan, Jan. 19, 1852, Buchanan MSS.; *Illinois State Register*, Feb. 5, 1852.

[2] *United States Democratic Review*, vol. xxx, p. 12.

[3] *Ibid.*, p. 12.

[4] *Ibid.*, pp. 61-63.

[5] *Ibid.*, p. 87.

bance had not the February number contained another article on the "Presidency and the *Review*". It declared that the Democratic party needed a candidate with a policy. It referred to the dismal failure of Taylor , a "no policy" candidate, and protested against the Democrats nominating a similar candidate such as General Butler; this statement was qualified by the addendum: "We use the name merely to represent the class, General Butler being a good sample of the no-policy statesman". Then followed a bitter arraignment of Butler's past career, making it ridiculous by playing up the fact that he voted for himself in 1848. The article admitted that the attack in the January number had been levelled against the Kentuckian. The conclusion stated that the *Review* was not controlled by any clique or person, that the statesman described in the preceding issue was an ideal not an actuality.[1] The editor stoutly maintained that Douglas had no connection with the paper. George N. Sanders alone conducted it.[2]

These slanders upon the fair name of Kentucky and the dignity of one of her sons could not pass unchallenged. On March 3, John C. Breckinridge arose in the House and publicly rebuked the *Review*. In the course of this speech he charged that Douglas was responsible for, or at least entirely in accord with, the vicious course of the periodical. As proof of this he declared Douglas had signed a testimonial for the paper after the first of the articles had appeared.[3] Douglas' close friend, W. A. Richardson of Illinois, replied to this a few days later denying that Douglas had any connection with the *Review*. He stated that the testimonial had been signed before the January number ap-

[1] *Ibid.*, pp. 182 *et seq.*

[2] *Ibid.*, p. 187.

[3] *Cong. Globe*, 32nd Cong., 1 Sess., *Appendix*, p. 299.

peared. Unfortunately in the controversy that ensued it appeared that Richardson was in error with respect to the latter statement.[1]

Then followed the worst outrage. The March number contained an article entitled "Congress, the Presidency and the *Review*". Biting satire was hurled against Breckinridge, the *Washington Union,* Marcy and many others; no one was spared. Boastfully the *Review* nailed Douglas' colors to its masthead.[2] But it was too much. Only harm came to Douglas from this wild and brainless course.

In vain did Douglas' friends charge that this was a plot, that the proof sheets of the articles had been found in the possession of one of Douglas' enemies.[3] In vain did Marshall of California, on the floor of the House, denounce Breckinridge's attacks as malicious and declaim an extravagant tribute to the candidate of the Young Democracy.[4] Rats flee from a sinking ship. "Bill" Polk, Congressman from Tennessee found that after all, Young Democrat as he was, he could not bear to strike a blow at that old hero, Cass.[5] He was not alone.

Douglas maintained his swagger. He met Blair one day. "Now that Butler is used up you will support me?" Blair replied that his support would kill anybody, to which the senator returned, "I've got a strong constitution, I can stand anything."[6] But he couldn't. Attacks redoubled. He was too young, he ought to wait a term or two. Northerners objected to his jingo policy towards Cuba. South-

[1] *Cong. Globe,* 32nd Cong., 1 Sess., pp. 711-4.

[2] *U. S. Dem. Rev.,* vol. xxx, p. 202.

[3] Johnson, *Douglas,* p. 202.

[4] *Cong. Globe,* 32nd Cong., 1 Sess., *Appendix,* pp. 383-5.

[5] *Ibid.,* p. 420.

[6] Blair to Van Buren, April 30, 1852, Van Buren MSS.

erners were suspicious as to his stand on slavery, even southern friends had to admit, "He does not stand right on record, but what northern man does?"[1] Worst of all he was accused on all sides of being the candidate of that conglomeration of "adventurers, politicians, jobbers, lobby-members, loafers, letter writers, and patriots which call themselves 'Young America'". All the corrupt elements were his friends. One who may be suspected of being unfriendly to him wrote:

> Douglas the candidate of the cormorants of our party is now considered a dead cock in the pit, unless some throe in the agony of political death should enable him to kill off his opponents which is not likely to occur. He is a mere hotbed production a precocious politician warmed into and kept in existence by a set of interested plunderers that would in the event of success disembowel the treasury, disgrace the country and damn the party to all eternity that brought them into power. Those arms thrown about his neck along the street—reading pieces to him in the oyster cellar of a complimentary character which are to be sent off to some subsidized press for publication, then a drink, next a haugh, haugh, then some claim to be discussed by which they expect to practise some swindle upon the government. If you were here where you could see some of the persons engaged and the appliances brought to bear for the purpose of securing his election you would involuntarily denounce the whole concern a poor miserable, vile Bandetti and much fitter to occupy cells in the penitentiary than places of state.[2]

Douglas' last month was spent in strenuous conciliation and promises. He made attempts at ingratiating himself with Cass men, Buchanan men, Marcy men. He is reported to have promised all the offices at the disposal of the Presi-

[1] H. J. Harris to Jefferson Davis, Mar. 3, 1852, Davis MSS.

[2] Andrew Johnson to D. T. Patterson, Apr. 4, 1852, Johnson MSS.

dent from the cabinet to meanest clerk in efforts to show how advantageous it would be to support him. In vain—the powers were leagued against him. Illinois alone favored him. A past carelessly lived, slanderous attack and lobbyist support, the contempt of the southern chivalry for his humble origin, the jealousy of age for youth, these all had done their work.[1] But the end was not yet; Douglas' motto was *Resurgam*.

[1] Cole, A. C., *Centennial History of Illinois*, vol. iii, p. 106.

CHAPTER VIII

The Strength of Hidden Currents

Month after month, back and forth over the broad land the conflict raged. One day the advantage was with one commander, the next and it was gone. As time wore on the forces became more and more closely balanced and victory seemed impossible to any. But away, beyond the battle lines a group of guerilla chieftains were planning to step in and seize the fruits of the conflict from the hands of the warworn leaders. New England had entertained bright hopes of having one of her sons in the White House. The death of Woodbury had shattered that dream. Now her leaders must look elsewhere for a candidate. To many Butler of Kentucky appeared to be the best presidential timber, and the ex-Woodbury leaders began to make plans for endorsing him. As New England's representative they were desirous of nominating the Vice-President in the person of one of Woodbury's disciples, Franklin Pierce of New Hampshire, a man who though young had been the recipient of many political gifts. Handsome, engaging and a good speaker, to him, the son of one of New Hampshire's governors and Revolutionary heroes, honour came easily. His pleasing personality and his father's name had carried him to the legislature of New Hampshire, to Congress, and to the Senate. But one fault, however, had cut short his career at the capital. An inherited weakness for alcohol had made it necessary for him to leave the convivial center of riotous politics, and in 1842 he had resigned his seat in the upper house and returned to Concord to the practice of law.[1]

In furtherance of the plan of Butler and Pierce, New Hampshire launched a "boom". The Granite State Democracy was controlled by a group of Pierce's friends known as the "Concord Cabal", prominent among whom were Charles G. Atherton, Charles H. Peaslee, "Editor" Butterfield, ando others of lesser note. In the usual convention in June, 1851, they had nominated Levi Woodbury for President and Luke Woodbury for governor. Since then Levi had died of an abdominal abscess and Luke had hanged himself. These twin disasters had made imperative a new state convention for the nomination of a gubernatorial candidate. This body assembled on Jackson Day, 1852. Here to aid Pierce's chance of getting the Vice Presidency his name was presented "as worthy . . . . of high place among the names of the eminent citizens who will be conspicuously before the national convention." Some noticed that the office was not designated.[2]

When Pierce found himself thus placed before the people he was torn between ambition and fear of returning to the scene of his former temptations. Mrs. Pierce besides was very much opposed to going back to the capital. She was a timid, frail, retiring woman who had all too vivid memories of Washington, and her dread amounted almost to terror. For these reasons Pierce wrote to his close friend Atherton, delegate at large from New Hampshire to the Convention, that the use of his name before that body "would be utterly repugnant to [his] tastes and wishes".[3]

[1] Irelan, *Franklin Pierce*, pp. 18, 575; Field, *Memories of Many Men*, p. 158; McClure, *Recollections of Half a Century*, p. 82.

[2] *State Capitol Reporter*, Jan. 9, 1852, *New Hampshire Patriot*, Jan. 14, 1852, *Boston Post*, Jan. 10, 1852.

[3] Irelan, *Pierce*, p. 75.

In spite of the fact that the *New York Herald* predicted that Pierce would be heard of again,[1] and notwithstanding the widely quoted declaration of Colonel J. F. H. Claiborne, editor of a New Orleans paper, that the interests of the south would be as safe in Pierce's hands as in those of any southerner,[2] the incident seemed to be forgotten and Pierce's little day of newspaper comment faded into obscurity.

The mills of the gods were grinding slowly but surely. As we have seen on March 3, 1852, William O. Butler was politically murdered. A second death had robbed New England of a candidate. But this darkest hour was only the harbinger of the coming dawn.

Even before Butler's end, the knowing ones began to perceive that the many candidates were all hopeless. Some new man must emerge. Some possibly harked back to 1844. Where was another Polk? Edmund Burke essayed to be the Warwick and few men were more familiar with the field of politics than he was. He had served New Hampshire in Congress and Polk had appointed him Commissioner of Patents. From 1849 to 1850 he had been joint editor of the *Washington Union* with Ritchie. These positions had made necessary contact with politicians of every variety from everywhere, and Burke had used his opportunities well; there were not many with whom he was unacquainted. Now Burke had ambitions to return to Washington as a Senator; but he had enemies. He had never been sure of the good will of the Concord group.[3] If he could make Pierce president the latter might feel under obligations to Burke to aid his ambition. He had

[1] *N. Y. Herald*, Jan. 15, 1852.

[2] *State Capitol Reporter*, April 30, 1852; *N. C. Standard*, June 28, 1852.

[3] *V. Congressional Biographical Directory*. The Burke MSS. contain valuable material in regard to his early life. His daughter, Mrs. George H. Dana, supplied supplementary material.

been in Washington in the fall of 1851 where he had appeared to be all things to all men, being reported as suporting Buchanan, Marcy, Houston, and Douglas. He had leaned toward Cass after Woodbury's death, but now he was becoming more strongly convinced that Pierce was the man. To test this conclusion he decided in the spring to go to Washington once more and put his ear to the ground. On March 25, 1852, he arrived at the capital.[1]

He was not the only one looking for the yet unseen. His friend, Caleb Cushing of Massachusetts, Tyler Whig, Democrat, and at present justice of the supreme court of Massachusetts by appointment of a coalitionist, had also been surveying the field. Cushing in company with Paul R. George of Lowell, Massachusetts, brother of one of Pierce's law students, had made an extended tour through the west to look after land and railroad investments, and had sounded out sentiment there.[2] But he had not yet found the available man. Douglas to whom he had leaned had been killed by a surfeit of violent praise. Where else might he turn? Marcy seemed to offer superior qualifications and Cushing decided to inevstigate. Accordingly, accompanied by the ever present George, he arrived in New York in the last days of March. After several days of interviews with New York politicians he went in to Washington seemingly impressed with Marcy's desirability.[3]

Burke had not been idle. The fortnight after his arrival had been a busy one. He stayed at the house frequented

[1] Gilmore to Buchanan, Jan. 25, 1852, Buchanan MSS., Burke to Welles, Nov. 5, 1851, Welles MSS.; H. K. Smith to Marcy, Jan. 28, 1852, Stryker to Marcy, Mar. 13, 1852, Marcy MSS.; *Baltimore Sun*, March 26, 1852.

[2] George, *Paul R. George, passim. Chicago Democrat*, Sept. 24, 1851.

[3] Thomas to Marcy, Mar. 25, 1852, Brodhead to Marcy, April 1, 1852, Marcy MSS.

by John S. Barbour, chairman of the Virginia Democratic Convention, and other prominent Virginians. Here he consulted with many as to Pierce's availability for his wide knowledge of politicians gave him excellent opportunities. He consorted with Virginians, with New Yorkers, and men from all sections and everywhere he got the same reply—if the other candidates could not win and Pierce would accept he would be just the man. He could even please both factions in New York. Burke was impressed by these possibilities and he laid the matter before the New Hampshire Congressional delegation and other men from that State then in Washington. Senator Bradbury from Maine who had gone to Bowdoin with Pierce became enthusiastic about him, and directed all his energies toward interesting others. Then Cushing arrived from New York, and it may be presumed that Burke was quick to confer with him. However, there was one stumbling block: Pierce had publicly declined to be a candidate. This must be removed somehow. About April 9 both Burke and Pierce's friend, Major Benjamin B. French, wrote him an account of their investigation and asked him to allow his friends to push his cause. Pierce replied to them both on April 12 and 13 that when, and only when, all other candidates were used up would he consent to go before the Convention. He definitely placed the matter in the hands of his New Hampshire friends, Burke, French, Atherton, Hibbard, Peaslee and Senator Norris. He did not seem to think that his chances were worth much. But aid was coming from another scource.[1]

The Mexican war, like all other enterprises of the Washington government of the period, was deeply tinged with

[1] Burke to Pierce, Apr. 9, Pierce to Burke, Apr. 13, 1852, Pierce MSS. B. B. French to Burke, Sept. 17, 1852, Burke MSS.

party politics. The Democratic party was in power but lack of Democratic generals made it necessary to appoint two Whigs, Scott and Taylor, to command the major expeditions of the war. For the brigade commands, however, there were plenty of deserving Democrats, so Major General Scott had for his brigadiers men who were politically opposed to him. Prominent in this group were Pillow, Pierce, Cushing, Seymour, Quitman and Davis. As might have been expected Scott's irascible temper brought on quarrels which political differences did nothing to heal. The most important of these quarrels, as far as results went, was one between Scott and Pillow which brought about Pillow's trial by court-martial upon charges preferred by Scott. Pillow was acquitted but he continued to cherish a hearty desire for revenge. When, therefore, Scott began to become a prominent candidate for the Whig nomination for the presidency Pillow determined to do what he could to build up the Democratic power in order to make its candidate sure of defeating Scott; incidentally he hoped to be chosen Vice President himself.[1]

Pillow had never forgotten the Convention of 1844 where, according to his own opinion, he had nominated Polk.[2] He felt himself to be a political power. He started to rally all those who had been brother officers in the Mexican War. He began a series of visits to different men but he was most active in his native state, Tennessee. He had a powerful ally in the person of his brother-in-law, Aaron V. Brown. The objective was the control of the state convention and a nomination to the Vice-Presidency by that body. Pillow's forces were joined with those of Douglas, and the Marcy men were friendly. Buchanan's

[1] A. O. P. Nicholson to John P. Heiss, Nov. 30, 1851, *Tennessee Historical Magazine*, vol. ii, p. 227.

[2] McCormac, *James K. Polk*, p. 240.

friends, on the other hand, were of the group antagonistic to the Pillow-Brown forces. They succeded in defeating these plans in so far as no instructions were given to the delegation, and Pillow and Trousdale, a Buchanan man, were both recommended as suitable candidates for the Vice-Presidency.[1] After this defeat, and with the coming of spring, Pillow decided to make a pilgrimage to the Mecca of political life. He arrived in Washington on April 11.

Here he met Cushing, Burke, and the other politicians in charge of the Pierce boom. He became enthusiastic about Pierce's chances and began to consider schemes for Pierce and Pillow.[2] Cushing and Pillow soon departed northward to see Pierce and on the way planned to do as much missionary work as possible, especially among their companions in arms in the late Mexican embroglio. Between April 20th and 24th they left Washington for New York. Here they talked with Marcy's friends and spoke of going up to see Marcy. However they managed to put it off until Pillow should return from a trip he was going to make into New England, and the conference was never held.[3] Shortly after this visit a long biography of Pillow appeared in the *New York Herald* in which the military glory of that intrepid soldier was exploited at the expense of Major General Scott.[4] Pillow and Cushing then went into New England stopping in Connecticut to see their

[1] Alfred Balch to A. J. Donelson, Dec. 28, 1851, Donelson MSS.; Marcy to Buchanan, Nov. 24, 1851, Buchanan MSS.; Cave Johnson to Marcy, Dec. 5, 1851, Pan. 14, 1852, Marcy MSS. *Washington Union*, Jan. 25, 1852.

[2] *Baltimore Sun*, Apr. 12, 1852, Pillow to Burke, Sept. 4, 1852, Burke MSS. and explanatory note in *State Capitol Reporter*, Oct. 29, 1853.

[3] Campbell to Marcy, April 13 and May 8, 1852, Cushing to Marcy, April 20, 1852, Stryker to Marcy, April 25, 28, 1852, Marcy MSS.

[4] *N. Y. Herald*, May 6, 1852.

former comrade, Brigadier General Thomas L. Seymour.[1] At Boston they held conference with politicians including Governor Boutwell, and on April 30 they visited Pierce at Concord. After conference they returned to Boston on the following day and soon thereafter Pillow left for Washington.[2] He stopped in Philadelphia and there emphasized the necessity of maintaining the time-honored two-thirds rule in the coming convention. He left Philadelphia on May 13 and went immediately to the capital.[3]

Meanwhile Burke had been adroitly suggesting Pierce's claims for consideration in case the others should be impossible. He spoke of his adherence to the Compromise, his friendship for the south, his desire that she should have her rights and his soundness on the tariff and on rivers and harbors. He secured the services of Francis J. Grund, a veteran newspaper correspondent, who wrote letters to the independent papers, the *Baltimore Sun* and the *Philadelphia Ledger,* cleverly suggesting Pierce's availability. He made rapprochments with Cass, Douglas, and Marcy leaders, and as the situation became more tense, his work began to make a greater impression. About May 1 he left Washington to lay plans in New England.[4]

He stopped in Boston on his way and had an interview with Benjamin F. Hallett. The Massachusetts delegation

[1] *Augusta Age,* May 6, 1852.

[2] Boutwell, *Reminiscences,* vol. i, p. 121; *State Capitol Reporter,* May 4, 1852; *New Hampshire Statesman,* May 22, June 12, 1852, Trenton (N. J.) *State Gazette,* June 8, 1852; Henry Wilson to Sumner, May 4, 1852, Sumner MSS.

[3] McKibben to Buchanan, May 12, 1852, Cadwallader to Buchanan, May 20, 1852, Buchanan MSS. Snow to Marcy, May 22, 1852, Marcy MSS.; Washington Union, May 15, 1852.

[4] *State Capitol Reporter,* Oct. 22, 1853, *N. H. Statesman,* Oct. 29, 1853; Shields to Burke, May 3, 1852, Horatio Seymour to Burke, Aug. 27, 1852, Burke MSS.

was divided. One element, that of Cushing and his coalition friends, were in the Pierce movement with Burke, but a larger portion under the lead of Hallett and Greene, were for Cass. Burke felt the need of union in New England, and as New Hampshire and some of the Maine delegation (through Bradbury's influence) were agreed he wanted Massachusetts solid.[1] If this could be brought about he felt that Vermont, Connecticut (with Seymour's assistance) and Rhode Island would come around when needed. Consequently he was rejoiced when Hallett acquiesced in his suggestion that in case Cass, whom they both wanted, should be killed off, they go for Pierce. Confident now that New Hampshire, Maine and Massachusetts had reached an understanding he went home to plan the final steps.

He had written Pierce prior to leaving Washington detailing what had been done, but Pierce was away on circuit and did not receive the letter until May 9 He replied stating a wish to see Burke and proposing a meeting at Newport, Burke's home. Inclement weather delayed this, however, and Burke was invited to a meeting of the delegation held at Concord, May 17, for a last conference before their leaving for Washington; Burke was unable to get to Concord for this but he wrote an outline of a plan of action which was substantially followed. Pierce was determined that his name should only be used as a last resort to harmonize the Convention. This fell in with the scheme agreed upon, namely, that Pierce was not to be a candidate; he had declined—let that stand. His name was not to be before the Convention. The delegates favorable to him were to vote for Cass, Buchanan ,Douglas, some for one, some for others—in fact they were to be all things to all men until the hour arrived. Meanwhile Pierce's availability

[1] B. F. Hallett to Burke, Aug. 28, 1852, Burke MSS.

as a last resort was to be quietly circulated by all. To show his genuine acquiescence in the Compromise he was to write a letter addressed to Colonel Lally glowingly endorsing the measure though disclaiming the idea that his name was to be before the Convention.[1] This was to be ready for circulation at Baltimore and the Scott letter was to be ignored. Pierce came over to Newport and had a final interview with Burke. The plan was perfected. The New Hampshire, Maine and Massachusetts delegates gradually appeared in Washington and Baltimore each quietly preaching the gospel of the new dispensation which was to be the salvation of the Democratic party.[2]

[1] Pierce to Burke, May 10, 12, 17, 1852, Burke MSS.; Irelan, *Pierce*, p. 76.

[2] Little of this got into the newspapers. Now and then a side remark would appear as to Pierce's possible chance. Pillow's advocacy of Pierce and Pillow led to some comment—but most were so intent on pressing their favorites and so well were the plans kept that few realized what was going on. *N. Y. Herald*, May 25, 1852, *Lawrence Sentinel* copied by the *State Capitol Reporter*, May 21, 1852, *Lowell Courier* copied by the *State Capitol Reporter*, May 11, 1852, *Indiana State Journal*, May 19, 1852, cited in *Indiana Magazine of History*, vol. xi, p. 317.

CHAPTER IX

THE CRISIS SAFELY PASSED

THE scene shifts from Washington to Baltimore. During the last two weeks of May the capital had been in turmoil. Delegates were arriving daily and no efforts were spared by the friends of the various candidates to lead them to see the true light. It is stated that even Presidential aspirants participated in disgusting scenes in oyster-cellar and barroom. There the electioneering resembled "a vulgar barbecue where county offices were solicited." Baltimore was but an intensified duplicate. The city was crowded. Besides some six hundred delegates there were any number of hangers-on, spectators, political scavengers. The hotels were packed to suffocation, the lobbies were filled with crowds dimly discernible through tobacco smoke. Guffaws, quarrels, heated arguments were punctuated by the hissing of spitoons. Everywhere was noise, confusion and intoxication. For the next few days many slept little and ate less, but drank much.[1]

Friends of the candidates had their headquarters in which centered delegates and workers. To these and to all comers were dispensed all manner of eatables and drinkables—on the principle that the way to a man's vote was through his stomach. Cass men had no regular headquarters or organization but individuals like Jesse D. Bright, General Aaron Ward of New York, and Simon Cameron were mov-

[1] *Cincinnati Gazette,* June 9, 1852; Field, *Memories of Many Men,* p. 157; *v.* p. 130, notes 1-4.

ing through the melée endeavoring to influence a vote here and there. Dickinson's rooms at Barnum's Hotel made another Cass center.[1] Buchanan men were at Caroll Hall. The delegates from Pennsylvania had issued an address setting forth his availability and circulated many copies of it. Also they distributed thousands of handbills inviting everyone to call at headquarters.[2] Marcy men were well prepared. They lodged at the Eutaw House. The work was in charge of Seymour, Skinner and Corning, who carried a letter from Marcy giving them full authority to act for him. They got the *Baltimore Sun* to publish his letters of the previous year written to Judge Fine. These documents showed how safe Marcy was on the Compromise. Five hundred extra copies of this number were procured for distribution. But the delegation from the Empire State was divided.[3] Everywhere Douglas men were the most active. They had command of much money and no stone was left unturned. His friends were willing to promise anything and everything. Young America neither slumbered nor slept.[4] It was apparent to unprejudiced observers that the principal contestants were so evenly matched that probably a dark horse would win the race. To some it seemed that Butler had the best chance, to others, Marcy or Houston or Douglas. Meanwhile Burke and his allies were busy with their propaganda.

[1] *Biographical Review of Broome County*, pp. 410-11; *N. Y. Herald*, June 1 and 2, 1852.

[2] Van Dyke to Buchanan, May 29, 1852, Buchanan MSS.; *Augusta Age*, June 3, 1852; *N. Y. Herald*, June 2, 1852; *Baltimore American*, June 1, 1852.

[3] *N. Y. Herald*, June 1-2, 1852; *Baltimore Sun*, June 1, 1852; Marcy to Seymour, Skinner and Corning, May 24, 1852, Wetmore to Marcy, June 5, 1852, Marcy MSS.

[4] *N. Y. Herald*, June 1-4, 1852; *Puritan Recorder* (Boston), June 17, 1852; Pruyn to Marcy, June 2, 1852, Wetmore to Marcy, June 5, 1852, Marcy MSS.

On Monday evening, May 31, a monster mass-meeting was held in Monument Square where there were fireworks and oratory. Many delegations held final caucuses to agree upon details of action. All night long there was ceaseless activity and the dawning day found it little abated.

At twelve o'clock noon on Tuesday, June 1, 1852, Benjamin F. Hallett of Massachusetts, Chairman of the Democratic National Committee mounted the rostrum of the hall of the Maryland Institute and called to order this convention as a symbol of the "union of the Democratic party throughout the Union" met "to preserve and maintain that Union." The confusion was great, seats had been provided for two hundred and ninety-six delegates, the number of the electoral votes, but some states sent enormous delegations, Virginia for example sent sixty-nine men to cast her fifteen votes. This practice augmented the number of delegates present to nearly seven hundred, plus members of Congress and the entire legislature of Maryland. A roaring mob is perhaps the best characterization of the convention when called to order. In the midst of the tumult, General Romulus M. Saunders of North Carolina was made temporary chairman and a Baltimore clergyman "addressed the Throne of Grace" in a petition "that plenteous streams of mercy and love may descend upon this convention" Then a committe for permanent organization was selected, and as there were contesting delegations from several states a committee on credentials was also chosen, in both cases consisting of one delegate from each state. This accomplished, the convention adjourned until 5 P. M.[1]

At a little before six the Convention came together and

[1] The account of the convention unless otherwise noted is taken from two editions of published proceedings. One was printed by Robert Armstrong and the other was reported and published by Wm. Hincks and F. H. Smith.

after much complaint as to the fact that the accommodations for the delegates were not large enough, Jacob M. Thompson chairman of the Organization Committee, brought in a report naming John W. Davis of Indiana for President of the Convention and reaffirming the two-thirds rule. This report was adopted, Davis took the chair adjuring the Convention "to cultivate harmony, conciliate compromise—everthing for principles, nothing for men." Creighton of Ohio then moved to reconsider the vote on the two-thirds rule, which motion Payne of Virgina moved to lay on the table. In the resulting vote only Ohio and three delegates from New York voted against maintaining this time-honored custom. When the result was known ex-President Van Buren's son, Smith, let out a war-whoop of joy that resounded through the hall.[1] The Convention adjourned and the first day was over, but the electioneering never ceased.

At ten Wednesday morning, June 2, the Convention again assembled amid the same confusion and resolutions were passed providing for a platform committee and a committee to select the new Democratic General Committee. Then Philips of Alabama introduced a resolution endorsing the Compromise and Charlich of New York an amendment making the endorsement of the Fugitive Slave Act much stronger. Bright of Indiana moved a similar resolution. These were all referred to the Resolutions Committee not yet appointed.

Coming together for the second session of that day the delegates found the hall rearranged with ample accommodations provided. After the appointment of a Platform Committee a motion was made to proceed to ballot. Immediately an attempt was made to have the platform ad-

[1] Blair to Van Buren, June 1, 1852, Van Buren MSS.

opted first; this was strenuously opposed. Wise of Virginia, Nabers of Mississippi and Robinson of Indiana made the principal speeches for the motion, while Soulé of Louisiana and Floyd spoke against it. It was an attempt of those opposed to an endorsement of the Compromise, largely Buchanan men, to fight that question out first. The vote taken showed that the opinion was that such a fight might destroy the Convention, and that the Douglas, Cass, Marcy and New England delegates had combined to defeat the move.[1] "Principles, not men" was defeated 155-123.

Next in the order of business was the report of the Committee on Credentials which had been organized with Edmund Burke as chairman. This consisted of a list of delegates and decisions on the various contested seats. All contests had been of a minor variety except those from Georgia and Massachusetts. The states rights and union delegations from Georgia were both admitted; as the states rights group was the larger it could outvote the union aggregation and make it powerless. But Masachusetts was not so easily disposed of. Here Robert Rantoul, Jr., had been regularly nominated by the Democratic Convention of the second district. However, Rantoul, though a loyal Democrat, had been in favor of coalition and the hunkers called an irregular convention to nominate a "pure" delegate. The committee majority declared in favor of the contestant, Lord, but a minority submitted a dissenting report. Decision by the convention was postponed till the morrow. The second day was over and no balloting had been accomplished. Outside the hall the missionaries were ceaselessly active.

[1] It is significant that the Dickinson faction in New York did not vote with the other Cass delegations but cast its lot with the southern rights delegates.

In the morning the Convention applied the steam roller and Rantoul, though regularly elected, was unseated, 194-83. The Marcy delegation from New York, the delegates from Ohio, New Jersey, a majority from Illinois, Iowa, Wisconsin and Rhode Island, together with small minorities from other northern states alone protested. The southern delegations were adamant and they carried two-thirds of New England with them.[1] This disposed of, the Convention proceeded to ballot. Two hundred and eighty-eight votes were the whole number and 197 was to be the fateful quota necessary to nominate.

During the morning eight ballots were cast and Cass was in the lead, mustering 119 votes. His strength lay in New England, Ohio, Kentucky,[2] and Michigan, and besides he had the votes of New Jersey, Delaware, Maryland, Louisiana, Missouri, and the Dickinson minority of New York. This support was too varied and his prospects were none too bright. Then came Buchanan with as many as 95, mustering a compact phalanx from Pennsylvania and the south. Douglas rose from 20 to 34 and was steadily advancing. He started with Illinois and a majority from Florida and was soon joined by Arkansas, Vermont and most of California. Marcy with 23 votes from New York and one or two others was the only other candidate of prominence. Lane had Indiana, but that delegation was going to use him only until the winner should appear.

[1] Rantoul declared later that he had been unseated because he refused to promise the credentials committee that he would support the platform before he saw it. A correspondent of the *N. Y. Herald* said this action was taken, against the better judgment of southern leaders, to gratify Hallett's spite against coalitionists. *Cong. Globe*, 32nd Cong., 1st Sess., p. 558, *N. Y. Herald*, June 16, 1852.

[2] Butler's friends had decided to support Cass first in accordance with the former's wishes. He had written a letter giving way to the Michigan Senator, *Augusta Age*, June 3, 1852.

Butler, Houston, Dickinson, Dodge of Wisconsin, and Weller of California received a vote or so now and then.

Meeting again at four, nine more ballots were cast without incident except that the breaking of a settee in the gallery created the impression that the structure was coming down; this caused a small panic. These ballots showed that Cass was weakening, Buchanan was remaining stationary, and Douglas was gaining. Cass lost Missouri to Douglas and went down to 98 as the latter reached 51. Thus passed Thursday.

Friday morning brought the Convention together again at nine o'clock. The night had been spent in caucus and consultation; threat, cajolery, pleading, promise, money, liquor, all had been at work.[1] The platform committee had completed its task, and its chairman, Aaron V. Brown would have reported a summary of its deliberations, had he not been called to order. Ill-feeling in the Virginia delegation precipitated a hot debate. Douglas men such as Floyd and Claiborne appealed to the Convention to decide against the unit rule so they might no longer be bound to vote for Buchanan. After angry speeches, the chairman finally ruled that this was a matter for each delegation to decide for itself. The balloting showed surprising results. Cass fell from 99 to 33, losing practically everything except Michigan, 13 from Ohio and his New York minority, Douglas went on up to 80 gaining Rhode Island, Wisconsin, Iowa, Louisiana, and a majority from Massachusetts and Tennessee, but Buchanan made the phenomenal spurt. By the twenty-second ballot he had 104; New Jersey had come over and he had made gains in New England. Then did the Buchanan leaders implore the Marcy men to come to their aid promising return support if Buchanan failed to carry. Marcy's managers refused to the anger and disgust

[1] *V.* p. 129 n.

of the Pennsylvanians. The New Yorkers were certain that Buchanan could get no more votes because he was the second choice of no northern state and he already had practically all the south. Also if the Marcy delegates were released from their instructions, those in charge felt that some of them would not feel bound to return to Marcy. Thus his essential New York nucleus would be destroyed and he could stand no chance of being run before the Convention. Now Marcy had the enmity of the Pennsylvanians as well as of the Dickinsonians.[1] Then Butler started a little boom when Kentucky went for him, and by the twenty-fifth ballot he had Deleware and a majority of New Hampshire and Maryland.

The afternoon session of Friday brought seven more ballots. Buchanan lost decidedly, falling back to 72, Butler failed and Douglas began to climb. He got back Missouri and broke into the south by securing four votes from North Carolina. He reached 92. Then fear began to take hold of the hearts of his enemies. Cass had failed, Buchanan had failed, and in a tired convention Douglas was looming large. In desperation they turned to Cass. He had fallen far even losing his Ohio majority and had only 27 votes. On the thirtieth Maryland came back, on the thirty-first Delaware, Ohio, Tennessee and Indian voted for him and his 27 increased to 65. Now the southern "Buchaneers" feared a landslide and Virginia attempted to adjourn—but it was no use. The thirty-second brought New Hampshire, New Jersey and Kentucky under the Cass banner and on the thirty-third they were joined by Louisiana, Missouri and a majority from Massachusetts. He was now at 123, but efforts to adjourn were successful. Cass' friends were jubilant, but his enemies were determined.

[1] Thomas to Marcy, Stryker to Marcy, June 7, 1852, Marcy MSS.; Johnson to Buchanan, June 8, 1852, Buchanan MSS.

A feeling of crisis was everywhere. Two days had been spent in balloting without result. The old fear that the Convention would break up without a choice and destroy the party's chance of success had haunted many during that second day. Now it seemed that in order to avert this dire calamity or its alternative, the nomination of Douglas, the delegates were in desperation going to choose Cass again. His meteoric rise in the last few ballots indicated such a danger. The Buchanan men were determined to prevent this.

Cass was too unreliable to be depended upon by the southerners. His squatter sovereignty doctrine was ambiguous and dangerous. Besides he had been defeated once and another disaster must not be invited. Buchanan's Pennsylvania friends knew if Cass were nominated Cameron would triumph over them. They were fairly confident that with their firm nucleus of seventy-eight votes they could prevent Cass' choice. But if they did this again would it not mean that the Convention would break up in despair? It was for them to provide an alternative. Pennsylvania invited representatives from the Virginia, North Carolina, Georgia,[1] Alabama and Mississippi delegations to meet at Caroll Hall. Here they planned far into the night. They decided that Buchanan could not be nominated until every other possible candidate had been tried and had been proven a failure. When the futility of any other choice had been demonstrated then they could stage a successful rally for Buchanan. To them Pierce, Butler and Marcy seemed the only candidates remaining. It was decided that

[1] In the Georgia delegation the southern rights men were mostly for Douglas and the union wing for Cass. In order to defeat Douglas, the Cass men joined with several Buchanan men and cast the vote of the state for the Pennsylvanian. This, they claimed, defeated Douglas, *Toombs Corr.*, pp. 298-302.

Pennsylvania, Georgia and Alabama would remain steadfast for Buchanan, but that Virginia, North Carolina and Mississippi would experiment with the others. Pierce and Marcy were to be tried first as Butler's friends felt he would have a better chance after all the northern men had failed. At the conclusion of these deliberations each committee reported to its delegation. Virginia, North Carolina and Mississippi must select new preferences.[1]

Early the next morning Virginia met to take action on the report of her committee. Friends of Dickinson in the Virginia delegation had been urging that the "Old Dominion" vote for him. Many thought that if Dickinson were tried and after him Marcy the New York delegation might be grateful and later come in with them for Buchanan. In fact Virginia had been on the point of voting for Dickinson the day before but at his earnest request they had postponed it. Now, however, as they were going to shelve Buchanan temporarily they decided to try Dickinson first. So with this determination they emerged from their consultation room. Dickinson's lieutenant, Birdsall, who had been awaiting their decision immediately hurried to the hall to tell his chief.[2]

Dickinson's state of mind was not pleasant. The last days had been filled with urging on the part of friends to become a candidate. Cass, it was argued, could never suc-

[1] Wise to Pierce, June 22, 1852, Pierce MSS. (N. H. Hist. Soc.), Articles from the *Richmond Enquirer* and *Richmond Republican* undated, one signed W. F. R. (W. F. Ritchie) in Pierce's scrapbook in the N. H. Hist. Soc.

[2] *Ibid.*, Gilmore to Buchanan, June 6, 1852, Parker to Buchanan, Nov. 12, 1852, Cave Johnson to Buchanan, June 8, 1852, Buchanan MSS.; Davis to Marcy, June 26, 1852, Marcy MSS.; Stanton, H. B., *Random Recollections* (3rd ed.), pp. 180-2; *New York Hards and Softs—Which is the True Democracy*, pp. 34-36; *Biographical Review of Broome County, N. Y.*, pp. 410-11.

ceed now. A new candidate must come forward, why not himself? Virginia was friendly; his loyalty to Cass would bring over the latter's supporters. But Dickinson had endured months of constant accusation. It had been charged that he was disloyal to Cass, that he was using his name only to purchase his own ambitions. Cass had given no one authority to withdraw his name, and as the balloting had closed the night before Cass had been rallying. If he took Virginia's offer now he would never be able to convince his enemies that he had not been unfaithful to his friend in order to advance himself. What could he do—and yet his action might mean Marcy's victory. In this position he turned to Birdsall with mind made us. "I cannot receive the vote at this stage of the Convention." [1]

The reassembling delgates were tense and fatigued. Chairman Davis was so hoarse and ill that he could no longer preside and Irwin of Alabama was in his place. The roll of the thirty-fourth ballot was called: Maine, New Hampshire, Vermont, Massachusetts, Rhode Island, Connecticut, New York, New Jersey, Pennsylvania, Deleware, Maryland—no change. "Virginia casts her fifteen votes for Daniel S. Dickinson." Dobbin of North Carolina starts to follow when Dickinson gets the floor. He pays glowing tribute to Virginia, he explains his position as a Cass delegate, he declares Virginia's vote to be but a compliment, Virginia surely will not ask him to accept her vote and desert his friends. Eloquently he implores the glorious "Old Dominion" to join him in supporting Cass. It is a touching scene as the bouquets of fair Maryland descend upon him from the galleries. But the balloting goes on.[2] Virginia withdraws for consultation.

[1] *Ibid.*

[2] *Ibid.*; Dickinson, *Dickinson*, vol. ii, pp. 470-2.

This demonstration of loyalty to one for whom the delegation had no use was not to Virginia's liking. The delegates decided to drop Dickinson immediately. Who was to be next? The Pierce leaven had been at work and Burke's efforts were taking effect. John S. Barbour was for Pierce and had talked to many of the delegation in his favor; also he was bitterly opposed to Marcy who had once decided against him in a pension claim case.[1] William A. Harris and Barbour's son were favorable to Pierce. Other delegates, Chastain White of Hanover and Charles Mason of Prince George, were willing to give him a trial. Wise's old friend, Caleb Cushing, and Major French had been urging their candidate upon him and the ground was prepared.[2] But how did the dark horse stand on the slavery question? Harris had been to the New Hampshire delegation and there procured Pierce's letter to Lally. This endorsement of the Compromise was read to the Virginia delegation together with a letter from a former editor of the *Fredericksburg Recorder* vouching for his orthodoxy. The ballot was taken, six districts went for Pierce, one for Butler, two for Marcy, three for Douglas, two for Cass and one equally divided. Six districts changed to Pierce and to him was the vote to go.[3] Virginia reentered the hall.

The thirty-fifth ballot was called. Cass gained Rhode

[1] Campbell to Marcy, June 7, 1852; J. F. Lee to Marcy, June 9, 1852, Marcy MSS.

[2] Wise and Pierce had not been friendly since the Cilley duel. Cilley and Pierce had been schoolmates at Bowdoin. When Wise acted as second to Cilley's opponent in the duel of 1838, Pierce and others felt that Wise was largely responsible for Cilley's death. Scrapbook—Class of 1825, Bowdoin College.

[3] *V.* p. 138, n. 1 and in addition, unidentified article in Pierce Scrap Book presumably by John M. Daniel. Wm. A. Harris to Burke, Aug. 16, 1852, Burke MSS., B. F. Butler to Wm. C. Todd, May 2, 1891 (this letter was supplied through the kindness of Prof. C. M. Fuess of Andover, Mass., Cushing's biographer).

Island and reached his maximum, 131. Virginia voted for Pierce. North Carolina, following the plan of the conference, started Marcy in spite of a vigorous Pierce minority led by Saunders.[1] Mississippi folowed as Jacob Thompson spoke fervently in Marcy's favor. Georgia went for Douglas. Only Maine, New Hampshire and Massachusetts delegates followed Virginia's lead and Pierce stood still for ten ballots with but 29 votes. But Marcy was climbing. Alabama, Georgia, Connecticut, a majority in Massachusetts, New Jersey, Tennessee wheeled into line until by the forty-sixth he had 98. His friends felt that the time had come—that the prize was in his grasp. But no—the Cass men and the Buchanan men remembered how the Marcyites had refused to aid them when their candidates were rising. With scorn Pennsylvania turned a deaf ear to their pleas and went off to urge Virginia to continue to vote for Pierce. Would Virginia stick to Pierce or would she change to Marcy. If only the Dickinson phalanx would unite New York upon Marcy! If this could be done the other states would follow. Buchanan men in the Virginia delegation were ready to go for Marcy and only the influence of John S. Barbour was holding them to Pierce. On the forty-second New York went out and then Seymour suggested applying the unit rule. Threats of personal violence and political reprisal on his chances for governor made him withdraw his obnoxious proposal. Dickinson would not yield. New York would not unite. Marcy's chance was slipping.[2]

[1] R. M. Saunders to Burke, Aug. 14, 1852, *State Capitol Reporter* (weekly), Oct. 29, 1853.

[2] *Boston Post*, June 5, 1852; Stanton, *Recollections* (3rd ed.), pp. 180-2. Marcy to Isaac Davis, June 16, Isaac Davis MSS.; Wetmore to Marcy, June 17, 1852, Marcy MSS. Also Marcy men had bitterly offended western friends of Cass by refusing to pay Cass a complimentary vote after his chances were gone. They, too, would not come to Marcy. T. A. Osborne to Marcy, Aug. 24, 1852, Marcy MSS.

Other agencies had been active. The New Hampshire men were making appeals to delegation after delegation, emphasizing Pierce's availabilty and the claims of New England to name the candidate. New England had never had a presidential nominee on the Democratic ticket. Would such a nomination not help redeem the Whig states there? New Hampshire had ever gone democratic; who had a better right to be heard now? Burke's wide acquaintance stood him in good stead; there was hardly a delegation in which he did not know someone. Not till the forty-sixth ballot did these arguments seem to have effect. Then Kentucky retired and returning voted for Pierce. On the forty-seventh Maryland and four from Massachusetts joined that column. Then the New York delegation went to consult and when they came back they endeavored to adjourn. But it was impossible. The forty-eighth ballot revealed Rhode Island and six Massachusetts delegates in the Pierce ranks, and he now had Maine, New Hampshire, eleven from Massachusetts, Rhode Island, Maryland, Kentucky and Virginia.[1] The Old Dominion was still holding to Pierce, urged on by Pennsylvania and other delegations which promised to come as soon as they could decently abandon their own men. Douglas men in the Virginia delegation now thought they could get the state for him and they demanded a consultation; in this demand they were joined by some Buchanan men who were ready for Marcy. Barbour, however, was firm for Pierce and revealed that North Carolina

[1] W. B. Lawrence to Burke, Aug. 11, 1852, B. F. Hallett to Burke, Aug. 28, 1852, Burke MSS., H. E. Staughton to Burke, Aug. 20, 1852, *State Capitol Reporter* (weekly), Oct. 29, 1853. Pierce's friendship for Dorr and his revolutionary activities in 1842 stood him in good stead in gaining Rhode Island. Also *v.* Hamlin, *Hamlin*, p. 258; *State Capitol Reporter*, Oct. 22, 1853; *N. H. Statesman*, Oct. 29, 1853; *Arkansas* (Little Rock), *Whig*, Dec. 1, 1853, *Minneapolis Journal*, Dec. 16, 1903.

and Georgia were coming in on the next ballot. This destroyed Marcy's last chance.[1] Surely he was unfortunate in his enemies.

Then comes the roll-call of the forty-ninth. From Maine, through New England, down the middle states to Virginia, there is no change, but when "North Carolina" is called, James C. Dobbin arises to utter words that are to make a president. He galvanizes the exhausted convention with an eloquent speech in which he casts the vote of his state for Pierce. The psychological moment has been well chosen. Georgia, Mississippi, Tennessee declare for the new leader. The confusion grows. New York will not change because Dickinson insists on a consultation, the Empire State withdraws.[2] A short calm ensues, Davis reenters and resumes the chair. Pennsylvania retires. Alabama votes for Pierce. Illinois retires. Then above the tumult Vermont and New Jersey are heard. They are changing to Pierce! Indiana is back. Bright has the floor; he lauds Lane, he praises Cass, but these men are hopeless, "Indiana casts her mite, thirteen votes, now, as she will in November next, as sure as the sun will rise and set on that day, for General Franklin Pierce." New York returns, Seymour withdraws Marcy and casts his votes for Pierce. Dickinson speaks for Pierce. But the climax arrives when Pennsylvania casts her votes for Pierce.[3] Then the other states fall in line. Chairman Davis with all the fervor of an evangelist announcing a convert reads, "Cass 2, Douglas 2, Butler 1, Houston 1, Franklin Pierce of New Hampshire (God bless him) 282 votes." One hundred and

[1] Pierce scrap book, articles already cited.

[2] Skinner to Marcy, Aug. 3, 1852, Marcy MSS.

[3] Nathan Clifford of Maine, a Buchanan man, had been urging Pennsylvania to go for Pierce in preference to Marcy and was influential at this point. Clifford, *Nathan Clifford, Democrat*, pp. 253-261.

one guns proclaim the results abroad. Now can the nerve-racked convention take a respite. The crisis is passed.

That afternoon Buchanan men were accorded the priviledge of nominating the Vice-President in the person of William R. King of Alabama, president pro tem of the Senate, a tall, prim, wig-topped mediocrity, then in the clutches of a fatal malady.[1] The platform was placed before a dwindling and inattentive convention, hurriedly read through, then passed without comment. This document was the usual statement of democratic principles. It adroitly avoided trouble on the Compromise by failing to proclaim its finality, but pleased all by merely promising steadfast adherence to it and resistance to the renewal of any agitation on the subject.

The convention was over. Everyone was in good spirits. Cass men rejoiced that Douglas and Buchanan were defeated. Buchanan and Douglas men were jubilant at Cass' downfall. Dickinson found satisfaction in Marcy's defeat. Young America felt they had won a victory. No one knew Pierce very well; he personally had thwarted no one's ambitions. He was reported safe on all dangerous questions.[2] All could hail his nomination with sincere congratulation. His name had saved the convention from possible dissolution and the party from disruption.

And where is the new leader? Pierce had come down to Boston to await the outcome, torn between desire and apprehension. The tense days pass—the balloting goes on and his name is not mentioned—perhaps this apprehension is needless. But on June 5th his name is presented. All

[1] Burke to Pierce, June 6, 1852, Pierce MSS.; Gilmore to Buchanan, June 6, 1852, Buchanan MSS. King was so ill that he went to Cuba after the election. Here he was sworn in as vice-president in March and returned to Alabama where he died early in April, 1853.

[2] Blair to Van Buren, June 5, 1852, Van Buren MSS.

that morning incoming telegraphic reports show that it gains no support. Mrs. Pierce breathes more easily. After dinner they enter a carriage to drive to beautiful Mt. Auburn. In the peace of this city of the dead they can enjoy the calm assurance of an evil escaped. The afternoon wears away. A messenger bursts into the lobby of the Tremont House. "Pierce is nominated!" "Where is Pierce?" ask his friends. Colonel Barnes jumps on horseback and rides to find him. He meets the carriage returning to Boston. The news is told. Mrs. Pierce faints, the General stammers his unbelief—but it is true.[1]

Monster ratification meetings immediately followed in all parts of the country. The committee of notification breaking their usual custom of writing the news decided to inform Pierce in person. Accordingy J. S. Barbour, Alpheus Felch, Pierre Soulé, and Jacob Thompson arrived in Concord on June 17.[2] At noon they formally handed

[1] *N. Y. Herald*, June 7, 1852; *N. H. Patriot*, June 16, 1852. Even Pierce's small son shared the dislike of Washington as evidenced by a letter which he wrote his mother: "Edward has just brought the news from Boston that father is a candidate for the presidency. I hope he won't be elected, for I should not like to live in Washington and I know you would not either." Clipping in Class of 1824 Scrap Book, Bowdoin College Library; Field, *Memories of Many Men*, p. 159.

[2] The appointment of the notification committee caused more ill feeling between the Marcy and Dickinson factions. Corning, chairman of the New York delegation, was to offer the resolution for the appointment of this committee and Angel, the secretary of the delegation wrote it out and sent it to the chair endorsed to the effect that Corning was the mover. However while the latter was attempting to get the floor Dickinson went up front and made the motion. Dickinson's friends expected that he would consequently be appointed chairman. The presiding officer followed the endorsement on the motion and appointed Corning. He was called to New York before the committee decided to go to New Hampshire and when informed of their decision it was too late for him to meet them. *Albany Argus*, Oct. 6, 1852; Angel to E. C. West, Oct. 1, 1852, Hallett to Marcy, July 24, 1852, Marcy MSS.

Pierce the notification and he presented his acceptance. The wires flashed abroad his hearty thanks and enthusiastic endorsement of the platform and the Compromise.[1] With all factions united and hopeful and the party solid, the campaign is on. Henceforth there is to be no East nor West, no North nor South.

[1] *N. H. Patriot*, June 23, 1852.

CHAPTER X

The Campaign

The convention safely passed without secession, the leaders drew breath again and turned their attention to the conduct of the campaign for Pierce's election. There were few clouds on the horizon as far as internal dissension was concerned. The southern rights men were satisfied with Pierce; they had suggested him to the convention and their turn from Buchanan had made his nomination possible. The union Democrats seemed satisfied with the Compromise endorsement of the platform. In the free-soil ranks the *New York Evening Post* was supporting Pierce while Rantoul, lately rejected by the convention, had expressed a desire to see the party triumphant.[1]

With an outwardly harmonious party, the campaign got under way. The National Democratic Executive Committee which had general charge, organized with Robert McLane of Maryland as chairman, and B. B. French as treasurer. It appointed a resident committee to remain at headquarters in Washington and adjourned, as each member had charge of the campaign in his own state. Before separating, they passed a resolution emplowering each member of the national committee to collect not less than one hundred dollars from each Congressional district in his state for the purpose of defraying the Committee's expenses.[2]

[1] Godwin, Park, *Biography of William Cullen Bryant*, vol. ii, pp. 62-63; Rantoul to Sumner, June 13, 1852, Sumner MSS.

[2] B. F. Hallett to Isaac Davis, July 5, 1852, Davis MSS. There were 233 Congressmen, so a fund of about $20,000 was expected.

The newly appointed resident committee was composed of William M. Gwin of California, chairman, A. P. Edgerton of Ohio, secretary, C. H. Peaslee of New Hampshire, J. W. Forney, and A. G. Penn of Louisiana, with R. T. Morsell as chief clerk. This committee with the aid of the money to be raised in accordance with the above plan, were to prepare and publish documents with which to flood the country.[1] These were for the purpose of refuting Whig slanders, attacking Whig principles and candidates, and converting men to the Pierce faith. Congress also remained in session until August thirty-first and the Democratic members endeavored to help on the campaign by their speeches. On the floors of Congress much campaign material was manufactured at public expense.

The organizations in the states were to see that the proper enthusiasm was worked up. Their hands were full for they were to arrange for meetings everywhere, in order that the orators of the party might inspiringly paint the past, present and future glories of the Democracy. Their activities were expensive; enthusiasm was sometimes hard to create unaided; money must be raised; the party must be properly advertised; and documents issued by the national committee must be scattered everywhere. In fine, local organizations must permeate even the remotest and most lonely hamlets. Only so organized could they successfully repel the onslaughts of the enemy.

The Whig sneer of "Who is Franklin Pierce?" called for immediate rebuttal. At Pierce's personal request, his friend, Nathaniel Hawthorne, prepared a biography, as did C. Edwards Lester and B. B. French; one in pamphlet form

[1] Circular letter of the committee, Sept. 21, 1852, Davis MSS.; *Washington Union*, July 4, 1852; Grant Green to J. C. Breckinridge, July 30, 1852; Breckinridge MSS.; E. Burke to Pierce, June (?), 1852, Pierce MSS.

was also prepared for distribution by the resident committee..[1] To influence the German vote the services of a Swedish scholar, G. C. Hebbe, were secured; he was to write pamphlets in foreign languages and use his influence with foreign-born editors. He was also to go out west and take the stump among the Scandinavian population there.[2] To aid this work of publicity, an organization in New York City, called the Jefferson Union, was formed. It prepared about a score of "Papers of the People" which were widely distributed. The *New York Evening Post* issued a weekly pamphlet of information, the *Washington Union* and the *Boston Post,* as well as many other newspapers, published weekly campaign numbers, and the Democratic press throughout the country featured articles and editorials. In this way the United States mail bore to every portion of the Union lives of Pierce and King in English and German, copies of the platform, the Virginia and Kentucky resolutions and other Democratic gospels; fulsome praise of Pierce, condemnation of Scott and the Whigs, indignant rebuttal of charges against the party and its candidate and reams of song and machine-made verse:

[1] Burke to Pierce, June (?), 1852, Pierce MSS.; Pierce asked the historian Bancroft to write a history of parties showing how the Whigs had been found wanting, Pierce to Bancroft, June 30, 1852, Bancroft MSS.

[2] Burke to Pierce, June (?), 1852 and G. C. Hebbe to Burke, July 15, 1852, Pierce MSS. There was some anxiety over the foreign vote. Burke had shortly before been asked by Kossuth to become Hungarian agent in the United States. He and Hebbe were endeavoring to get Kossuth to endorse Peirce, knowing his influence with the German vote. Kossuth was alive to his political advantages. He desired a pledge of American aid in his next European revolt. Pierce publicly expressed gratitude at the material aid rendered in the American Revolution by the patriots of Europe. He declared the United States would never forget this. However, he would commit himself no further and Kossuth never came out openly for him. The foreign vote did not become a campaign problem. Kossuth to Burke, May 25, 1852, Burke MSS.; Pierce letter to Philadelphia Committee, June 30, 1852, printed clipping in Pierce scrap book.

Fling forth our banner gallantly
And let the people sing—
Hurrah for old Democracy—
Hurrah for Pierce and King.
Come brave Locos—
Gallant men and true,
The Whigs were Polked in 44
We'll Pierce in 52.[1]

However it was felt that a deluge of printers' ink alone would not elect Pierce. There must be enthusiasm induced by spread-eagle oratory and other means. In various parts of the country Granite Clubs were organized. These raised "Hickory Poles to the honor of the Young Hickory of the Granite Hills",[2] provided reading rooms and centers for distribution of documents and held meetings where they were thrilled by oratory and liquid refreshment. One of the largest mass-meetings was the grand rally held by Tammany Hall at its annual Fourth of July celebration. Here was read a letter from Martin Van Buren endorsing the candidate.[3] On July 26 another great meeting was held at Newburgh, New York, at which John Van Buren and John A. Dix spoke, the former declaring that there was no longer any free soil party in New York.[4] On August 19 a big meeting was held at Hillsborough, New Hampshire. The New Hampshire leaders attempted to organize this barbecue on a mammoth scale and it was attended by a host of prominent men.[5] Several large mass-meetings were held in Pennsylvania at one of which Buchanan contributed a dull and interminable effort.[6] Enthusiasm perhaps

[1] *Indiana Magazine of History*, vol. xii, p. 45.

[2] *Washington Union*, July 24, 1852.

[3] Martin Van Buren to Tammany Hall, July 1, 1852, Van Buren MSS.; *New York Herald*, July 5, 1852.

[4] *Ibid.*, July 27, 1852.

[5] *Ibid.*, Aug. 20, 1852; *Washington Union*, Aug. 21, 1852.

[6] Buchanan, *Works*, vol. viii, p. 460.

reached its highest pitch at a Tammany Hall rally on September 3. Here Douglas spoke, and Cass, in order to demonstrate that he was not an old fogy, felt called upon to tear off collar, coat and vest. In his shirt sleeves he denounced Whiggism and socialism, declaring that under the free love standards of the latter group it would be a wise woman who knew her own husband.[1] In spite of these attempts the campaign lagged, enthusiasm was isolated and sporadic.

Congress felt called upon to take a hand. The party organ, as usual, needed overhauling. Since the withdrawal of Donelson it had been owned solely by Armstrong and edited by Charles Eames. His efforts were so feeble and lifeless, and he was so obviously pro-southern and anti-barnburner that it was deemed necessary to get another editor.[2] Even at the convention the New Hampshire delegation had consulted Marcy's New York friends as to a proper successor.[3] Edmund Burke, the New Hampshire Warwick, had been Ritchie's assistant and the logical man for the place. He was much talked of and was willing to assume the responsibility but a rumor was widely circulated, especially in Washington, that he was unfriendly to Pierce. This seems to have resulted from his ancient quarrel with Pierce's leading Concord friends. In spite of ample evidence of Burke's loyalty to Pierce and his services in bringing about the nomination he failed to receive the position, presumably because of the opposition of the Concord group.[4]

[1] *New York Herald*, Sept. 3, 1852; Slidell to Buchanan, Sept. 15, 1852, Buchanan MSS.; *Evening Post Document no. 10.*

[2] Campbell to Marcy, Sept. 21, 1852, Marcy MSS. Just when Donelson severed his financial connection with the paper is not known. Forney to Bancroft, July 8, 1852, Bancroft MSS.

[3] Thomas to Marcy, June 7, 1852, Marcy MSS.

[4] Burke to Pierce, June 8, 1852, Pierce MSS.; Jas. W. Bradbury to Burke, July 20, Aug. 19, 1852, Bright to Burke, July 7, 1852, Burke MSS.

Besides a new editor, the *Union* needed financial support. It will be remembered that Donelson had expected large printing jobs which he had failed to get. Now that the convention was over and Donelson had withdrawn, another attempt was going to be made to subsidize the party organ from the public treasury. On July 6 a Democratic Congressional caucus appointed a committee of ten to consider the editorial conduct of the *Union,* financial support for it, and the general welfare of the party; in addition it was to make a report on organization for the campaign.[1] This committee, composed of William H. Polk, Bright, Soulé, Hamilton, Toucey, Jenkins, Rusk, Stuart, Harris and Bayard voted, 8-2, that the printer, A. Boyd Hamilton, by his carelessness, lack of promptness and failure to keep to his agreement, had forfeited his contract. They proposed to the caucus, July 8, that a bill, already drawn up by the joint printing committee and a select committee of the house, be passed. This provided that each house elect its own printer. The committee recommended no action on a new editor; it was thought better to wait until the president was chosen and then find out his preference.[2] Shortly thereafter, Robert Armstrong was elected printer of both houses, Hamilton was indemnified and "Father" Ritchie had his long promised claim honored by Congressional appropriation.[3] John W. Forney took over the editorial management of the *Union* for the period of the campaign with the aid of Eames and Roger A. Pryor of Virginia. His salary was to be $5,000.[4]

[1] *N. Y. Herald,* July 8, 1852.

[2] *Cong. Globe,* 32nd Cong., 1st Sess., p. 1794.

[3] *Cong. Globe,* 32nd Cong., 1st Sess., pp. 1884, 2020, 2196, 2206, 2257, 2324, 2353, 2355, 2387, 2393-2401, 2473, xiii.

[4] Brawley to Buchanan, Sept. 22, 1852, Buchanan MSS.; *Washington Union,* Aug. 28, 1852.

Putting the *Union* in order was not the only Congressional contribution. Many speeches made on the floor of Congress for campaign purposes were distributed by the Resident Committee. Many like Douglas made addresses in various centers within a considerable radius of Washington, and after adjournment on August 31, the country was stumped by the returning members. Here again Douglas was prominent, making a large number of addresses all the way from New York to St. Louis.[1]

But what was the burden of all these speeches? What were the issues of this campaign? Not slavery; for the Democrats and Whigs had both endorsed the Compromise settlement. Not the glorious principles of '98; they stirred no enthusiasm. Not the bank; in spite of Democratic warnings, there was no longer any danger of one: nor internal improvements; the western Democrats were as eager for them as the Whigs. Nor the tariff; the country was prosperous, no one seemed anxious to change the prevailing law. Foreign policy was a possibility; Douglas and Young America tried to raise enthusiasm by demanding Cuba, expressing violent sympathy for Hungary and Ireland, and stressing the need for the Pacific trade with Japan and China. They condemned Fillmore's apology to Spain and the Clayton-Bulwer treaty which they denounced as truckling to Great Britain.[2] Imperialism and anglophobia, however, struck no responsive chord. Charges of graft and extravagance against the Whigs were tried; the Galphin Case was well aired; but no one seemed greatly exercised about corruption in high places.[3] In fact, in spite of their

[1] *Ibid.*, Sept. 8, 1852.

[2] Burke to Pierce, June 14, 1852, Pierce MSS.; Douglas, *pamphlet speeches*, especially the Richmond speech of July 9, and one at Tammany Hall, September 3, *New York Herald*, Sept. 4.

[3] *Speech of Gilbert Dean, M. C. from New York*, in the House of

slogan—" Principles, not men ", the Democrats were almost immediately outmanoeuvred and put on the defensive by the Whig campaign of personalities.

Thes slanderous attacks started immediately after the nomination. On June 7, the *Philadelphia Ledger* blossomed out with the charge that Pierce was anti-Catholic. The New Hampshire constitution of 1792 still in effect provided that only Protestants could hold office. In 1850 a constitutional convention presided over by Pierce had stricken out this qualification. The voters, however, had refused to ratify the change. Now it charged that Pierce had been hostile to the amendment and had influenced the Democratic state electorate, generally in the majority, to vote it down. This was immediately denied by Charles O'Conor, a very prominent Catholic layman of New York City in a speech at the ratification meeting of Tammany on June 9. It was later shown that Pierce had been in favor of the change and that it had failed because a two-thirds vote was necessary or 10,000 more than the Democratic vote. The candidate himself denied any hostility to Catholics in a public letter widely published.[1] This charge nevertheless frequently reappeared as vain attempts were made to prejudice the Catholic vote against Pierce.

On June 10, the *Tribune* published a scurrilous letter charging the Democratic candidate with gross intemper-

Representatives, Aug. 23, 1852; pamphlet *The Galphin Case*. The Galphin Case was a claim paid during the Taylor administration by the Secretary of the Treasury acting on an opinion of the Attorney-General. This claim netted the Secretary of War $95,000 and improper conduct and collusion were freely charged. Taylor himself was blamed. Rhodes, *op. cit.*, vol. i, pp. 202-205.

[1] *Washington Union*, June 9, Aug. 14, 1852; *Newark Daily Advertiser*, June 16, 1852; *New York Herald*, Sept. 1, 27, Oct. 9, 1852. An attempt was made to draw Archbishop Hughes of New York into the controversy and to persuade him to advise the church how to vote. In a dignified public letter, the Archbishop refused, *ibid.*, Sept. 27, 1852.

ance. For this the editor apoligized the next day saying that "Pierce is not a temperance man in our sense of the term but we know nothing in regard to his habits that should subject him to public reprehension." This drunkenness charge was much exploited and called forth a flood of testimonials of the candidate's moral character as a citizen, lawyer and Sunday-school teacher. These, it may be noted, all came from Concord friends and none from former political associates in Washington. Few, outside of the professional prohibitionists of the time cared much whether he drank or not, and the "Maine law" did not get into the campaign.[1]

Not having roused public sentiment against intemperance the Whig journals next tried cowardice. Pierce's military glory consisted of "two somersaults and a faint." He had run away from the firing line and had fainted from fear. He had had his face slapped by a brother officer and failed to resent it. He would not accept a commission as Brigadier-General without six months pay in advance and rations for man and horse. How compare this poltroon with the glorious hero of Chepultepec, Winfield Scott! These charges were also proved false. Scott's own report of Pierce's actions, the testimonials of many of his comrades in arms and a letter from Marcy procured by Edmund Burke showed that the candidate had gone into battle against physician's orders while suffering from a fever and in the engagement had been overcome with exhaustion. The cowardice charge fell flat.[2]

To the accusations of religious intolerance, drunkenness and cowardice was added the crowning charge of abolition-

[1] *N. Y. Tribune*, June 10, 11, 1852; *Washington Union*, July 15, 23, 1852.

[2] *Washington Union*, Aug. 21, 1852, *Cincinnati Gazette*, Nov. 22, 1852; pamphlet, *Vindication of the Military Character and services of General Franklin Pierce by his companion in arms in Mexico.*

ism. On June 17, the *National Era,* abolition organ, published an article entitled "A Brief Chapter from the Life of Franklin Pierce". It endeavored to prove that Pierce was really friendly to abolitionism because he was supported by such men as Van Buren, Dix and Henry B. Stanton. It also published a speech which Pierce had made on January 1, 1852 at New Boston, N. H. In this he was reported to have said that the Fugitive Slave Act was loathsome and opposed to moral right and that he would never aid in rendering up a fugitive. This article was given wide circulation in a pamphlet entitled "Franklin Pierce and his Abolition Allies" which Whig Congressmen franked broadcast to the number of over 50,000 copies. This version of his New Boston speech Pierce branded as false in a public letter. This brought out testimony to the effect that the version was true. The controversy narrowed down to a point of veracity between Pierce and some of those who heard the speech; an independent with Pierce leanings, like the editor of the *New York Herald,* believed that Pierce had said it in haste and repented at leisure. To offset further this Whig broadside a pamphlet with the same title was prepared in which ex-Governor Brown of Mississippi set forth conclusively how real abolitionists like Sumner and Hale had repudiated Pierce. Publicity was also given to the fact that in 1851 the candidate had been prominent in calling a new Democratic gubernatorial convention in New Hampshire which discarded a regularly nominated candidate because he had expressed decided anti-slavery views, retracted them and then declared the retraction forced by the hunkers.[1] As it was generally known that Pierce be-

[1] *Washington Union*, Aug. 15, 1852; *New York Herald*, July 20, 22, Aug. 5, 10, 1852; *Hunter Corr.*, pp. 146-7; *N. H. Patriot*, Feb. 13, 20, 1851; J. W. McKnew to Breckinridge, Sept. 21, 1852, Breckinridge MSS.; *Cong. Globe Appendix*, 32nd Cong., 1st Sess., p. 1090; Pamphlets (2) *Franklin Pierce and his Abolition Allies*; Hawthorne, *Life of Pierce*, pp. 116-119.

lieved that slaves were property and that the government was bound to protect their owners in their property rights, these abolition charges convinced only those who wished to be convinced.

Pierce's legislative record was another weapon wielded against him. It was largely a negative record. He had been eight years in Congress with no legislative measures and few speeches to his credit. He had voted against five rivers and harbors acts signed by Jackson and Van Buren, as well as minor internal improvements. In fact most of his votes had been in the negative. This opposition to rivers and harbors would, it was feared, alienate western Democrats. This was not to be, however. Many, like Stuart of Michigan, felt that Pierce, the executive head of all the United States, would be guided by different motives than Pierce, the representative of an inland country constituency.[1]

Finally Pierce was spread upon the broad page of the press as a friend of our traditional enemy, England, as one in sympathy with aristocracy. British papers were favoring Pierce and August Belmont, Rothschild's agent, was active in his behalf—consequently it was assumed that European gold was buying up votes for Pierce. These charges seem to have been little heeded.[2]

The Democratic managers and editors in their turn opened their batteries upon the Whig candidate, Winfield Scott. The Whigs boasted much of his military reputation. To dispel the glamour attaching to his name the Democrats ridiculed him as "Old Fuss and Feathers" and spoke much of two phrases he had used during the late war, namely "a

[1] Forney to Bancroft, July 8, 1852, Bancroft MSS:; pamphlet, *The Presidency: Winfield Scott and Franklin Pierce; Their Qualifications and Fitness for that High Office.*

[2] *N. Y. Herald*, Oct. 12, 27, 1852.

hasty plate of soup", and "firing on the rear". These caused much merriment and aided Scott's own personal peculiarities and vanities in making him ridiculous. Then when he went on a stumping tour into Kentucky and back his speeches showed that he was not especially happy as a campaign orator, a fact emphasized by the Democratic press. Various letters from Scott were published showing that he was opposed to foreigners, hostile to Catholics, ignorant of the Constitution, in favor of a bankrupt law, and, worse, a national bank. They purported to show his "incompetency, aristocracy and persevering efforts against naturalization laws". Another pamphlet was prepared showing the *Dangers of Electing an Incompetent Man President*. This portrayed Taylor's weakness as an executive and gave the details of the Galphin fraud. "Why", said Douglas, "should we make a good general into a bad president." F. P. Blair, Sr., dug up a mass of facts which he put into a pamphlet called a *Memoir of General Scott from records contemporaneous with the events*. In this he showed that Scott had quarreled with most of his officers, had been recalled from Florida in 1836 and in the last war had been engaged in a lengthy dispute with Secretary of War Marcy. Also at Marcy's suggestion Scott's accounts were investigated by Congress but no irregularities were found. This petty sniping was not of a character to develop enthusiasm and the campaign drifted. Indeed the *New York Herald* aptly remarked that there was more interest in New York in the Women's Rights Convention, Fourierism and the rivalries of two foreign concert singers.[1]

[1] Pamphlets: *The Political Letters and Writings of General Scott*, *The Dangers of Electing an incompetent man President*, *Memoir of General Scott*; Buchanan, *Works*, vol. viii, p. 460; Blair to Van Buren, Aug. 16, Sept. 30, 1852, Van Buren MSS.; Dean to Marcy, July 27, Marcy to Campbell, July 30, Dean to Marcy, Aug. 14, Campbell to Marcy, Aug. 25, Marcy to Campbell, Sept. (?), 1852, Marcy MSS.; *N. Y. Herald*, Sept. 10, 17, 1852.

Lack of enthusiasm was not the only difficulty that the Democrats had to face. There were some rebellious groups within the ranks. In spite of the fact that Blair, Benton, the Van Burens and the New York Barnburners supported Pierce, Senator Chase, Hale and Sumner would not get behind him. Chase wote in vain to Martin Van Buren and Benjamin F. Butler of New York to rally to the standard of '48. They replied that the slavery question was settled; there was no need for further agitation. But the "die-hards" and free-soilers persisted and John P. Hale and George W. Julian were nominated for President and Vice-President. This movement caused some apprehension but it proved harmless. Hale and Julian could not retain the vote of Van Buren and Adams.[1]

In the south, too, there was some lack of harmony. Cobb's Union party in Georgia was one focal point. Before the Baltimore Convention the majority of the Georgia Democracy, known as the Southern Rights Democrats, had held a convention, March 31, which, besides choosing delegates to the convention, had, against the advice of MacDonald, their most prominent leader, nominated an electoral ticket to support the nominee of the coming national gathering. The Cobb Union party had also sent delegates to the National Convention where they were received with the others. Their platform of the Compromise was adopted and they felt that they were as good Democrats as the southern rights men. Consequently Cobb and his lieutenants asked that a new state convention of both wings be held and a new electoral ticket nominated representing each. The radicals refused as they desired to keep the unionists

[1] S. P. Chase to Van Buren, June 27, 1852, Van Buren to Chase, July 7, Van Buren to Tammany Hall, July 1, Van Buren MSS.; Chase to Hamlin, Aug. 3, 1852, Chase MSS.; *N. Y. Herald*, Aug. 10, 1852; Preston King to Welles, June 12, 1852, Welles MSS.

out of fellowship. Therefore the latter met on July 15 and chose a separate Pierce and King electoral ticket of Democrats and Whigs. This action drove off most of their Whig support and left them a remnant. Feeling between the two wings of the Democracy was very bitter extending even into social life. Pressure was brought to bear upon the unionists by prominent Democrats for the sake of harmony, and by August 10 the executive committee realized that their cause was hopeless. They decided to issue an address disbanding the party and withdrawing the ticket. This made the southern rights men more friendly, and in a last attempt at amalgamation a convention of union men met September 18 to act on the overtures of the radicals. These were found to be polite but unyielding on any vital point, and the convention ratified the action of the executive committee and the party was no more. Certain friends of Cobb in northern Georgia in the Tugalo district refused to abide by the decision and soon put in the field another Pierce and King ticket known as the Tugalo ticket. In spite of the apprehensions of many the southern rights Pierce and King ticket carried the state polling 33,-843 votes, though the Tugalos mustered 5,733.[1]

In Alabama there was also some trouble, this time from the rabid southern rights group led by William L. Yancey. That group in their March, 1852, convention had declined to cooperate with either of the two parties by sending delegates to the national conventions and determined to maintain their organization until after the results of these meetings were known. Pursuant to these resolutions the convention reassembled July 12 and determined to appoint a

[1] *Washington Union*, July 11, 22, Aug. 28, Sept. 4, 21, 1852 (often incorrect); *N. Y. Herald*, July 8, 19, 1852; *Hunter Corr.*, p. 148, *Toombs Corr.*, pp. 302-21; Ritchie to W. R. King, Aug. 26, 1852, Pierce MSS.; Phillips, *Robert Toombs*, pp. 108-10.

committee to correspond with Pierce and Scott as to their attitude toward southern rights. They were to reconvene when these replies were received. Scott sent a non-committal reply and Pierce ignored them, so when they came together again on September 13 they nominated George M. Troup of Georgia and John A. Quitman of Mississippi for President and Vice-President. Troup accepted but declared he should support Pierce. This ticket carried little weight, and most southern rights men supported Pierce, who easily carried the state with 26,881 votes while Troup only received 2,174 votes from bitter enders like Yancey. This ticket was less popular elsewhere in the south, in Troup's home state it received 119 votes and elsewhere less.[1]

Lack of harmony was not confined to the South. New York was a storm center. How to raise campaign funds was the chief trouble. Marcy's friend, Thomas, had surveyed the situation and was worried. When Peaslee visited New York in July they discussed the situation. Peaslee told Thomas that George N. Sanders had been to see him and told him that if George Law and Pierce could come to an understanding Law would furnish all the money necessary for the campaign. Thomas impressed upon Peaslee the fact that if Law should be countenanced by Pierce, nothing would be done by the respectable element in New York in support of the ticket. Thomas then introduced Peaslee to various party workers including Samuel J. Tilden and efforts were made to raise some money. But it was slow work. Many of Marcy's opponents refused to contribute. Many were away for the summer. There were so many state offices depending on the result of the state elections

[1] *N. Y. Herald*, July 8, 18, Sept. 14, 1852; *Washington Union*, Sept. 15, 1852; DuBose, *Wm. L. Yancey*, p. 268, Hodgson, *Cradle of the Confederacy*, pp. 326-337, Harden, *Troup*, pp. 529-30.

that much money was reserved for carrying primaries, city and state elections. As the national committee were counting on New York for funds this was embarrassing. Two weeks later Thomas sent for aid and Robert McLane, the chairman, and Peaslee came to New York. Here representatives of all cliques were invited to meet at the Astor House on July 31 and confer. Only Flagg, Kelly and Tilden, all barnburners, came. After consultation it was decided to let each one raise what he could as an individual; organization was dispensed with. Other difficulties piled up. Thomas' activities aroused the jealousy of the national committeeman, Beekman, a barnburner. He complained to McLane that Thomas was absorbing his functions. However, as Beekman had been holding off because he wanted Congressman Dean placed on the resident committee, he got little sympathy from Washington. Tammany, too, was cold, and instead of raising money, actually asked the national committe for $10,000 for state campaign expenses. Thomas and Tilden after much work succeeded in raising $1,100 by the middle of August, but could see prospects of only $400 additional. As this was less than half the state's quota they had reason to be discouraged.[1] Finally at the opportune moment Belmont stepped in and contributed a large sum to the national committee. Thus the matter of funds was taken care of.[2]

These difficulties led some to fear that the hards were going to bolt the ticket in New York, especially as they had just been defeated again in the state convention. The Marcy men learned from Pierce's intimate, Atherton, that Birdsall, Dickinson's henchman, had been to Pierce demanding pledges that Marcy would not be considered as predominant in New York. Atherton further stated that

[1] Thomas to Marcy, July 19, 29, 31, Aug. 14, 1852, Marcy MSS.

[2] C. H. Peaslee to Marcy, May 9, 1853, *ibid.*

Pierce had not only refused these pledges but had told Birdsall that if the state ticket were defeated he would know why. Every effort was made to whip the disgruntled hards into line. They need not have feared, however, as the state ticket ran 2,000 votes ahead of Pierce.[1]

There was another revolt in New England. As the Massachusetts state convention of September 8 approached certain ultra-hunkers like Bradford and Austin wished to break the coalition with the free-soilers which of late had been winning victories. They pressed this in spite of the fact that Benjamin F. Butler and others who had returned from the Hillsboro rally had reported that the general sentiment among leaders from all quarters was that the coalition should be maintained; it was felt that in no other way could Massachusetts be rescued from the Whigs. Nevertheless Bradford and Austin introduced a resolution at the convention dissolving the agreement. When this was voted down two to one, these men withdrew with about a hundred followers known as the "Fitchburg seceders". They found aid and comfort in the attitude of Pierce's friend, Edmund Burke. He wrote an article in the *New Hampshire Argus and Spectator* condemning coalition and declaring Pierce would not look with favor upon it. As Pierce was intimate with Cushing and Greene, the managers who had preserved the coalition at Fitchburg, Burke was probably mistaken. Pierce never really favored him with his confidence. This matter caused a stir in New England and it was feared that such unnecessary antagonism would only make votes for Hale.[2]

[1] S. B. Jewett to Marcy, Oct. 19, Thomas to Marcy, Oct. 21, 22, 25, Marcy to Berret, Oct. 27, 1852, Marcy MSS.

[2] *N. H. Daily Patriot*, Sept. 9, 1852; *N. Y. Herald*, Oct. 11, 1852; unsigned and unaddressed letter in B. F. Butler's handwriting, Aug. 20, 1852, Moses Bates, Jr., to Benj. F. Butler, Sept. 25, 1852, Benj. F. Butler MSS.; Bradford to Marcy, Feb. 22, 1853, Marcy MSS.

In spite of these numerous Democratic difficulties, the Whigs were so rent with dissentions themselves that they were unable to pursue their advantage. Many of that party felt that Webster, the great nationalist, should have been the candidate. This was especially true in the south. There many leaders, prominent among them being Stephens and Toombs of Georgia, felt that Scott had been nominated and Webster defeated by the manipulations of Seward and the free soil group. The domination of these men the Compromise Whigs refused to own. On July 3 Toombs got up in the House and declared that the Whig party was under the control of the free soil element, and that the election of Scott would reopen sectional strife. On the same day Stephens, Toombs and other southern union Whigs published a letter repudiating Scott and declining to support him. Gentry of Tennesse, one of the signers, gave up all hope and flamboyantly declared in the House:

> I will go home. In a sequestered valley in the state of Tennessee, there is a smiling farm with bubbling fountains, covered with rich pasturage and fat flocks and all that is needful for the occupation and enjoyment of a man of uncorrupted tastes. I will go there and pray for "Rome".

Some of these supported Pierce while others, especially in Georgia and North Carolina, joined with certain disaffected ones in Massachusetts in nominating Webster at public meetings. Webster electoral tickets were formed in several states. In spite of the fact that Webster advised his friends to vote for Pierce, and notwithstanding the fact that he died a few days before the election, several thousand votes were cast for him. In New York, Fillmore's defeat cooled the enthusiasm of the sliver grays, Seward's enemies.[1] Various prominent and semi-promin-

[1] Pamphlet: *M. P. Gentry's speech with Stephens-Toombs letter attached*; Ogg, *Webster*, p. 408.

ent Whigs gained praise from the Democratic journals by announcing publicly their support of Pierce.[1] These defections combined with Scott's individual peculiarities and anti-foreign tendencies did much to break the morale of the Whig party.

What had Pierce been doing during these months of the campaign? He had spent the time quietly at Concord, Rye Beach and Boston. He had received many visitors. Already those who were curious as well as many who hoped for favors and office were seeking out him upon whom their hopes rested. In addition there were conferences with his managers who came to make reports and give and take advice. His part was almost wholly quiescent. He wrote a few letters in order to settle doubts about some of his views and made four short speeches in New Hampshire, but they were like most of his efforts, glittering but vague, and void of real meaning. During September and October he was reported as nervous and discouraged, and he kept his agents busy. Charles L. Woodbury, the George brothers, Hibbard, Arherton, Peaslee, and Upham travelled back and forth, especially in New York and Pennsylvania, observing, speaking, reporting.[2]

The hard work of the campaign was carried on by the Democratic Resident Committee at Washington. This body had dwindled to three, Peaslee, Forney and Penn. These had been industriously at work with a staff of about thirty clerks. Their chief occupation was sending out campaign documents, often as many as 5,000 a day, to everyone who was thought to have the least interest in

[1] Among these were Senator Wm. Wright of N. J. and Thos. L. Clingman, M. C. from North Carolina, *Washington Union*, June 30, *N. Y. Herald*, Oct. 14, 1852.

[2] Thomas to Marcy, Sept. 13, Oct. 11, 20, 21, 22, 23, 1852, John H. George to Marcy, Sept. 14, Oct. 14, 1852, Marcy MSS.; Irelan, *Pierce*, pp. 106-8; Field, *Memories*, pp. 160-2.

them. They made frequent appeals for address lists and every effort was made to keep in touch with the leaders in all portions of the country. In order to stir up a little activity the committee sent out a circular on September 18, asking for detailed reports, urging care in establishing a thorough organization to ensure a large attendance at the polls and warning against any excess of confidence. Then as reports had been coming in that Whig postmasters were not delivering Democratic documents, the committee sent out a check list asking those receiving this list to report whether all their documents had been delivered. When Scott had been on his stumping tour for a few days they sent out another circular, October 9, showing that the Democratic vote had been steadily growing and that all state elections except that in Vermont had been successful. The Democrats had carried Maine, Missouri, New Hampshire, North Carolina, Rhode Island, Texas, Arkansas, Connecticut and Iowa with an aggregate majority of 48,242. On October 22 they sent forth their final appeal. They declared that

> Within a few days there has been a grand conclave of the active men of the Scott party in Philadelphia and New York and that large sums of money have been raised to dispatch secret emissaries to every nook and corner of these states to provide bounties for recruiting service—to prostitute the base—to keep a rendezvous in every village and pay the sergeants and corporals in their service—to hire bullies to intimidate and drive from the polls the weak-hearted and to bring every Whig voter to the ballot-box.

They appealed to all to be active and bring out a full vote, especially if the weather were to be unpleasant.[1]

[1] *Washington Union*, July 4, Sept. 29, 1852; Peaslee to Breckinridge, Sept. 18, Forney to Breckinridge, Sept. 28, 1852, J. C. Breckinridge MSS.; Dean to Marcy, Aug. 14, 1852, Marcy MSS.; a file of the circular letters of the committee is preserved in the Isaac Davis MSS.

On November 2 the vote was cast. Pierce and King were elected, carrying all the states except Vermont, Massachusetts, Kentucky and Tennessee. This sweeping victory in the electoral college in its appearance, however, belied actualities. Analysis of the returns shows that the Whig vote decreased but very little; only in the strong southern rights states of Alabama, Florida, Georgia, and Mississippi was there a marked falling off. The loss of but a small percentage of votes in other states was what deprived Scott of their electoral votes. Indeed the relatively slight shift can be seen from the fact that in 1848 the Whigs obtained 48 percent of the vote while in 1852 this dropped only to 44 percent. The Whig party was by no means numerically dead. Pierce's majority over all candidates throughout the country was barely 30,000 in a total of 3,100,000.[1]

Thus Pierce was elected not through any particular qualification of his own, except "availability", not because of astute political management on the part of his henchmen, but by force of circumstances. Since the "Hurrah and Hallelujah Campaign" of 1840, there had occurred a series of crises which had wrecked the political nerves of the country. The tension had nearly precipitated disunion in

[1] Whig Almanac, 1854. Moore, *Schuyler Colfax*, p. 59.

The vote was:

Pierce	1,587,256
Scott	1,384,577
Hale	157,296
Webster	7,425
Troup	3,300
Broome (American)	4,485
Goodel (Abolition)	75
	3,144,414

1850 and in 1852 the county was undergoing a natural reaction. There was little to choose between the candidates and parties, and the country was too prosperous to be interested in a battle without issues. Since Jackson's time the country had been normally Democratic, consequently the natural result had followed—Pierce had been elected. During the campaign the politicians had seen the necessity for uniting for the spoils and, with few exceptions, all Democrats, free soil, union and southern rights, had joined hands to win the election. Victory had resulted from union. Would the Democratic politicians profit by the lesson? Would the harmony last?

CHAPTER XI

The Cabinet

By eleven o'clock on the evening of Election Day, Franklin Pierce knew that he was to be the next President of the United States. He allowed no demonstration of congratulation in Concord that night, and the next morning he went quietly away to the old homestead at Hillsborough. The thoughts which came to him and the emotions that he experienced during the next few days were unknown to any but himself; on November 5 he returned to Concord nerved to his new task. And it was a task. During the next four months he must choose a cabinet, formulate his policies and incorporate them in his inaugural address. Upon the success or failure of these creations depended in large measure the maintenance of party harmony and strength. These problems were in themselves difficult of solution, but circumstances made them thrice difficult. The President-elect was continually distracted. He was the legitimate prey for any and all who might desire to receive office or give advice. Concord became a shrine for the faithful and thither many a hopeful pilgrim wended his way. There many made their devotions and came away with the bitter sweet recollection of a hearty welcome, a pleasant smile—and no satisfaction.

In Concord, New Hampshire, then, Pierce settled down to work out his problems. His chief adviser was ex-Senator Charles G. Atherton, a long time confidential friend who during his congressional career had been the sponsor of the famous "gag resolution".[1] Pierce planned to have him in the Senate as his spokesman. With difficulty his friends secured his election by the New Hampshire legislature on November 25.[2] Another close friend of Pierce was Judge Josiah Minot, his law partner, who also managed his property. The President-elect depended upon him in a great many ways and decided to give him a position in the Treasury so that he might be near him. John H. George, chairman of the state committee, was going to take charge of his law practice. Congressman Charles H. Peaslee was also a close friend, and Peaslee's nephew, Sidney Webster, who had been a law student of Pierce, was going to Washington as private secretary to the new executive. These were the local confidants of the President-elect, and they as well as Pierce were deluged with applications and advice. Their movements were watched with cat-like intentness by the press—in fact they became oracles whose every move was portentous. However, in spite of their importance in the public eye, none of them, with the possible exception of Atherton and Webster, seems to have known anything of Pierce's real plans or intentions, so close did he keep his own counsel.

The seat of the more important activities of this period was not Concord. This little capital was too small, everyone could be too closely watched, pilgrims could be too easily identified and advertised. Boston, the metropolis of New England, was only about seventy miles away and could be reached by a three hour railroad journey. Here the arrival and sojourn of prominent men was less notice-

[1] Corning, *Amos Tuck*, p. 63.

[2] The Pierce wing of the New Hampshire Democracy were by no means dominant and it was with difficulty that enough of their opponents were persuaded to vote for Atherton, *Boston Atlas*, Nov. 27, 1852, *N. Y. Herald*, Dec. 4, 1852; Thomas to Marcy, Nov. 27, 1852, Marcy MSS.

able. Consequently Pierce went there as often as two or three times a week, staying sometimes at the home of his wife's uncle, Amos Lawrence, or more often at the Tremont House. Here he saw the more important pilgrims, and here he held many important conferences with Cushing, Greene, Woodbury and others.[1]

In these surroundings Pierce set out to choose his cabinet. In order to maintain harmony all elements must be satisfied. Compromise supporters, free soilers, states rights men, the factions of Cass, Buchanan and Douglas, all demanded a friend in the President's council. By the appointment of seven men, Pierce was called upon to usher in the millenium.

Naturally many were interested in his choice and some statement or announcement was eagerly awaited. Speculation was rife. On December 8 there appeared an editorial article in the *New Hampshire Patriot* on the cabinet. This was generally considered to have been "inspired". It declared that "unity" was to be the keynote, no portion of the party was to be proscribed, previous office holders such as members of Polk's cabinet still would be eligible, the Baltimore platform was to be the only test. Pierce, so the article ran, was open to suggestion. This pronouncement indicated that anybody and everybody who had voted for Pierce was to be in good standing with the new administration. With this the curious had to be satisfied. Meanwhile Pierce was struggling with knotty problems.[2]

New York politics, as usual, presented the most difficult puzzle. Pierce wished to unite and harmonize the party there by means of appointments. He felt that the Empire State should be represented in his body of advisers, but whom should he choose? There were at least three men of

[1] *Diary and Correspondence of Amos Lawrence*, p. 335.

[2] *Washington Union*, Dec. 22; *N. Y. Herald*, Dec. 19, 20, 1852; Blair to J. Van Buren, Dec. 19, 1852, Van Buren MSS.

cabinet stature, William L. Marcy, soft, Daniel S. Dickinson, hard, and John A. Dix, barnburner. This matter occupied Pierce's mind immediately. Marcy in his congratulatory note of November 7 stated his intention of spending the winter in the West Indies with his consumptive son. The public press put the date of his departure at November 13. Quick action was necessary if Pierce wished his advice, so the President-elect requested the ex-Secretary of War to meet him in Boston, November 11. On the day appointed they had a long interview in which Pierce made it clear that he would like to have Marcy in his cabinet but as they both realized, because of the latter's enemies in New York, such an appointment would be unwise.[1]

Pierce's own choice sems to have been his friend and boyhood companion, John A. Dix. But there were other considerations, and powerful influences were being brought to bear on the matter. Immediately after the election the General Committee of the Democratic Party of New York City appointed a group of hards with Augustus Schell as chairman to proceed to Concord and offer Pierce the hospitality of the city. This was probably made an excuse to provide an opportunity for a political visit, perhaps to urge Dickinson's claims. They arrived in Concord on November 11 and there met Pierce on the way to the railroad station. On learning from him that he was going to Boston they decided to go also and have their interview in that place. During the railroad journey while talking over New York's cabinet possibilities Pierce is reported to have declined to state whom he favored, but to have declared that Marcy had the privilege of saying who should

[1] Pierce to Marcy, Nov. 9, 1852, Marcy to Berret, Jan. 15, 1853, Marcy to Wetmore, Jan. 19, 1853, Marcy MSS.; Slidell to Buchanan, Dec. 19, 1852, Buchanan MSS.; Marcy to Bancroft, Nov. 10, 1852, Bancroft MSS.

not be appointed. That evening when they were ushered into the presence of the President-elect at the Tremont House they found him talking with their principal opponent, W. L. Marcy. Their dream of a confidential interview vanished.[1]

The next New York move was from the other side. Governor-elect Seymour and Erastus Corning of Albany went up to Concord, November 26, to press Marcy's name and to urge Pierce to make an announcement of his cabinet plans for New York before the legislature met in January; this they thought would aid them in asserting their dominance in the party. In spite of their pressure the President-elect refused to announce any candidates before he left for Washington. They came away with the impression that Dix would be the man—largely because of Pierce's objection to others.[2]

Then on December 1 the electors of the several states met in their respective state capitals and cast their votes. The New York factional fight entered even this harmless formality. Dickinson's friends had been circulating a petition praying the President-elect to appoint their leader to the cabinet. They requested signatures on the ground that Pierce desired such a petition sent to him. To offset this the Marcy members of the New York electoral college, who numbered twenty-two of the thirty-five, after casting the states' vote for Pierce, delegated Pruyn to write to the President-elect on behalf of the electors. In this letter they intended to recommend Marcy in general terms without mentioning his name. Friends of Marcy, however, complained that the letter sent endorsed Dix.[3]

[1] F. Byrdsall to Buchanan, Nov. 24, 1852, Buchanan MSS.; Thomas to Marcy, Nov. 20, 24, 1852, Marcy MSS.

[2] J. V. L. Pruyn to Marcy, Nov. 23, 27, 1852, Seymour to Marcy, Dec. 1, 1852, Marcy MSS.; *N. Y. Herald*, Nov. 28, Dec. 12, 1852.

[3] Seymour to Marcy, Dec. 1, 1852, Pruyn to Marcy, Dec. 1, 1852, H. K. Smith to Marcy, Dec. 7, 1852, Marcy MSS.

Meanwhile, Pierce had been sounding out opinion elsewhere through his friend, Peaslee. He saw Blair and inquired of him how Van Buren, Benton and the old Jacksonians felt about a cabinet member. The consensus of opinion among them seemed to be that Dix was the man.[1] Thus fortified by his own predelections, the advice of the Jacksonians, the barnburners, and the free soilers, Pierce determined upon Dix as a representative of these groups.[2] Consequently in an interview with Dix he offered him a place or at least suggested such a possibility.[3] For the time being New York was disposed of.

Another problem was satisfying Pennsylvania. The Keystone state like New York had its famous man, James Buchanan, a veteran in cabinet service. Pierce evidently did not want him in the cabinet, but on the other had did not wish to antagonize him by neglecting to consult him. The anti-Buchanan men were out in full force while some of his friends were making a strong drive to get him appointed and thus assist their leadership in state politics. Other "Buchaneers" were pushing James Campbell who had been defeated by the Cameronians for state office. On

[1] Blair to Van Buren, Nov. 25, 1852, Van Buren MSS. Van Buren did not commit himself openly but wrote a draft of a letter for Blair to sign and send to Pierce advising him to appoint no presidential possibilities in the cabinet. Blair accompanied this with a letter to Peaslee strongly urging Dix.

[2] The friends of Dickinson even seemed willing to take Dix rather than Marcy, consequently the appointment would seem to have some healing power in New York as Marcy's friends did not care to oppose Dix. There is reason to believe also that Marcy suggested Dix. Pruyn to Marcy, Nov. 27, 1852, Marcy, unaddressed, Nov. 17, 1852, Marcy to Berrett, Jan. 15, 1853, Thomas to Marcy, Jan. 18, 1853, Marcy MSS.

[3] Date not mentioned in Dix, *Memoirs*, vol. i, p. 271. Dix lectured in Boston, Nov. 29, and it may have been then. *N. Y. Herald*, Dec. 9, 1852; Stanton, *Random Recollection* (2nd edition), p. 90.

December 7 Pierce wrote to Buchanan, he suggested that Buchanan might concur with him in the belief that no former cabinet officers ought to be reappointed. However, he desired his advice and suggestions, especially as regards Pennsylvania affairs. This epistle gave Buchanan an opportunity to agree. Buchanan immediately replied that Pierce's statement of views relieved him of no little anxiety—he had feared he might be appointed to the cabinet in the "laborious and responsible position" which he formerly occupied. He advised the President-elect to leave New England and get better acquainted with views in other sections. For a cabinet position he urged Campbell or ex-Governor David R. Porter. Upon the receipt of this Pierce expressed "sincere gratitude" which there is no doubt he felt. For the next two months both Pennsylvania factions made every effort to get Campbell or his opponent, George M. Dallas, into the next cabinet.[1]

A third problem was the representative of the southern rights group. For advice he turned to his old army associate, Jefferson Davis. On December 7 he wrote him desiring an interview in regard to opinion in the south and the formation of the cabinet. As he was uncertain whether Davis would accept a cabinet position he declared that he did not desire to offer him one, but that he would like to talk with him as a friend knowing that he would receive from him a "friend's free and useful suggestions". He asked him to telegraph when he could come and follow this by a letter. These messages, however, were not to be addressed to Pierce but were to be sent to Col C. G. Greene.

[1] H. D. Gilpin to Van Buren, Nov. 9, 1852, Van Buren MSS.; Thomas to Marcy, Dec. 23, 1852, Feb. 16, 1853, Timothy Jenkins to Marcy, Jan. 3, 1853, Marcy MSS.; Buchanan, *Works*, vol. viii, pp. 492-500; Van Dyke to Buchanan, Feb. 1, 1853, Buchanan to Gilmore, Jan. 18, 1853, Buchanan MSS.; *New Orleans Weekly Delta*, Mar. 13, 1853; *N. Y. Herald*, Jan. 3, 1853.

Thus the fact of communication between Davis and the President-elect would be kept secret. Davis replied, December 27, that illness in his family made a visit north impossible.[1]

While awaiting Davis' answer Pierce was considering a fourth problem. Who was to represent the Union Compromise Democrats, special followers of Cass? He did not communicate with Cass, but early in December A. O. P. Nicholson, editor of the *Nashville Union,* an old associate, came to confer with him.[2] Nicholson was close to Cass. A few days later, December 1, he had the benefit of a consultation with Senator Shields and Senator Gwin, who were closely identified with the Cass wing; the latter advised him to seek the advice and the approval of the Congressional leaders.[3] Sometime during this period it may be supposed Nicholson was offered a position in the cabinet.[4]

Meanwhile without waiting for word from Davis, Pierce decided to confer with Robert M. T. Hunter, Senator from Virginia, and a powerful southern rights politician. Although recognition of this faction was not very pleasing to Nicholson and the Cass men Pierce got Nicholson to take a message to Hunter asking him to come to Boston for consultation. Nicholson did so leaving for New England again on the 19th of December. On Christmas eve, Hunter arrived in Boston. Christmas day Pierce spent in con-

[1] Pierce to Davis, Dec. 7, 1852, Jan. 12, 1853, Pierce MSS.

[2] Thomas to Marcy, Dec. 7, 1852, Marcy MSS.

[3] Cass to Cobb, Dec. 18, 1852, *Toombs Corr.*, p. 322, Blair to Van Buren, 27 Dec., 1852, Van Buren MSS.

[4] The evidence on this point is the undocumented statements in Appleton's *Biographical Encyclopedia* and Caldwell, *Bench and Bar of Tennessee*, p. 230, and the following statement in a letter of Blair to Van Buren, Dec. 27, 1852: "Nicholson . . . has been plying between Washington and Concord several times and gives out that he is to be of the cabinet." Also *Nashville Union*, March 8, 1853.

sultation at the Tremont House with Cushing, Atherton, Nicholson and Hunter. The upshot was that Hunter went home with the offer of a cabinet position.[1]

During this month of December Pierce had also decided on Caleb Cushing, another personal friend and Mexican War associate. As a member of the cabinet he would represent New England and be pleasing to the south, especially to the group in that section which had supported Tyler.[2] Thus by the first of the year Pierce seems to have definitely decided upon Dix, Hunter, Cushing and Nicholson, the first a free soiler who would harmonize New York, the second a southern states rightsman, and the third a New Englander and a Cass-Union Compromise man.

With these tentatively decided on, and perhaps others, Pierce thought it wise to test opinion. His friend Peaslee had already done a little scouting and so had P. R. George, who had carried New Hampshire's electoral vote to Washington. Now Senator-elect Atherton and Sidney Webster arrived in Washington on January 6. Atherton conversed with a number of politicians but it was charged that this group was made up principally of free soilers and Soulé. He suggested the merits of a Dix-Hunter combination. His visit was cut short by the death of his father and on January 9 he left Washington. What report he made at

[1] Thomas to Marcy, Dec. 20, 27, 1852, Wetmore to Marcy, Dec. 28, 1852, Campbell to Marcy, Dec. 31, 1852, Marcy MSS.; Blair to Van Buren, Dec. 27, 1852, Van Buren MSS.; *N. Y. Herald*, Dec. 24, 26, 28, 30, 1852, Jan. 3, 1853, *Boston Atlas*, Dec. 28, 1852.

[2] Webster, *Franklin Pierce and his Administration*, p. 52; Wise later claimed the credit for Cushing's appointment though his usual extravagant claims of his accomplishment lead this to be taken with a grain of salt. Wise to Hunter, Apr. 16, 1853, *Hunter Corr.*, p. 156. Cushing was debarred from further consultation with Pierce because the former was quarantined by an attack of scarlet fever from Jan. 2, 1853 until late in February. Information supplied by C. M. Fuess, Cushing's biographer.

his conference with Pierce on January 17 is not known. However, his visit set loose a vast amount of speculation and the fire-eating senators, Mason, Atchison and Butler, as well as many others, were wroth over the appointment of Dix the party traitor of 1848.[1] A storm of protest came from the south against him.[2]

In the midst of these consultations occurred a tragedy which drove thought of the cabinet and all else from the mind of the President-elect. On January 6 Pierce's little boy was killed before his parents' eyes in a railroad accident.[3] This awful shock prostrated Mrs. Pierce, and Pierce himself had a terrible heart-ache to bear along with the burdens of his new position. Everyone sympathized with him and for a space he had a respite from the importunities of office seekers.

Scarcely had Pierce recovered in a measure from this shock when he received a letter from Hunter declining a cabinet position. His family were much opposed to his taking such a responsibility and he had just been reelected to the Senate where as chairman of the finance committee he occupied an important place.[4] This refusal and the storm of southern protest against Dix combined with the activities of certain New York politicians were going to make necessary a recasting of the slate.

The newly elected state administration in New York

[1] *N. Y. Herald*, Jan. 5, 1853; *Boston Atlas*, Jan. 10, 13, 1853; Thomas to Marcy, Jan. 11, 16, 1853, Berret to Marcy, Jan. 14, 1853, Marcy MSS.; Blair to Van Buren, Jan. 11, 1853, Van Buren MSS.

[2] Powell to Breckinridge, Feb. 5, 1853, Breckinridge MSS.; King to Welles, Dec. 29, 1852, Welles MSS.; Eames to Marcy, Nov. 25, 1852, Thomas to Marcy, Dec. 20, Jan. 4, 13, 15, 16, 1853, Berret to Marcy, Jan. 14, 1853, Jenkins to Marcy, Jan. 22, 1853, Marcy MSS.; *N. Y. Herald*, Dec. 31, 1852.

[3] *N. Y. Herald*, Jan. 7, 1853.

[4] Hunter, *R. M. T. Hunter*, pp. 107-8.

was dominated by Marcy's friends and they were determined to maintain control of the party. Marcy's lieutenants, Thomas, Stryker and Cutting, went to Washington where they looked over the ground. There Thomas learned that Dickinson had written his friends not to endorse Dix, that any such action would be a violation of all principle. Then on January 19, Pruyn went up to Concord for a private interview with Pierce. In this he impressed upon the President-elect the ease whereby he might settle the Dix-Dickinson feud by the appointment of Marcy. While there, Pierce showed Pruyn a telegram from Beardsley and Pierson announcing their coming to present a petition in favor of Dickinson signed by a majority of Democrats in the legislature.[1] Pierce invited Pruyn to stay and meet them but he declined and went on to Boston where he met Cagger, Church, Chatfield and Wright who were going up to explain away this Dickinson petition. It so happened that these two delegations arrived on January 21 and Pierce used a little device of which he was fond—he caused both delegations to see him at once. By this plan he got out of a private interview with either and both factions adjourned to the Eagle Hotel to partake of an oyster supper. They all went home the next day, each side rejoicing at the other's discomfiture.[2]

New York was not the only state that pressed its claimants. Buchanan's faction in Pennsylvania continued to press Campbell while his opponents were just as intent on Dallas. Various electoral colleges had endorsed favorite

[1] A Marcy man declared that but few had signed this until it became apparent that Dix was going to be appointed and then rather than have him a number signed for Dickinson. Jenkins to Marcy, Jan. 22, 1853, Marcy MSS.

[2] Thomas to Marcy, Jan. 13, 15, 16, 18, 1853, Pruyn to Marcy, Jan. 18, 21, 1853, Marcy MSS.; *N. Y. Herald*, Jan. 22, 23, 1853.

sons. North Carolina had endorsed James C. Dobbin,[1] Virginia had recommended J. S. Barbour in spite of the fact that he was an intemperate invalid who could only move on crutches,[2] Ohio had set the seal of its approval on Samuel Medary. This friend of Douglas was very anxious to get in; he had the endorsement not only of the electors of Ohio but also of the representatives of that state; he had persuaded the opposing faction in his state to withdraw opposition and had been to Concord to press his claim. Atherton was reported to have gone back to Concord with his various recommendations in his pocket to submit to Pierce.[3] F. P. Blair had written to Peaslee (who showed the letter to Pierce) recommending Dix, Houston and Peaslee, and later had spoken well of Guthrie, also he had let it be known to Pierce that he was again willing to enter the editorial sanctum to defend Pierce and restore the principles of Jacksonian Democracy.[4] Henry A. Wise wrote early to Paul R. George, condemning the appointment of Dix, pouring vitriol on the Floyd-Bailey faction of Douglas men in Virginia, advising the President to leave New York out, recommending Hunter, Cushing in glowing terms, and Bright.[5] Benton to the delight of F. P. Blair, Sr., urged Montgomery Blair for Attorney General.[6] Governor Powell of Kentucky recommended James Guthrie.[7] Many had their claims pressed, the list was long—John B. Floyd

[1] *Ga. Hist. Quarterly*, vol. vi, no. 1.

[2] *Boston Atlas*, Jan. 17, 1853, *N. Y. Express*, Jan. 7, 1853.

[3] Chase to Hamlin, Feb. 15, 1853, Chase MSS. Day to Chase, Dec. 9, 1852, Blair to Van Buren, Dec. 27, 1852, Jan. 3, 11, 1853, Van Buren MSS.

[4] Blair to Van Buren, Nov. 25, 27, Dec. 18, 27, Van Buren MSS.

[5] Wise to P. R. George, Dec. 11, 1852, Pierce MSS. (N. H. Hist. Soc.).

[6] Blair to Van Buren, Dec. 18, 1852, Van Buren MSS.; Blair to Rives, Nov. 6, 1852, Rives MSS.

[7] Powell to Breckinridge, Feb. 10, 1853, Breckinridge MSS.

of Virginia, Howell Cobb and John P. King of Georgia, Jacob Thompson and Jefferson Davis of Mississippi, John Slidell of Louisiana, William Medill of Ohio, Robert Strange of North Carolina, Governor Robert McClelland of Michigan, Louis McLane of Maryland, and many others. William H. Polk and Edward C. Marshall, friends of Douglas and Young America, had been to Concord,[1] and numerous other self-appointed delegations had flocked there. Out of all these multitudinous and often conflicting forces Pierce had to select the remainder of his cabinet.

Hunter had declined and Nicholson had decided not to serve. The pressure was so strong against Dix that Pierce called him to Concord and told him how impossible it was for him to be appointed; Dix could only agree with this opinion whereupon Pierce showed him his inaugural and Dix expressed his approval.[2] These places must be filled. On February 2 and again on the 18th Pierce sent urgent telegrams to Davis to come to Washington as soon as possible, stating no object. He was slated for Secretary of War.[3] On February 6 Sidney Webster wrote a mysterious note to Marcy asking him to be in Washington by the 18th or 20th.[4] Marcly was to be Secretary of State. James Campbell of Pennsylvania received notes saying that Pierce would confer with him on his way through Philadelphia.[5] Governor McClelland of Michigan was invited to enter the cabinet on the advice of Nicholson and the Cass men.[6]

[1] *N. Y. Herald*, Feb. 3, 1853.

[2] Dix, *Memoirs*, vol. i, p. 272; Dix to Ludlow, Aug. 28, 1853, Marcy MSS.

[3] Greene to Davis, Feb. 2, 18, 1853, Pierce MSS.

[4] Webster to Marcy, Feb. 6, 1853, Marcy MSS.

[5] Campbell to Buchanan, Feb. 13, 1853, Buchanan MSS.

[6] There was some southern protest against McClelland because he had voted for the Wilmot Proviso but he circulated papers showing that

James C. Dobbin of North Carolina and James Guthrie of Kentucky were to be Secretaries of the Navy and the Treasury. The slate was complete. The policies of the new administration had been formulated in an inaugural address.

With these preparations made, Pierce bade goodbye to Concord on February 14. He was accompanied by his secretary, Sidney Webster, and his bodyguard, Sergt. O'Neil. He was pale, careworn, thin, and evidently very nervous, and on the journey declined all public receptions. At Philadelphia he conferred with Campbell as to entering the cabinet. He received his acceptance and his approval of the inaugural.[1] He finally reached Washington February 21.[2] Here he found Marcy, Guthrie, Dobbin and McClelland awaiting him and he conferred with each.[3] He showed them the inaugural and stated that these were to be the principles of the new administration. Would they agree to stand firmly upon them? All assented. On February 22 a committee of Congress waited on the new leader to inform him that the electoral vote had been duly counted before a joint session of Congress in February 9 and that he had been declared elected.[4] All was ready for the inauguration. Then the public would learn the policy and personnel of the new administration.

he had presided over a Democratic State convention in 1850 which had endorsed the Compromise, and that as a candidate for governor in the late campaign he had run on a platform decidedly in favor of the Compromise. *Richmond Enquirer*, March 4, 1853, Parker to Breckinridge, June, 1853, Breckinridge MSS.

[1] Campbell to Buchanan, Feb. 25, 1853, Buchanan MSS.; Webster, *Franklin Pierce and his Administration*, p. 51.

[2] *N. Y. Herald*, Feb. 15, 17, 18, 22, 1853, Thomas to Marcy, Feb. 17, 1853, Marcy MSS.

[3] Davis did not arrive in Washington until March 5 and was much averse to entering the cabinet. However, Pierce persuaded him. Davis, *Rise and Fall of the Confederacy*, vol. i, pp. 22-3.

[4] *Washington Union*, Feb. 24, 1853.

The fourth of March 1853, was a day of snow and sleet. At noon Pierce appeared on the steps of the east front of the capitol and instead of taking the usual oath made an affirmation. Then he delivered his inaugural. This speech was a mixture of bad taste in personal allusions and pomposity in empty phrases yet it clearly indicated certain principles. The foreign policy was to be imperialistic; Cuba was to be acquired and new lines of trade were to be opened. American rights abroad were to be maintained and the Monroe Doctrine was reaffirmed. This was a foreign policy very pleasing to imperialists and jingoists such as the slavery advocates and Young Americans. As to domestic policy, announcement was made that the victors were to have the spoils, the Whigs must go; but Pierce was under no obligations as to office, all were eligible who were efficient. The central government was to stay strictly within its constitutional limits, the states were to be unhampered in their spheres. Finally, the Union under the Compromise was to be paramount, the measures of 1850 were held to be " strictly constitutional " and must be " unhesitatingly carried into effect ". This domestic programme which forecast no new measures was pleasing to the rank and file of politicians and was deemed by the Compromise men to show that the new President was of their beliefs. Imperialists, business men, professional politicians, Compromise men, all were satisfied. Pierce was going to be a safe man.[1]

On March 7 the President's cabinet was announced and the names confirmed by the senate. Then it was learned that the lists which had been appearing in the press since February 25 were substantially correct.[2]

The Secretary of State was to be William L. Marcy.

[1] Richardson, *Messages and Papers of the Presidents*, vol. v, pp. 197-203.

[2] *Washington Union*, March 8, 1853.

His problem was to conduct the foreign affairs of the nation so as to acquire Cuba, bring about better commercial relations with all countries and maintain the Monroe Doctrine. Besides this he was expected to unite the New York Democracy in support of the administration. This was a difficult task especially as he had little knowledge of foreign affairs and had the bitter enmity of the Dickinson faction.

The Secretary of the Treasury was to be James Guthrie of Kentucky. He was a tall square-shouldered, awkward man with the appearance of a farmer and a sleepy drawl which led people to believe he was slow. However, he was an excellent business man, a good executive who had amassed a fortune, a hard worker who shunned society and had little reputation outside of Kentucky. He was appointed as a southern Unionist and as Blair spoke well of him he was thought to propitiate Blair's group. Pierce had never met him till a few days before the inauguration.[1]

The Secretary of War, Jefferson Davis, was a quiet, reserved, unapproachable, though high-strung, southern gentleman who suffered from neuralgia. His training at West Point and in the army had given him the soldier's narrowness of viewpoint and the martinet's idea of discipline. His masterful manner often overruled less persistent men with wiser plans. He was Pierce's close friend and the representative of the southern rights group.

Caleb Cushing, Attorney-General, was a New England lawyer and politician who had had a varied experience. A Whig in 1840, he had left the main party and became one of Tyler's corporal's guard. Thence he had gone into the Democratic party. He had been opposed to coalition in Massachusetts in 1851, in the fall of the same year he had

[1] Webster, *Administration of Franklin Pierce*, p. 54; Clay, *A Belle of the Fifties*, p. 70.

prevented the passage of resolution condemning it and had been appointed a justice of the Supreme Court of Massachusetts by a coalition administration. He was a man of high intellectual attainments whose mental outlook had deprived him of the power to judge a question as to whether it was right or wrong according to the common standard or to perceive that most people were largely emotional. For this reason he was a bad political adviser. He was a widower and lived in retirement. He was a personal friend of Pierce and was chosen as a New England man who would not injure the susceptibilities of southern leaders. This appointment was anathema to all New Englanders with free soil leanings.[1]

James C. Dobbin, a small man, with an intellectual face, a hardworking administrator of great kindliness of nature, was to be in charge of the Navy. He confined himself to his duties to such a degree that he died immediately upon leaving office. He had made the speech which had turned the tide in favor of Pierce at the Baltimore Covention and was appointed with Guthrie as a southern unionist to balance Davis. He had no reputation or influence outside of his state.[2]

James Campbell of Pennsylvania, Postmaster-General, was another unknown man, not a leader. He had been a successful lawyer and city politician. He had been defeated for state office, it was claimed, by the treachery of the Cameronians, and this appointment was at once a solace and a reward to the Buchanan faction.[3]

Robert McClelland, lately Governor of Michigan, completed the slate as Secretary of the Interior. He was a

[1] Clay, *op. cit.*, p. 64; Parker, *Reminiscences of Rufus Choate*, p. 285; Boutwell, *Reminiscences*, vol. i, p. 119.

[2] Clay, *op. cit.*, p. 65.

[3] *Ibid.*, p. 64.

man of forbidding demeanor who tended strictly to business. He had voted for the Wilmot proviso and repented of it; he was a friend of Cass. He was appointed to fill the triple role of satisfying the free soilers, the northwest and the friends of Cass. He, also, had not been heard of before outside of his own state circle.[1]

This cabinet evoked little unfavorable comment. Still certain groups were covertly dissatisfied. Free soilers felt they had no representative, southern rights men thought that the Compromise men had too many, the Compromise men resented the appointment of any but themselves. Douglas' friends were slighted altogether, thus were they punished for their leaders presumptuous and too ardent campaign against the "Old Fogies".[2] But it was too early for outward signs of dissatisfaction; there were many other plums to be distributed.

[1] One report had it that McClelland had expected the Post Office and when he was asked to take the Interior, he and Cass demurred decidedly. The Post Office department had control of much patronage, and to have it under the control of a friend was a great advantage to a prospective presidential candidate. Parker to Buchanan, Feb. 26, 1853, Buchanan MSS.; Clay, *op. cit.*, p. 64; *Life of Zachariah Chandler*, p. 83.

[2] A. Campbell to Marcy, Dec. 10, 1852, Marcy MSS.

CHAPTER XII

The Distribution of the Spoils

The President and his cabinet found themselves confronted by an enormous task. It was neither the administration of government nor the formulation of new policies, it was the distribution of the spoils. For four years the doors of the government departments had been closed to deserving Democrats. These had been lean years, but now there were offices worth $50,000,000 a year to be distributed to the faithful, and the faithful were on hand. Washington was a seething mass of importunity. From all portions of the country had been gathering an ever increasing horde of office-seekers, each with a well-developed sense of capacity, and each loaded with credentials. Some had definitely in mind what they wanted—others were not particular, willing in fact to take anything. Every hotel and boarding house was filled, every ante-room was crowded, every man who might by the farthest stretch of the imagination be conceived to have influence was besieged for letters to this one or that; the newly-appointed cabinet members were hounded from dawn to dark—and after, and the President was well-nigh overwhelmed by the multitude who daily sought admission to the Executive Mansion to press their claims and demonstrate their peculiar fitness for serving the Republic.

Just what were they so anxious for? The stakes were the government offices, positions so numerous that a list of them filled over one thousand octavo pages. But in spite of the gross amount paid in salaries, the places were so numerous that only a relatively small proportion netted over two thousand dollars annually. The stipends were about equal to or less than those paid to the average young clerk or book-keeper. Besides this the work did not give training for anything else, the tenure was insecure, and the result was that generally after four or eight years of struggle to keep alive on insufficient money in an unhealthful climate, the office holder was turned adrift with nothing, unfit for anything else.[1] Nevertheless the stream poured on into Washington lured by the tinsel of a government job.

The major spoils, however, were worth something. All the offices, with the exception of the territorial positions were classified under the seven departments. Under the Secretary of State were an assistant secretary and chief clerk, twelve major representatives of foreign courts whose salaries were $9,000, fifteen chargés d'affairs each receiving $4,500 and one commissioner whose pay amounted to $5,000. Besides there were numerous consuls and minor diplomatic offices.

The Secretary of the Treasury had under him an assistant secretary, chief clerk, two comptrollers, six auditors, the treasurer, register of the treasury, solicitor of the treasury, and commissioner of customs in Washington, whose salaries ranged around $3,000. Besides there were six assistant treasurers, five mint directors and nearly one thousand revenue officials ranging from collectors of ports to night watchmen at the customs houses. These were distributed among the states.

The Interior Department had the commissioners of patents, pensions and Indian affairs, and the superintendents of the census, printing and land office, as well as surveyors, registers, receivers of the public lands, and many agents.

[1] *N. Y. Herald*, March 15, 1853.

The War and Navy had few plums to offer but the Department of Justice had the district attorneys and marshals as well as the district judges who were appointed for life. The Post Office Department was the bonanza as it had three-quarters of the whole number of appointments. In the hands of the administration was the distribution of all these jobs. In spite of the large number of offices there were many more applicants than could possibly be accommodated. Consequently many difficult problems arose.

Taking care of most of the horde of applicants, though fatiguing, was not difficult. Their papers were placed on file and they were assured that they would receive careful attention. Thereupon they went away, the great majority to wait in vain. There were many who could not be put off thus. Senators and Representatives of influence had political debts to collect; some of these creditors were most importunate in their demands upon the administration for patronage to their friends. Others who had done good service in electing Pierce must be rewarded. The President and the Cabinet had their own friends whom they wished to favor. In fact, often several who were too powerful to be brushed aside asked for the same thing. Thus the dispensers of patronage tackled the task with the knowledge that for every friend satisfied the adminstration would make ten enemies.

Pierce previous to his inauguration had determined on his policy in regard to the patronage. The purpose of its manipulation was to build up a strong party organization which would not only ensure continued Democratic success but would aid Pierce's ambitions for 1856. The Baltimore platform of 1852 had been acquiesced in by all sections of the party, and from this harmony had come victory. To Pierce, therefore, it seemed the obvious and practical way to declare bygones to be bygones, to ignore all past distinctions, and to require only that appointees should have supported this platform. In other words, a new era would be dated from June 6, 1852. This policy he had presented to the members of his cabinet for approval before sending in their names to the Senate, and had announced it publicly in his inaugural address.[1]

With this general rule the Administration attacked the problem. It was immediately decided that the large offices at the capital were to be distributed as equally as possible among the various sections. Each member of the administration was to look after his special friends and the patronage in his state,[2] while the remainder of the offices throughout the states was to be left to the Democratic Senators and Representatives concerned; [3] if there were no Democrats in Congress from any state the local leaders or national committeemen had the privilege of making the necessary recommendations.[4] This system was worked out by the president and cabinet in their frequent meetings during the first months of the administration—in all this time little else but patronage business was transacted.[5] Meanwhile many were on the anxious seat and the press was filled with rumors. The Compromise Union Democrats felt that now was the day of their harvest when their steadfast loyalty would receive a fitting reward.

[1] In this policy of lookng no further back may perhaps be seen the hand of Caleb Cushng, who had been most intimate with the President-elect during this formative period. He had been of many groups and only by starting anew could he have regular standing.

[2] Marcy's papers reveal the fact that nearly every one of his close friends and frequent correspondents received an office. Also see James Guthrie to Joseph Holt, *circa* June, 1853, Holt MSS. for a description of how each state was allotted a certain number of each class of office. H. B. Stanton to Marcy, April 16, 1853, Marcy to H. B. Stanton, May 2, 1853, Marcy MSS.

[3] *Illinois State Register*, June 9, 1853; Parish, *G. W. Jones*, p. 186.

[4] D. A. Smalley to Marcy, March 22, 1853, Marcy MSS.

[5] *N. Y. Herald*, April 22, 1853; Curtis, *Buchanan*, vol. ii, p. 81.

On the fifteenth of March the Boston appointments were published. Peaslee, the close friend of the President, was made collector of the port, in spite of the fact that he was from New Hampshire; Hallett and Greene respectively became district attorney and naval officer.[1] Also the President's intimate friend, N. G. Upham, was made claims commissioner, under the Treaty of 1853 with Great Britain, and Marcy's chief aide, J. A. Thomas, was appointed solicitor on behalf of the United States before this commission.[2] The President's friend and biographer, Hawthorne, became consul at Liverpool.

Political service and friendship, however, were not to be the only criteria. Peter G. Washington, who had worked himself up from an $800 clerk to Sixth Auditor of the Treasury, was made Assistant Secretary. Selah R. Hobbie, long Assistant Postmaster-General, was reappointed, and John Randolph Clay and Theodore S. Fay, who had both been in the diplomatic service under Whig and Democratic administrations became Minister to Peru and Chargé to Switzerland respectively.[3] J. D. B. DeBow, editor of *DeBow's Review* was made Superintendent of the Census.[4] John Wilson, a Whig, was retained as Commissioner of the Land Office because of long and efficient service. This was done at the earnest solicitation of Senators Cass, Downs and Gwin, in spite of the fact that Willis A. Gorman, a prominent Hoosier Democrat, wanted it.[5]

These appointments were all measurably satisfactory, but the first cloud appeared on the horizon when John A. Camp-

[1] *Washington Union*, March 15, 19, 1853.

[2] *Washington Union*, March 25, 1853; *State Capital Reporter*, March 29, 1853.

[3] *New Orleans Weekly Delta*, March 27, April 10, 1853; *New York Herald*, March 16, 1853.

[4] *Washington Union*, March 16, 1853.

[5] *New Orleans Weekly Delta*, April 10, 1853.

bell of Alabama, a prominent states rights advocate, was appointed to a vacancy on the Supreme Court. This was considered by the unionists as a blow which was hardly softened by the appointment of John Slidell, one of their number, to the Central American mission.[1] All these appointments, made between March 8 and April 1, were confirmed by the Senate with no opposition.

During the time in which these less important selections had been made the President and Cabinet were struggling with appointments in the important states wherein there was schism, New York, Pennsylvania and Louisiana. The purpose of the administration was to heal these breaches and create an unified party. After much arranging and rearranging the completed slate was made public, March 29. In New York Dickinson, leader of the hards was made collector while Dix, prominent barnburner, became subtreasurer, and Redfield, soft, was appointed naval officer; of the nine important offices each faction had three.[2] This arrangement was acquiesced in by the moderates of all three branches, but Dickinson complicated matters by declining,[3] and in the Senate there was trouble. Certain hunkers and southerners were so opposed to Dix's free soil antecedents that Bright of Indiana, Brodhead of Pennsylvania, Rusk of Texas, Atchison of Missouri, Mason of Virginia, Butler of South Carolina, Thompson of New Jersey, all voted against the administration, scarcely a month after its inauguration.[4] Neverthelesss Dix was con-

[1] *N. Y. Herald*, March 22, 1853; *Washington Union*, April 1, 1853. Slidell refused the place. He wished a mission in Europe, Slidell to Buchanan, Sept. 25, 1852, Buchanan MSS.

[2] *Washington Union*, April 3, 1853. See Marcy MSS. for an idea of the difficulty of coming to an agreement especially when Marcy's friends expected all the good positions.

[3] J. A. Thomas to Marcy, April 12, 1853, Marcy MSS.; *N. Y. Herald*, April 1, 1853.

[4] *Washington Union*, April 12, 1853.

firmed and Greene C. Bronson, another hard, was made collector. Peace seemed to reign once more in the Empire State.

In Pennsylvania the appointments were generally satisfactory though Buchanan complained that all whom he had recommended had been turned down.[1] In Louisiana the factions, headed by Slidell and Soulé, each received half of the offices and Soulé himself, at Davis' suggestion and over Marcy's protest, was sent as minister to the Court of Spain.[2]

No sooner had these three troublesome problems been solved when it became necessary to take up the question of the diplomatic service. These appointments had been laid aside for the time being partly because the domestic patronage required so much attention and partly because the terms of the diplomats did not begin until July 1.[3] The desire of the administration to obtain Cuba was well-known, and the first thought was given to the selection of ministers to England, France and Spain by whom the negotiations would have to be conducted. Acording to the usually well-informed *New York Herald,* as early as March 12 the President and Cabinet had decided to give these missions to Pennsylvania, New York and Louisiana. In reality sometime after Pierce had found it undersirable to appoint John A. Dix to the cabinet he had offered him the French mission. However, the appointment was not announced and Pierce did not communicate further with Dix.[4] Soulé was

[1] *N. Y. Herald,* March 30, 1853; Buchanan to James Campbell, March 31, 1853, Buchanan MSS.

[2] *New Orleans Weekly Delta,* May 1, 1853. Upon Soulé's appointment and resignation from the Senate Slidell was elected to that body. Solon Borland, Senator from Arkansas, received Slidell's declined Central American mission. Slidell to Buchanan, Mar. 30, 1853, Buchanan MSS.; *N. Y. Herald,* Apr. 9, 1853, *Washington Union,* Apr. 23, 1853; Dodd, *Jefferson Davis,* p. 137.

[3] *N. Y. Herald,* May 3, 1853.

[4] Dix, *Memoirs,* vol. i, p. 273.

chosen for the Spanish mission. His foreign connections, his knowledge of Europe, his ardent desire for Cuba and his negotiations in Spain in 1846 made him seem well-fitted for the task.[1] Then Pierce offered the British post to Buchanan as an expert in foreign affairs. The latter was not anxious to accept the position. It was an onorous and expensive duty. Also it would make more ill-feeling in the Pennsylvania ranks; this was undesirable especially if he had any hopes of 1856. Pennsylvania already had the Postmaster-Generalship and if the British Mission also was credited to the patronage account of that state there would be no other jobs for Keystone politicians. Buchanan would be accused of keeping many of his followers from office by accepting one himself. After a conference at Washington this difficulty was straightened out. Pierce assured Buchanan that he was chosen from the nation at large and his acceptance would deprive none of the deserving Democrats in Pennsylvania of office. After Soulé's confirmation on April 7 the Senate which had been in special session decided to adjourn, but at Buchanan's urgent request—he was averse to sailing to England without having his appointment ratified—the President notified enough senators to wait over until April 11. On that day Buchanan's nomination was confirmed.[2] From this date nothing more was announced until May 24. Then the complete list appeared. It was apparent that Virginia had carried off the lion's share. Pierce could not forget her influence in nominating him. Upon the recommendation of John Y. Mason, Henry A. Wise and others to whom Pierce felt especially indebted, Henry Bedinger had been appointed minister to Denmark, Richard K. Meade, chargé to Sardinia, Shelton

[1] *N. H. Statesman*, Dec. 12, 1852.

[2] Curtis, *Buchanan*, vol. ii, pp. 76-92 *passim*; Buchanan, *Works*, vol. viii, pp. 493-512 *passim*.

K. Leake, commissioner to the Sandwich Islands, Robert G. Scott, author of the famous Scott letter, consul at Rio Janiero, and B. Jennings Wise, son of Henry A. Wise, secretary of the legation at Berlin.[1] The President had also made diplomats of several of his friends. Thomas N. Seymour, Governor of Connecticut, and William H. Bissell, members of congress from Illinois, former army associates in Mexico, were appointed respectively minister to Russia and chargé to Argentine, while Charles L. Woodbury was made chargé to Bolivia.[2] Robert Dale Owen at the instance of the Indiana delegation was appointed chargé to the Two Sicilies largely, it was said, to free the Democratic organization of Indiana from him and his socialistic views.[3] August Belmont, too, got his reward. As soon as the election was over he persuaded many of his friends to bespeak for him the chargéship at Naples—he urged that his relationship with certain members of the Spanish and Neopolitan governments would give him the inside track in negotiations for Cuba. Buchanan, Slidell and Peaslee backed him strongly, the latter disclosing to Pierce and Marcy that when the campaign committee had been almost without funds during the last election, Belmont had contributed a large sum. These arguments had their weight and while not appointed to Naples he was made chargé to Holland which was quite as satisfactory to him.[4]

[1] John Y. Mason to Marcy, Mar. 10, 1853, Marcy MSS. Wise to Buchanan, Mar. 19, April 9, 24, May 2, 11, 1853, Buchanan MSS., Buchanan to Wise, June 1, 1853, Buchanan MSS. (L. C.). Tyler, *Times of the Tylers'*, vol. ii, p. 504. Wise had been summoned to Washington and offered a full mission. He decided he couldn't afford it and recommended Buchanan, meanwhile earnestly desiring a place for his son.

[2] Philadelphia *Public Ledger*, May 28, 1853.

[3] R. D. Owen to N. P. Trist, July 7, 1852, Trist MSS., *N. Y. Herald*, Nov. 6, 1853.

[4] August Belmont to Geo. N. Sanders, Mar. 21, 1853, Sanders MSS. Buchanan to Marcy, Mar. 8, 1853, P. M. Wetmore to Marcy, April 6,

At the earnest instance of Howell Cobb, the most prominent southern union Democrat, Henry R. Jackson of Georgia was made chargé to Austria.[1] The rest of the billets were distributed among the states with some attempt at equitable apportionment. It was significant that no appointment was made to the French court in spite of Pierce's offer to Dix.

Having disposed of most of the patronage it was found that as usual the party organ needed attention. *The Washington Union* was never in a satisfactory condition. Armstrong was financing it and Charles Eames and Roger A. Pryor were editing it after a fashion. Pierce suggested that his friend, A. O. P. Nicholson of Tennessee, take over Donelson's share of the concern. This was arranged and about July 1 Nicholson settled down to edit the paper [2] and reap the rewards of the government printing.[3]

Thus the healing balm of the patronage had been applied to the wounds of the Democracy, the organ had been tuned. Calhoun once remarked on the "cohesive power of the public plunder"

1853, Isaac Townsend to Marcy, C. W. Lawrence to Marcy, R. Withers to Marcy, April 6, 1853, C. H. Peaslee to Marcy, May 9, 1853, W. J. Staples to Marcy, Nov. 26, 1852, Marcy MSS., Belmont to Buchanan, Nov. 22, 1852, Jan. 28, 1853, Mar. 7, April 22, May 28, Buchanan MSS.

[1] Howell Cobb to Marcy, April 25, 1853, Marcy MSS. Henry K. Jackson to Marcy, June 1, 1853, *ibid.*

[2] Pryor had been forced out because of an editorial lauding the Czar which would never do in a democracy and Nicholson soon forced out Eames who received the chargéship to Venezuela as solace. Nicholson had as his assistant Harvey Watterson of Tennessee. *Nashville Union,* Mar. 8, 1853; *Memphis Daliy Eagle and Enquirer,* Mar. 19, 1853; *N. Y. Herald,* June 17, 25, July 1, 1853; *Indiana Daily State Sentinel,* June 23, 1853, *Phila. Public Ledger,* May 3, Nov. 22, 1853; Henry Watterson to the author, June 15, 1921; Pryor, *Reminiscences of Peace and War,* pp. 15 and 16; Nicholson to Pierce, Mar. 27 and June 3, 1857 Pierce MSS.

[3] Nicholson received $123,500 for the Congressional printing alone during the next two years—as well as many fees for miscellaneous government printing. A great deal of this was clear profit. *Official Register,* 1855.

JAMES CAMPBELL

JEFFERSON DAVIS

CHAPTER XIII

THE COHESIVE POWER OF THE PUBLIC PLUNDER

THE policy of the administration soon bore fruit. It was of a different variety than had been expected. Protests came from the south. In that section the Union Democrats such as Cobb, Downs, Clemens, and Foote had expected to receive the lion's share. But John A. Campbell had been appointed to the highest tribunal of the nation and Soulé, Borland, Gadsden and Trousdale had been offered foreign missions. These men were an offense unto all Compromise supporters—they were secessionists. Editorials appeared in the union papers and protesting letters were sent to Washington. The President was accused of throwing overboard the Baltimore platform of 1852, of giving the union men the principles and the states rights men the spoils.[1] The *Union* countered with the statement that union men such as Slidell and Jackson had been named to important posts, and that the state officers had been divided evenly; as for Soulé, Gadsden, Trousdale, Borland—their eminent fitness put them above politics.[2] The truth of the matter was that the administration considered this union party in the south to be largely Whig; this was true, and

[1] *Philadelphia Public Ledger*, April 12, 1853; *Mobile Daily Advertiser*, Mar. 26, April 10, May 18, 1853; *Natchez Courier*, Mar. 31, April 14, April 15, April 29, 1853; *N. Y. Herald*, June 3, 27, 1853; Howell Cobb to Marcy, April 25, H. K. Jackson to Marcy, June 1, G. W. Jones to Marcy, May 19, Geo. S. Houston to Marcy, July 9, 1853, Marcy MSS.; *New Hampshire Patriot*, June 15, 1853.

[2] *Washington Union*, June 25, 1853.

consequently as the large majority of the party in the south belonged to the southern rights group, Pierce, in his policy of forgetting the past, naturally gave the most to the larger group.[1] Some unionists, like G. W. Jones of Tennessee, underestimating the talents of such men as Soulé solaced themselves with the thought that all these fire-eaters would do less harm abroad than in the Senate.[2] Cobb, too, remained faithful, extinguishing a move to revive the Union party.[3] He, however, wrote some strong letters to Washington. His eye was on the future, the United States Senate and higher, places afforded only to those who remained regular. The action of these leaders, however, was not sufficient to stop the charges that the administration had deserted Cobb, Foote and Clemens and that it was traitorous to the cause.

In the north the hunkers were wroth. Dix was in the sub-treasury in New York City. Ex-free-soilers received office in New England. Douglas and the Illinois delegation had nominated an ex-free-soil advocate for district attorney and the northern Illinois appointments had been made from the friends of John Wentworth, a notorious anti-slavery man.[4] These selections proved to the conservative southern Democracy that Pierce was pushing aside the Baltimore platform and welcoming the free-soil element. This cry was echoed in the south and Compromise papers declared that the President was forming a coalition of free soil and states rights men and was leaving his union supporters out in the cold.[5] Men like Buchanan began to

[1] *N. O. Weekly Delta*, May 1, 1853.

[2] G. W. Jones to Marcy, May 17, 1853, Marcy MSS.

[3] *Wash. Union*, May 1, 1853, Cobb to Marcy, April 25, Marcy MSS.

[4] *Weekly Alton Telegraph*, April 29, 1853; *Mobile Daily Advertiser*, May 6, 1853; Cole, *Centennial Hist. of Ill.*, vol. iii, p. 112.

[5] *Mobile Daily Advertiser*, May 13, 1853.

believe that in this way Pierce was attempting to build up a machine to manufacture his second nomination.[1] In all probability there was no thought of such a coalition. Pierce was steadfastly ignoring past schism.

In the west some felt that their section was not receiving its share of the plums, and a comparison of the numbers allotted to the various sections shows upon what grounds that was founded.[2] In Indiana the Democracy was torn in two; Governor Wright and Senator Pettit were disputing state leadership with Senator Bright. The Wright-Pettit forces found their recommendations ignored and declared that Bright and the hunkers had the presidential ear; even so, Bright was disaffected because, so the *Union* claimed, a recommendation of his had been ignored, and he had already bolted Dix.[3] In Ohio, the war between the "Miamis" (barnburners) and "Sawbucks" (hunkers) led by Samuel Medary and ex-Governor Allen respectively, was bitter and the hunkers declared that the appointments were controlled by their opponents.[4] In Illinois, the hunkers declared that Douglas had sold out to Wentworth and had recommended free soilers. Douglas and Shields, on the other hand, the two senators, had almost threatened the administration to get a foreign mission for an Illinois man, David L. Gregg, and then succeeded in obtaining it only after the place had been declined by a Virginian. Also

[1] Buchanan to Wise, June 1, 1853, Buchanan MSS. (L. C.); Curtis, *Buchanan*, vol. ii, p. 80.

[2] F. J. Grund to Marcy, April 9, 1853, Marcy MSS.; *Indiana Daily State Sentinel*, March 29, April 9, 1853.

[3] John Pettit to Marcy, Mar., 1853, April 18, 1853, W. J. Brown to Marcy, April 16, 1853, Marcy MSS.; *New Orleans Weekly Delta*, May 8, 1853.

[4] Wm. Trevitt to Marcy, May 10, 1853, Marcy MSS.; *New Orleans Weekly Delta*, April 10, 1853; *N. Y. Herald*, July 21, 1853.

Douglas had failed to get a relative a job. Apparently certain leaders in the West were none too well satisfied.[1]

This discontent seemed to have little apparent effect during the spring. The party was markedly successful in the spring elections in New Hampshire, Connecticut, South Carolina, Rhode Island, Louisiana and Virginia. Thirty-one Democratic Congressmen were elected as compared with one Whig, a net gain of eight.[2] So far there had been only protest, but signs of revolt were becoming ominous.

The first real outbreak came from the President's own state. Here the Concord "Regency" had been getting the offices. Atherton was Senator, Peaslee, collector of the port of Boston, George, District Attorney. Burke, on the other hand, had received no mark of appreciation of his services in the convention and his faction, the "Old Guard", had been neglected. Besides the President was careless about the antecedents of the men whom he appointed, he did not inquire as to whether they had been free-soilers or not. During his campaign for Pierce's nomination Burke had repeatedly declared that Pierce was "national" and untainted by "free-soilism", and now greatly to Burke's chagrin he was abandoning this national ground and appointing sectional men. This policy seemed to Burke to be a direct repudiation of the pledges made for Pierce by his friends. He was not a man to accept this repudiation without a struggle. When the state convention met June 9, 1853, Burke was made president of that body and chairman of the committee on resolutions. He took the opportunity then afforded him to drop "a gentle hint

[1] *Alton Weekly Telegraph*, April 29, 1853; S. A. Douglas to Marcy, March 10, undated, James Shields to Marcy, June 7, July 16, 1853, Marcy MSS.; Cole, *op. cit.*, p. 112.

[2] *Whig Almanac*, 1854; *Washington Union*, June 7, 1853, the figures in the *Union* are incorrect.

to the President" of the inadvisability of putting too many free soilers in office. This "gentle hint" consisted of a resolution rebuking Pierce for his neglect of the truly national Democrats and his appointment of coalitionists. The sharpness of this article was softened but it was passed and remained to be alluded to by the President's opponents. The legislature tried to nullify this action by passing a resolution endorsing Pierce but the Old Guard succeeded in keeping out of it any mention of appointments. Then began an abusive newspaper controversy between Butterfield's *New Hampshire Patriot,* the organ of the regency, and a rival paper, friendly to Burke, known as the *State Capitol Reporter.* Recriminations were exchanged continuously. Pierce's friends were openly branded as free soilers, tainted with actual corruption and were shown to be closely connected with the rising railroad corporations as their counsel. On the other hand, Burke was charged with being a disappointed, unfaithful and even dishonest "sorehead". From August to October Burke edited a page of the *State Capitol Reporter* called the "Old Guard". Therein he laid bare some of the details of Pierce's nomination and also successfully refuted the charge that he had been disloyal. This whole matter did no immediate harm to the party in that state; the vote remained about the same. It did strengthen animosities which were to bear fruit in the coming years and aid the ruin of a strong organization. Nationally the controversy was much copied in factional and Whig papers so that Pierce himself showed up in a bad light as a leader; altogether it was damaging to his national prestige.[1]

Elsewhere a more disastrous storm was breaking. New

[1] *New Hampshire State Capitol Reporter* and *New Hampshire Patriot,* June-Nov., 1853; *New York Herald,* July 3, 1853; *N. Y. Times,* July 1, 1853.

York, the scene of schism and reunion, reunion and schism since the days of George Clinton, was about to become again a field of battle. Pierce and Marcy felt that when the New York slate was appointed and confirmed trouble in the Empire State among hards, softs and barnburners would be amicably settled to the satisfaction of all. But the consequences of two decades of bitter political strife could not be averted by the distribution of offices.

The hards refused to accept this as a solution, and Dickinson declined the remunerative post of collector of the port. He made Augustus Schell his candidate [1] but the place was given to another hard, Greene C. Bronson.[2] This was done with the approbation of the softs [3] and Bronson was "instructed" by the administration to give equal recognition in his appointments to all factions. This fact was semi-officially announced in articles in the *Washington Union* and the *New York Evening Post* by John L. O'Sullivan, barnburner and disciple of "Young America", who acted as the special go-between for the President and the New York leaders of his denomination.[4] At the same time, however, Marcy wrote Bronson that he would in no wise interfere with his appointments or make recommendations.[5] Under these circumstances the collector's office was occupied by a nervous, crotchety old man with a bad cough who, it was predicted, would be the horror of business men.[6] As Cochran, a barnburner, was surveyor of the port, it was desired that there should be cooperation between

[1] Thomas to Marcy, April 8, 1853, Marcy MSS.

[2] *N. Y. Herald*, April 9, 1853.

[3] Thomas to Marcy, April 9, 1853, Marcy MSS.

[4] Tilden to Marcy, June 21, John Van Buren to Marcy, Oct. 17, 1853, *ibid.*

[5] Marcy to Bronson, April 21, 1853, *ibid.*

[6] Tilden to Marcy, Apr. 9, Thomas to Marcy, May 17, 1853, *ibid.*

Bronson and himself in the filling of the several hundred offices at their disposal. Bronson, however, was otherwise minded and late in June sent his list to the secretary of the treasury for approval without submitting it to Cochran, although the latter had sent Bronson his slate, approved by the barnburners, accompanied by O'Sullivan's article as a tactful reminder.[1] Marcy was flooded with complaints. Cagger, a prominent barnburner of Albany, wrote that none of that group had been appointed by Bronson.[2] Fernando Wood, soon to be notorious, at that time a powerful soft politician in New York City, wrote that the barnburners and hards were being appointed by Cochran and Bronson respectively, but that the soft group was nowhere. He threatened to let the administrations, national and state, look elsewhere for their city support unless he was accommodated.[3] Besides, New York City and the Custom House were not the only seats of discontent.[4] There was bad feeling in the legislature.

Controversy over the enlargement of the state's canal system had been going on for many years. The barnburners favored a strictly economic, pay-as-you-go policy, while the hards were for a more extravagant expenditure involving the mortgaging of future revenue. The judging of a canal act unconstitutional by the Court of Appeals made some new legislation necessary, but the usual course of the legislative session of 1853 had gone by with a dead-

[1] Tilden to Marcy, June 21, Cochrane to Marcy, June 22, 1853, *ibid.*

[2] Cagger to Marcy, June 27, 1853, *ibid.*

[3] Wood to Marcy, July 1, 1853, *ibid.*

[4] Gov. Seymour later claimed that Bronson had been willing to cooperate until Sec. Guthrie had decided that he was not entitled to the fees of his office but only to the salary. This financial cut from $25,000 to $6,000 was too much for Bronson's loyalty. Seymour to Marcy, Oct. 24, 1853, *ibid.*

lock and no action. Consequently it was necessary for Governor Seymour to reconvene the legislature in May. The legislation he then recommended was a compromise between the position of the barnburners and the hards. This was staunchly supported by the barnburner-soft combination and was of such a character as really to rob the hards of any ground for opposition. If some new issue was not found the hards felt that there would no longer be any ground for them to take in a battle with the softs for leadership of the party. Therefore in order to create the needed issue, the hards dragged in national politics.[1]

In the regular session a series of three resolutions congratulating Pierce upon his inaugural had been introduced by the hards. These resolutions were phrased in a manner as distasteful as possible to the barnburners. They specifically approved of that part of Pierce's address which spoke for the acquisition of Cuba and congratulated the President on his statement that the Constitution recognized slavery, that the Compromise of 1850 was constitutional and that the Fugitive Slave Act must be enforced. The resolutions specifically pledged New York to aid in executing all laws including the obnoxious act. Because of their peculiar character these propositions had been allowed to slumber in committee. But on June 30 when the canal bills had been disposed of and the session was about to adjourn, an opportunity was seized. Many of the barnburners were absent so a combination of hards and Whigs called these resolutions from committee and hoped to pass them after they had forced the barnburners to vote against or swallow them. The result was not as was expected. The barnburners all voted for the first two resolutions and

[1] Whitford, N. E., *History of the Canal System of the State of New York*, vol. i, pp. 201-210; Marcy MSS., *passim, N. Y. Times*, June 1, 1853.

only four balked at pledging aid to the enforcement of the Fugitive Slave Act. However, as thirty-one barnburners were absent or had failed to vote, the hards claimed that they had bolted and were as unsound as ever on national questions. To disprove this the barnburners introduced a series of resolutions the next day. These condemned sectionalism, affirmed the Baltimore platform and congratulated the President upon his inaugural and the spirit of his administration. On July 8 this set was triumphantly passed and again the hards had failed.[1] But the breach was deeper.

This fight was made more bitter because the hards declared that the administration was discriminating against them. Congressmen of their faction complained that they were not given the proper authority over the patronage in their districts.[2] Marcy was seen to be the malign influence prejudicing Pierce. On the other hand, the barnburners were becoming impatient because Dix had not received the French mission and Daniel E. Sickles, prominent hard,[3] and George N. Sanders,[4] a bitter enemy of Marcy and the softs, had been appointed respectively secretary of the American Legation at London and consul at the same

[1] Seymour to Marcy, July 2, 1853, Marcy MSS.; *Washington Union*, July 6, 12, 22, 1853; *New York Herald*, July 3, 9, 1853; *Speech of Benj. Bailey to the Democratic Convention at Carmel, N. Y., Oct. 8, 1853; Speech of James E. Cooley at Syracuse, Nov. 1, 1853; New York Hards and Softs—Which is the true Democracy?* p. 42.

[2] *New York Herald*, July 13, 1853.

[3] *Washington Union*, July 31, 1853. This was done upon request of Sickles to Forney, the latter suggested him to Buchanan. Forney to Buchanan, July 16, 28, 1853, Buchanan MSS. Sickles' appointment was not an unmixed evil for Seymour wrote Marcy, "If there is any honorable way of getting him out of the country, I hope it will be done as I regard him as the most able and efficient of the Hard Shells." Seymour to Marcy, July 25, 1853, Marcy MSS.

[4] *New York Herald*, Aug. 18, 1853.

place.[1] Everything portended a conflict of unusual ferocity at the fall convention.

The hards won the first preliminary skirmish in these manoeuvers. On July 15 the state committee met in the Astor House to organize the plan for the fall meeting. Only eight attended, mostly hards, and the natural outcome was the election of Minor C. Story, hard, as chairman and the adoption of a series of hard resolutions similar to those introduced in the legislature.[2] This gave the hards an advantage, as the officers of this committee had full charge of the calling and preliminary organization of the state convention. They set September 12 and Syracuse as the date and place of meetings.

During August and early September the delegates to this convention were chosen at a series of primary meetings. These were the scene of sharp practice and fraud on both sides. The soft leaders sent out a letter warning their adherents that Whigs were going to attempt to vote in the primaries to aid the hards in breaking up the party.[3] Both sides wished to control the convention not only for tactical reasons but also because of the fact that some members of the state canal commission were to be nominated and the successful candidates, if elected, would have a voice in the

[1] In order to build up more favorable feeling toward itself the administration determined to establish a soft newspaper in New York City. The *Herald* and the *Journal of Commerce* were sympathetic with the hards, the *Evening Post* was too free soil. Forney was therefore slated to conduct this sheet and $85,000 was pledged in New York's financial district. The coming fight however prevented this idea from ever being carried out. Forney to Buchanan, Sept. 16, Nov. 21, 1853, Buchanan MSS.; Forney to J. C. Breckinridge, Sept. 20, 1853, Breckinridge MSS. Cochran to Marcy, Aug. 16, 1853, Marcy MSS., *N. Y. Herald*, July 30, 1853.

[2] *Washington Union*, July 20, 22, 1853; *N. Y. Times*, July 16, 1853.

[3] Cassidy and Vandyke to Marcy, Aug. 26, 1853, Marcy MSS.

awarding of canal contracts. It was evident that there would be many contested seats.

The day of the convention arrived. At the last minute the officers of the committee changed the location of the meeting and the softs learned of this but twenty minutes before the hour set. They rushed in a body to the newly designated place and there found the convention organizing and the door guarded by men hired for the purpose. It did not take the newly arrived members long to brush these aside. The convention, with hard officers elected, immediately adjourned. The softs, who had a large majority, were now ready to take charge, but when the afternoon session met, not a hard put in an appearance. In answer to a summons by a convention committee they refused to participate saying that their lives were not safe in the same hall with the softs and barnburners. Consequently each faction declared itself to be the regular convention and each nominated a ticket. In reality the barnburners and softs were in a majority and in a fair convention would dominate. The hards realized this, but were determined that they would no longer submit to conventions controlled by the heretics of '48 and the trimming, unprincipled softs. As they could not shake off this domination by regular means they had, as we have seen, adopted sterner measures. Their procedure, it was charged, had been planned in advance.[1]

The softs expected that their ticket would have the support of all the appointees of the Pierce régime. But to their astonishment they found they were mistaken. In reply to an invitation to attend a ratification meeting of the

[1] *New York Hards and Softs. Which is the true Democracy*, p. 45. *The Softs, the True Democracy of the State of New York*, pp. 15-34. Thomas to Marcy, Sept. 3, 1853, Cochran to Marcy, Sept. 15, 1853, Marcy MSS.

soft nominees at Tammany Hall, Bronson brusquely refused, saying he would "not approve nominations brought about by fraud and violence." O'Conor, the district attorney also refused, replying that he would "only support nominations made for the purpose of cementing national union—not those of a convention contaminated by adjulators who had nominated agitators." These letters were followed on September 26 by one from Bronson endorsing the bolter's ticket.[1] This was rebellion. Letters began to pour into Washington sent by softs who demanded Bronson's removal as a "bolter".[2]

Bronson was not the only writer to have his letters published. Dix had not yet been appointed minister to France. He was still in charge of the sub-treasury at New York City. His choice for a foreign post had been rumored about and had met with violent opposition. He was Dix, the barnburner, the free-soiler, the heretic of '48, the abolitionist. Southern leaders and papers, disliking his past course and fearing perhaps that he would not exert himself to aid in acquiring Cuba, brought all possible pressure to bear upon Pierce. But the President was Dix's friend and was, in addition, desirous of giving a prominent place to a barnburner. In hopes of placating the opposition in some way he put off the decision. Dix naturally was impatient and when it was intimated to Dix by his friend, Wm. H. Ludlow, who had just been to Washington, that the President was holding off because he was not sure of Dix's views, the latter forwarded to the President through Ludlow and Marcy some extracts from his speeches [3] and published a letter to a Dr. Garvin in Georgia. This letter, which ap-

[1] *N. Y. Herald*, Sept. 24, 27, 1853.

[2] *V.* Marcy MSS., September, 1853.

[3] Dix to Wm. H. Ludlow, Aug. 27, 1853, Ludlow to Marcy (with enclosures), Aug. 30, 1853, Marcy MSS.; Dix, *Memoirs*, vol. i, p. 276.

JAMES C. DOBBIN

ROBERT McCLELLAND

peared in the press on September 13, categorically denied any abolition taint; in it Dix stated that while he wished to keep slavery where it was he believed in the strict enforcement of the Fugitive Slave Act and adherence to the Compromise. On the 16th the *Herald* rumored that John Y. Mason of Virginia was going to receive the French post and on the 21st Dix wrote another more emphatic and more lengthy letter emphasizing his former statement.[1] In publishing this letter the *Washington Union* printed extracts from Dickinson's speeches in 1849 expressing the same sentiments for which Dix was condemned. This was done in spite of a letter published by Dickinson a few weeks before denying that he was a free soiler and showing how he had violated his legislative instructions to vote against the Wilmot Proviso.[2] A flurry of notes and two tickets certainly were demoralizing the New York Democracy.

The administration was not going to let the so-called partisan conduct of Bronson and O'Conor go unnoticed. Guthrie went to New York on September 24 where he conferred with Bronson. On his return to Washington he sent the collector a letter dated October 3 which it was rumored was written by Pierce. This contained the following statement, "It has so happened that your appointments have been very generally made from that portion of the party to which you now adhere. This you thought best calculated to secure union and harmony. That desirable object has failed to be obtained . . . . [and it is expected that] you will recognize [the barnburners] in the only way that will carry conviction with it." Such false rumors of the contents of this letter were circulated that Guthrie released it for publication on October 8.[3]

[1] *New York Herald*, Sept. 13-29, 1853.

[2] *Ibid.*, Sept. 16, 1853.

[3] *Ibid.*, September 25–October 8, 1853.

Three days later appeared John Y. Mason's appointment as minister to France. The President had yielded to Dix's enemies and through Jefferson Davis a few weeks before had offered the Virginian the foreign post.[1] The barnburners felt this deeply. To add to the troubled situation the *New York Herald* had broken out with violent attacks upon Pierce's government. James Gordon Bennett had solicited the French mission from the President,[2] and so far had lived in hopes. When it became apparent a week or two before the official announcement that Mason was to receive the appointment, Bennett was deeply chagrined. From then on the administration had no more bitter or malignant foe than this powerful organ of public opinion, perhaps the mightiest in the country at that time. The editorial columns charged Pierce with being a free soiler because of his rebuke to Bronson, the opponent of that wing. The editors especially ridiculed Jefferson Davis, the friend of states rights, declaring that he had endorsed John Van Buren and Preston King by remaining in the cabinet. Then Davis added his note to the collection. He stated that although willing to let bygones be bygones he no more approved of the utterances of John Van Buren and Preston King than he did of Dickinson's anti-slavery speeches of 1847-9 or Bronson's letter to the Van Buren ratification meeting of July 15, 1848. He closed saying, "Holding, as I do, that party organization is a necessary means to insure success to principles on which parties are formed, I cannot but lament the division which has, without recent cause, opened the old wounds in our party." Thereupon the *Herald* demanded that Pierce dismiss his present advisers and appoint a union cabinet.[3]

[1] John Y. Mason to Jefferson Davis, October 2, 1853, Davis MSS.

[2] Bennett to Pierce, Dec. 15, 1852, Pierce MSS.

[3] *N. Y. Herald*, Oct. 13, 1853.

On October 13 Guthrie arrived in New York, and about the same time came his assistant, PePter G. Washington.[1] Then more notes were added to the series. On October 17 Charles O'Conor wrote a letter to the *Washington Union* declaring that the free soilers had run the party too long and that true national democrats would stand it no longer.[2] On the same day Bronson replied to Guthrie.[3] In this letter he made the following points:

1. He was under no pledges as to appointing power.

2. The Secretary's letter inferred that he must go back of 1852 and enquire what a man's political antecedents were—the thing which he supposed was to be avoided.

3. The faction in dispute had received their fair share of appointments as most of the offices were in New York and Kings County where only one Democrat in seven was an 1848 free-soiler.

4. He had never desired or aided rupture but did not approve of the basis of the Union of 1849 which was the division of the spoils.

5. The national Democrats could win if they had a fair field but the *Washington Union* was against them.

6. The Secretary's letter had come after the rupture and ratification meetings and after his removal had been demanded and he had been defamed.

7. Then he had been required to submit his lists of appointments to the Secretary before making them, something which had never been done before, and which was required of no other collector.

8. Finally, in open defiance he refused to submit his appointments declaring that "the law and my commission have cast the burden [of appointments] upon me, and I cannot surrender it to another without a derelection of duty."

[1] *Ibid.*, Oct. 14, 17, 1853.

[2] *Ibid.*, Oct. 18, 1853.

[3] *Washington Union*, Oct. 20, 1853.

This, said the *Boston Times,* was the "greatest specimen of the sublimely impudent in epistolary writing." [1]

Even before these last two letters had appeared some of the leaders of the barnburners had begun to be impatient at the government's inaction; a month had gone by since the rupture and Bronson's bolt. On the 17th, the same day as the O'Conor and Bronson letters were written, John Van Buren, in a frank letter to Marcy, demanded that Bronson be removed. He detailed a long list of grievances and declared that if some action was not taken he would start on the stump denouncing the policy of the administration.[2] This was no idle threat for John Van Buren was vindictive and dangerous: he was one of the foremost orators in the state and could sway mass gatherings with ease. No administration would care needlessly to provoke him to stump against it.

On October 22 Guthrie took final action. He wrote, "My letter was intended to guard you against distinctions between democrats founded on local politics and local divisions . . . . the appointive power rests wholly in the Secretary of the Treasury, not in the collector. . . . You are removed by the President's direction." [3] Immediately Heman J. Redfield, soft hunker, was appointed to succeed Bronson; John J. Cisco, hard, became assistant-treasurer vice Dix resigned, J. R. Brodhead, barnburner, became naval officer vice Redfield and O'Sullivan, barnburner, chargé to Portugal.[4] Thus, officialy the matter ended to the satisfaction of nobody.

Barnburners, like John Van Buren, denounced Pierce's

[1] *Washington Union,* Oct. 23, 1853.

[2] J. Van Buren to Marcy, Oct. 17, 1853, Marcy MSS.

[3] *Washington Union,* Oct. 23, 1853.

[4] *N. Y. Herald,* Oct. 23, 1853; *Washington Union,* Oct. 23, 1853.

treatment of Dix, and emphatically asserted that Bronson should have been removed solely on the ground that he had left the party by bolting.[1] Softs, like Governor Seymour, were bitter about the appointment of such men as Sickles and Sanders and the neglect of "everyone who made active efforts" in New York in 1852 for the success of the party.[2] Hards, like Croswell, were indignant because the administration had bestowed its "entire confidence . . . . upon the chief instigators and actors in this state in the revolt of 1848, warming them into prurient and active life with the same spirit and with the same malignity that characterized their course then, to the . . . . unprecedented prescription of those who . . . . were true."[3] The best criticism perhaps was uttered by a friendly neutral, P. M. Wetmore, who wrote Marcy:

It seems to be that the great error the President has committed was in not removing Mr. Bronson for writing his first letter to the public meeting [in New York]—upon the express ground that he was using the influence of his official position to control state elections. This position would have given the President the vantage ground. On the contrary, Mr. Guthrie's first letter changes the whole aspect of the case and censures Bronson for not doing precisely what he ought not to have done—namely—interfering in political matters of a local nature. All past administrations have, of course, done the same thing and all others will continue to do the same—but no one has ever been so frank as this—and avowed under the hand of a secretary of the treasury that the government meant to control elections.[4]

[1] J. Van Buren to Marcy, Oct. 17, 1853, Marcy MSS.

[2] Seymour to Marcy, Nov. 5, 1853, *ibid.*

[3] Crosswell to Marcy, Nov. 5, 1853, *ibid.*

[4] Wetmore to Marcy, Nov. 2, 1853, *ibid.*

Denunciation, criticism and abuse were not confined to letter writing. The bolting ticket was conducting a vigorous campaign. Prominent on the stump was a violent and abusive orator, James E. Cooley, of the New York state senate. He was a disappointed office seeker [1] and his abuse knew no bounds. He even went so far as to attack the President himself in a very undignified and insulting way.[2] In this, however, he was not followed by most of the hards. They blamed the sins of the administration upon the cabinet and Marcy was the scapegoat. They pleaded loyalty to the President but charged that Marcy and the rest had sold out to the free soilers. In fact, this was their principal strain. The hards were true union men with national vision earnestly abjuring all sectional agitation; their opponents, on the other hand, were free soil agitators who by their propaganda would surely bring disaster to the beloved union. These assaults were not allowed to go unrepelled.

The charge that the administration appointed or favored free soilers was emphatically denied in public and in private. Marcy wrote " not one person of that character [free soiler] has been appointed unless by mistake: not one who did not stand at the last election upon the Baltimore platform; not one who was known or suspected to be unsound in his political faith," [3] and later he defined a free soiler, " I have reference to what men now *are* and you in making the charge probably refer to what they *were*. . . . You cannot exclude free soilers if you take in secessionists, they are equally sinful." [4] The *Washington Union* in its semi-of-

[1] Cooley to Marcy, March 10, 1853, *ibid*:; *Lafayette* (Indiana) *Journal*, Nov. 7, 1853.

[2] *Speech of James E. Cooley at Syracuse*, Nov. 1, 1853.

[3] Marcy to Bradford, July 23, 1853, Marcy MSS.

[4] Marcy to Pierson, Nov. 24, 1853, *ibid.*

ficial capacity stated, "It is manifest that the Democratic Party rallied in union with the primary purpose of putting down sectional dissention and controversy. . . . They determined and declared that unswerving and cordial fidelity to the national democratic creed, as now proclaimed, should work an amnesty for past political errors; and that no man should henceforth justly be denounced as a free soiler or a disunionist who in good faith had openly placed himself upon the Baltimore platform as his party ground, and then faithfully cooperated with the party organized to sustain it . . . . When the President came into power he found this question already settled to his hand. The conditions of membership of the democratic party had been decided by the people themselves."[1] This the hards declared was depriving those who had remained faithful of their just rewards. So the contest went merrily on. The whole affair was noticed in the press throughout the country and the disappointed in the party began to rally around the hunker standard in various states. The administration was denounced for having interfered in a state matter and it was charged oftener than ever that the Pierce government was not national but free soil. But the war of notes was not yet over.

The Democracy in Massachusetts was never in a very healthy condition. It was in itself of little importance until it joined in coalition with the free soilers. In spite of the success of this amalgamation, there were a certain element of "simon pure" Democrats, jealous of Hallett, Greene and Cushing. Prominent among these were S. D. Bradford and A. W. Austin who had led a secession from the convention of 1852 when a resolution condemning coalition had been defeated. These "Fitchburg Seceders" had refused to return to the party fold and on September 22, two con-

[1] *Washington Union*, Sept. 1, 1853.

ventions were held and two tickets nominated. The regular convention endorsed the administration and Cushing but said nothing about future coalition. The seceder's convention was the occasion of a bitter and absurd speech by Benjamin H. Barstow. He directed his fire against Cushing, the free soiler and coalitionist. He pointed out several federal appointments made from the free soil ranks. He demonstrated how Cushing had opposed Sumner's election to the Senate, or at least had made a show of doing so, and then had defeated an anti-coalition resolution in the convention of 1851. As his reward, he charged, Cushing had been appointed to the Massachusetts supreme bench by the coalition régime.[1] This species of attack was continuous.

As the state campaign advanced local Democratic leaders in Massachusets arranged coalitions in various counties. In one of the conventions which formed such an arrangement the chairman made a speech in which he alluded to Bronson's removal and drew the conclusion that evidently the national administration was not opposed to the Democrats of Massachusetts coalescing with free soilers on state matters.[2] Such statements combined with increasing coalition only added weight to the charges that the Pierce government was partial to free soilers. This notion could not be allowed to circulate unnoticed. Cushing wrote a note. On October 9 he addressed a letter to R. Frothingham, junior editor of the *Boston Post*. In part it read:

I perceive that in several counties of Massachusetts, coalition senatorial tickets have been formed of associated Democrats and free soilers. My judgment is that the Democrats

[1] *Speech of Benj. Barstow at Boston*, Sept. 22, 1853; *Boston Atlas*, Sept. 9, 1853; *N. H. State Capitol Reporter*, Sept. 30, 1853, *N. H. Patriot*, Sept. 28, 1853; A. W. Austin to Marcy, June 14, July 20, 1853, S. D. Bradford to Marcy, July 9, 1853, Marcy MSS.

[2] *N. Y. Herald*, Oct. 26, 1853.

who have participated in this have done worse than to commit a fatal error. They have abandoned a principle which is fundamental . . . . The dangerous element of abolitionism . . . . shall be crushed out, so far as this administration is concerned.[1]

This "ukase" only added to the burden of the administration. In it some detected glaring inconsistency. In New York Bronson was removed because he refused to recognize free soilers; in Massachusetts free soilers were to be crushed out. On the contrary, the administration used the same principle in both cases. The underlying idea was a united party of Democrats. In New York barnburners, a faction of Democrats, must be recognized in order to unite the party; in Massachusetts Democrats must not traffic with Whigs (as most of the free soil party had been of that persuasion); a united, purified party of loyal Democrats was the purpose in each instance. But logical as this procedure was it had the effect of adding another group to the body of the disaffected, namely, the free soilers, who objected to being "crushed out."

As 1853 was an off year the fall elections could not exhibit any general tendencies[2] but the only one of importance clearly demonstrated the results of schism. In New York the Whigs were easily triumphant. But what was worse from the point of view of the administration the head of the hard ticket of bolters received some 3700 more votes

[1] *Washington Union*, Nov. 1, 1853. Coalition in Missouri was likewise banned in a letter written by Campbell. Croswell to Marcy, Nov. 5, 1853, Marcy MSS.

[2] The elections during the summer and early fall had all been in the south, with the exception of Wisconsin, and in that section, the party had been uniformly successful gaining Congressmen in Maryland, South Carolina and Alabama, although there was a net loss of one in Tennessee. Governors were gained in Tennessee and Wisconsin. *Tribune Almanac*, 1854.

than the leader of the regulars.[1] This was considered by many as a rebuke to the Pierce government. Pierce and his cabinet attributed it, among themselves, to the apathy of their voters, claiming that the hards were aided by the votes of many silver-greys or anti-Seward Whigs. They complained that no enthusiasm could be worked up over the administration and that the hards by declaring they were the hunker party of 1848 had attracted soft votes by the old issue. The fact that the vote fell off 150,000 from the previous years total signifies to some extent the disgust manifested at the renewed quarrel.[1]

Public opinion was being educated against the administration. The *New York Herald* daily found ingenious ways for attacking and ridiculing the Pierce régime. In the capital Beverly Tucker of Virginia, a disappointed office seeker, had in September started a new paper called the *Sentinel* which preached states rights and hunker doctrines against the free soil tendency of the government. The New York Young Men's Democratic Club issued an address condemning the administration and promising to run a candidate against Pierce in 1856.[2] On November 14 a meeting was called at Washington for all those living in the District and the adjoining states who wished to congratulate the New York hards. This gathering was presided over by an associate of Tucker's and ended in a riot.[3] Finally, just before Congress assembled a general meeting of rejoicing was held by the hards themselves in New York

[1] The official returns later showed that the average vote of the administration ticket was larger but the other impression got abroad and its effect was too strong to be wiped out by contradiction, *ibid.*

[2] Seymour to Marcy, Nov. 24, 1853, Marcy MSS., Blair to Van Buren, Nov. 27, 1853, Beekman to Van Buren, Dec. 2, 1853, Van Buren MSS.

[3] *Washington Union*, Nov. 23, 1853.

[4] *N. Y. Herald*, Nov. 13, 15, 1853.

City. Congratulatory letters were read from Senator Weller of California, Governor Foote of Mississippi and other prominent Democrats.[1]

Meanwhile the southern unionists had been none too well satisfied with the appointments. They had felt that they had been sacrificed for the states rights element. Then in the fall Cobb and Foote had both been defeated for the Senate and in the latter case it was charged the administration, through Davis, had interfered against the union candidate.[2] But the last straw for them was an editorial in the issue of the *Union* for November 30. Here they read that the Democracy at the Baltimore convention had not approved or disapproved of the Compromise. The party had only acquiesced in it as a final settlement and formed a union which

> required no sacrifice of principles. It only required the exercise of forbearance and conciliation to effect a compromise on a middle ground and agree to 'let bygones be bygones' . . . . Whilst it did not undertake to decide whether the friends of the compromise or its opponents had been right, it furnished to both a common status on which all future attempts to reopen the slavery agitation could be resisted and [with] abolition in every phase . . . . expunged from the organization of the party . . . . [it] opened up the way to a restoration of those fraternal feelings between the North and South on which alone the Federal Union can be sustained.

This to be sure was the truth but to the deluded Compromise men it seemed the worst kind of repudiation. Their cherished dream of a party reorganized on their platform guided by their influence had vanished.

[1] *Washington Union*, Dec. 25, 1853; *Lexington* (Ky.) *Statesman*, Dec. 13, 1853.

[2] *Washington Union*, Dec. 24, 1853.

Thus the patronage had been distributed on the logical principle of perfect fairness to all, but all were by no means satisfied. The administration was but nine months old, yet southern unionists, northern hunkers, free soilers, westerners, these were passively dissatisfied or in open revolt. Why?

CHAPTER XIV

WHY?

ON March 4, 1853 Franklin Pierce entered office with the good will of an harmonious Democracy. As Congress assembled in December of that same year the feeling most prevalent within the party was one of dissatisfaction with the administration. The causes for this general attitude were to be found in the personalities of the men at the cabinet table including the President himself.

Pierce was a semi-brilliant man whose natural mental quickness made him superficial. He did not think deeply but considered simple and apparently real solutions sufficient for complex problems. This led him to believe that by treating all alike in the distribution of offices he could eradicate the animosities of years in a few months and harmonize hostile factions into a band of brothers. A second weakness in Pierce's character unfitted him to succed. His natural kindness of heart, his dislike of refusing any request and his desire for harmony led him to promise more than he could fulfill. The warmth with which he received seekers after favors seemed to them an assurance that all that was necessary to obtain was to ask. Furthermore because he did not openly take issue with those whose opinions he did not approve or whose requests he was not going to grant, he led most people to believe that he was in agreement with them and when he made his decision finally, there was much disappointment. He was charged with takrng the opinions of the last man he talked with. Such qualities of mind and such behavior spread abroad the impression of unreliability and made numerous enemies among those who felt he had deceived them.

Bodily weakness was also apparent. He had received a terrible shock in the tragic death of his son. This had affected Mrs. Pierce even more deeply and had produced in her a state of deep melancholy and ill-health which only accentuated her dislike for the capital. Then the wretched climate of Washington, the unhealthy situation of the White House, as well as the heavy responsibilities of office impaired the President's health during his first months as executive. All these misfortunes caused a return of Pierce's old habit of intemperance.[1]

Furthermore Pierce erred in the choice of his advisers. The council chosen to please all factions was a political blunder. A man of small reputation himself he drew around him too many as little known as he, associates recommended to him by the national men of the party. He was unable to realize that his nomination had been but an accident brought about by a few politicians and not the reward due to an eminent leader given unanimously by a worshipping party. He did not know, as others did, how little personal following he had, how little weight the name of Franklin Pierce, without the title of President, carried. Consequently, he could not realize how necessary it was, if he expected to assume any leadership or accomplish anything in Congress, to choose a strong cabinet of men who could command the influence and leadership he lacked. Rather he chose Dobbin, McClelland, Campbell and Guthrie, efficient officers to be sure, but quiet unassuming men,

[1] F. L. Burr to Welles, Sept. 15, 1853, Welles MSS.; Forney to Buchanan, July 16, 1853; Slidell to Buchanan, Jan. 14, 1854; C. L. Ward to Buchanan, Oct. 22, 1853; J. Glancy Jones to Buchanan, Oct. 3, 1853, Buchanan MSS.; A. Campbell to Marcy, Nov. 22, 1852, Marcy MSS.; *State Capitol Reporter*, April 22, 1853; Hamlin, *Life of Hamlin*, p. 261; Field, *Memories of Many Men*, pp. 159-165.

unknown beyond the borders of their states, with no influence or prestige politically or socially. Of the remaining three, Cushing was trusted by but a few and his influence in Congress was small, besides his legal and intellectual training seem to have deprived him of the ability to understand that most people are not rational beings; this made him a bad counsellor, for he could not estimate popular opinion. Marcy, perhaps the most astute politician in the group, seemed to have had his influence largely nullified by New York feuds and the attacks of the *New York Herald*. Davis alone could count on the confidence of any considerable amount of public opinion, but his was the narrow view of the man trained in military life. These were not the men best fitted for the task of harmonizing factions which could only be impressed by strength.

But these personalities were the natural product of the Democratic machine. With the development of the ideal of American democracy, there had come the development of the American politician. The gradual advance of the principle of universal manhood suffrage was accompanied by the growth in a growing number of the political manipulators. These pages have borne the record of their relation in 1850 to the party which stood for democracy and which had become powerful because of Andrew Jackson's appeal to the plain people. After Jackson's retirement the politicians had sought to conserve the popular enthusiasm over the retired leader for the party's use. The democratic ideas were embalmed in platforms and these remains were exhibited to the faithful at election times and on patriotic anniversaries. But those who then guided the party and planned its campaigns had lost the spirit of the doctrines they preached. As an historian of the period has said, they had become the priesthood of the cult who went through the forms and ceremonies seemingly without comprehension of their meaning. The ruling desire was a powerful nation, not that it might aid primarily the improvement of the condition of the common people, but that business might flourish and that more self-satisfaction and power might come to those who ruled.

To make the nation prosperous and to keep in power, these were the ideals of the Democracy as formulated by its leaders in 1850. These objects were to be accomplished by maintaining a powerful and smooth-running political machine carefully tended by political engineers. How difficult was the efficient regulation of this machine has been related above. For the politicians from the different sections had procured power and retained it by exploiting the needs, real and fancied, of their communities. By 1850 this had been done so long that these leaders had lost sight of the objectivity of these demands, these needs became subjective and personal. Criticism and argument over slavery, tariffs, public lands, internal improvements became personal and the politicians of one section had become actually jealous of those of another, and all were determined that no section's leaders should procure more than what seemed at the moment mathematically just. Consequently 1850 saw the "Democratic Machine" apparently about to be scrapped by personal jealousy and hate.

The clear-headed, the far-sighted, and, in many cases, the crafty in both sections saw the danger of destruction and sought for a means of removing the friction. These political engineers were essentially unmoral in the sense that moral issues appeared to them to have no value. Consequently they were willing to side-step all the principles involved in the conflict. They were to accomplish what they sought by a gentlemen's agreement to take notice of no debateable questions. Such disturbing elements were to be kept from the public and to make this possible press and platform were to be induced by all conceivable means to make no mention of these issues. Thus the first step of the problem was worked out and the shibboleth was "Finality of the Compromise".

With this platform laid down the next step was to find an available candidate pledged to it. Many sought the honor. Most of the seekers, being old in years and service confined their endeavors to demonstrating their availability to the manipulators of the various sections. This they attempted by correspondence and conference, by the work of friends and by publishing judiciously non-committal opinions that successfully carried out the great principle of dodging the issue. One who was younger and unable successfully to appeal to many politicians sought aid from the people by working some of the time in the open. But the honor was not for the seekers; at the eleventh hour the managers went elsewhere for their choice. After a campaign devoid of all issues except the safe one of personalities their choice became President and the Democracy was again in power.

So far all had gone well but the Democracy must stay in power. How was necessity to be made a surety? By arousing enthusiasm over the principles of democracy? By creating a program which would promote these ideals? No, simply by making the organization more perfect. The "Machine" must be rebuilt. Generally speaking, the organization of the party had been characterized by strict discipline, discipline maintained by a scheme of rewards and punishments. Faithful service had been the chief road to reward and independence and irregularity were generally stifled by severe penalties in the shape of loss of preferment. Leadership had been the prerogative of the elders, the younger men had been required to await their turn in patience. The will of the ruler, if expressed as the will of the majority by fair means or foul, must never be questioned. But such were conditions in 1852 that those who sought to control the party destiny decided that the party could be best solidified by wiping the slate clean, by throwing away all the scores of the old discipline, and by allowing those under a cloud to emerge and start on an equal footing with all the faithful. Under these conditions an era of good feeling and harmonious strength was to be made possible by distributing the $50,000,000 worth of patronage to the satisfaction of all politicians. The administration had not, however, been able to please all and there was open discontent ere nine months of the administration's life had been lived.

Moreover, a more dangerous consequence of this system was becoming apparent. The continued policy of dodging issues and the continual fear of displeasng someone was destroying the moral calibre of the leaders of the Democracy. They had not that *morale* of security which would have come from the knowledge that they had the enthusiastic backing of a considerable body of public opinion. In its place was an inferiority complex produced by their lack of any inspiring ethical or moral guiding principle. Consequently their experiences as politicians bred in the politicians' school unfitted them for producing and laying before Congress in December, 1853, any program which would inspire the masses with the feeling that here were leaders, men of greater strength and foresight than their fellows. But worse than this, the leaders had lost the power of recognizing the force of a moral issue and when the Kansas-Nebraska Bill was introduced on the political stage after such a prelude, these so-called heads of the government failed to realize its consequences and were unable to understand or to cope with the rising tide of moral indignation. Franklin Pierce, not Andrew Jackson, was in the White House, and Calhoun, Clay, and Webster were dead.

APPENDIX

Democratic Platform—1852

1. *Resolved,* That the American democracy place their trust in the intelligence, the patriotism, and the discriminating justice of the American people.

2. *Resolved,* That we regard this as a distinctive feature of our poltical creed, which we are proud to maintain before the world, as the great moral element in a form of government springing from and upheld by the popular will; and contrast it with the creed and practice of federalism, under whatever name or form, which seeks to palsy the will of the constituent, and which conceives no imposture too monstrous for the popular credulity.

3. *Resolved,* Therefore, that entertaining these views, the Democratic party of this Union, through the delegates assembled, in general convention of the states, coming together in a spirit of concord, of devotion to the doctrines and faith of a free representative government, and appealing to their fellow-citizeens for the rectitude of their intentions, renew and reassert before the American people, the declaration of principles avowed by them on a former occasion, when, in general convention, they presented their candidates for the popular suffrage.

4. *Resolved,* That the Federal government is one of limited powers, derived solely from the constitution, and the grants of power shown therein ought to be strictly construed by all the departments and agents of the government, and that it is inexpedient and dangerous to exercise doubtful constitutional powers.

5. *Resolved,* That the constitution does not confer upon the

general government the power to commence and carry on a general system of internal improvements.

6. *Resolved,* That the constitution does not confer authority upon the Federal government, directly or indirectly, to assume the debts of the several states, contracted for local internal improvements or other state purposes; nor would such assumption be just or expedient.

7. *Resolved,* That justice and sound policy forbid the Federal government to foster one branch of industry to the detriment of another, or to cherish the interests of one portion to the injury of another portion of our common country—that every citizen and every section of the country has a right to demand and insist upon an equality of rights and priviliges, and to complete an ample protection of persons and property from domestic violence or foreign aggression.

8. *Resolved,* That it is the duty of every branch of the government to enforce and practice the most rigid economy in conducting our public affairs, and that no more revenue ought to be raised than is required to defray the necessary expenses of the government, and for the gradual but certain extinction of the public debt.

9. *Resolved,* That Congress has no power to charter a National Bank; that we believe such an institution one of deadly hostility to the best interests of the country, dangerous to our republican institutions and the liberties of the people, and calculated to place the business of the country within the control of a concentrated money power, and that above the laws and will of the people; and that the results of Democratic legislation, in this and all other financial measures, upon which issues have been made between the two political parties of the country; have demonstrated to candid and practical men of all parties, their soundness, safety, and utility, in all business pursuits.

10. *Resolved,* That the separation of the moneys of the government from banking institutions is indispensable for the safety of the funds of the government and the rights of the people.

11. *Resolved,* That the liberal principles embodied by Jefferson in the Declaration of Independence, and sanctioned in the constitution, which makes ours the land of liberty and the asylum of the oppressed of every nation, have ever been cardinal principles in the Democratic faith; and every attempt to abridge the privilege of becoming citizens and the owners of the soil among us, ought to be resisted with the same spirit that swept the alien and sedition laws from our statute books.

12. *Resolved,* That Congress has no power under the constitution to interfere with, or control, the domestic institutions of the several states, and that such states are the sole and proper judges of everything appertaining to their own affairs, not prohibited by the constitution; that all efforts of the Abolitionists or others, made to induce Congress to interfere with questions of slavery, or to take incipient steps in relation thereto, are calculated to lead to the most alarming and dangerous consequences; and that all such efforts have an inevitable tendency to diminish the happiness of the people, and endanger the stability and permanency of the Union, and ought not to be countenanced by any friend of our political institutions.

13. *Resolved,* That the foregoing proposition covers, and is intended to embrace, the whole subject of slavery agitation in Congress; and therefore the Democratic party of the Union, standing on this national platform, will abide by, and adhere to, a faithful execution of the acts known as the Compromise measures settled by the last Congress, "the act for reclaiming fugitives from service labor" included; which act, being designed to carry out an express provision of the constitution, can not, with fidelity thereto, be repealed, nor so changed as to destroy or impair its efficiency.

14. *Resolved,* That the Democratic party will resist all attempts at renewing in Congress, or out of it, the agitation of the slavery question, under whatever shape or color the attempt may be made.

15. *Resolved,* That the proceeds of the public lands ought

to be sacredly applied to the national objects specified in the constitution; and that we are opposed to any law for the distribution of such proceeds among the states as alike inexpedient in policy and repugnant to the constitution.

16. *Resolved,* That we are decidedly opposed to taking from the President the qualified veto power, by which he is enabled, under restrictions and responsibilities amply sufficient to guard the public interests, to suspend the passage of a bill whose merits can not secure the approval of two-thirds of the Senate and House of Representatives, until the judgment of the people can be obtained thereon, and which has saved the American people from the corrupt and tyrannical domination of the bank of the United States, and from a corrupting system of general internal improvements.

17. *Resolved,* That the Democratic party will faithfully abide by and uphold the principles laid down in the Kentucky and Virginia resolutions of 1797 and 1798, and in the report of Mr. Madison to the Virginia Legislature in 1799; that it adopts these principles as constituting one of the main foundations of its political creed, and is resolved to carry them out in their obvious meaning and import.

18. *Resolved,* That the war with Mexico, upon all the principles of patriotism and the law of nations, was a just and necessary war on our part, in which no American citizen should have shown himself opposed to his country, and neither morally nor physically, by word or deed, given aid and comfort to the enemy.

19. *Resolved,* That we rejoice at the restoration of friendly relations with our sister Republic of Mexico, and earnestly desire for her all the blessings and prosperity which we enjoy under republican institutions, and we congratulate the American people on the results of that war which have so manifestly justified the policy and conduct of the Democratic party, and insured to the United States indemnity for the past and security for the future.

20. *Resolved,* That, in view of the condition of popular institutions in the old world, a high and sacred duty is devolved

with increased responsibility upon the Democracy of this country, as the party of the people, to uphold and maintain the rights of every state, and thereby the union of states, and to sustain and advance among them constitutional liberty, by continuing to resist all monopolies and exclusive legislation for the benefit of the few at the expense of the many and by a vigilant and constant adherence of those principles and compromises of the constitution which are broad enough and strong enough to embrace and uphold the Union as it is, and the Union as it would be, in the full expansion of the energies and capacity of this great and progressive people.

BIBLIOGRAPHY

A. Unpublished Manuscript Collections

George Bancroft MSS., Massachusetts Historical Society.
John C. Breckinridge MSS., L. of C.
Buchanan MSS., Pennsylvania Historical Society.
Buchanan MSS., L. of C.
Buchanan–Johnston MSS., L. of C.
Burke MSS., private collection.
B. F. Butler of Massachusetts MSS., private collection.
Salmon P. Chase MSS., L. of C.
William W. Corcoran MSS., L. of C.
Lewis S. Coryell MSS., Pennsylvania Historical Society.
Isaac Davis MSS., American Antiquarian Society.
Jefferson Davis MSS., L. of C.
Andrew J. Donelson MSS., L. of C.
Joseph Holt MSS., L. of C.
Andrew Johnson MSS., L. of C.
William L. Marcy MSS., L. of C.
Franklin Pierce MSS., L. of C.
Franklin Pierce MSS., New Hampshire Historical Society.
John C. Rives MSS., L. of C.
George N. Sanders MSS., L. of C.
Charles Sumner MSS., Harvard University Library.
Nicholas P. Trist MSS., L. of C.
Martin Van Buren MSS., L. of C.
Gideon Welles MSS., L. of C.

B. Published Personalia

The Works of James Buchanan, John Bassett Moore, ed., Philadelphia and London, 1908-10.

Clay's Private Correspondence, Calvin Colton, ed., New York, 1855.

Correspondence of Robert M. T. Hunter, Charles H. Ambler,, ed., *Annual Report of the American Historical Association*, 1916, vol. ii.

Diary of James K. Polk, M. M. Quaife, ed., Chicago, 1910.

Correspondence of Robert Toombs, Alexander H. Stephens and Howell Cobb, U. B. Phillips, ed., *Annual Report of the American Historical Association*, 1911, vol. ii.

C. Periodicals

I. NEWSPAPERS:

Alabama: *Mobile Daily Advertiser.* L. of C.
Arkansas: (Little Rock) *Whig.* L. of C.
District of Columbia: *Washington Union.* L. of C.
Illinois: *Weekly Alton Telegraph.* L. of C.
Chicago Democrat. L. of C.
State Register (Springfield). L. of C.
Indiana: *Daily State Sentinel* (Indianapolis). L. of C.
Lafayette Journal. L. of C.
Kentucky: *Lexington Statesman.* L. of C.
Louisiana: *New Orleans Weekly Delta.* N. Y. Pub. Lib.
Maine: *Augusta Age.* Maine State Library.
Maryland: *Baltimore American.* L. of C.
Baltimore Sun. L. of C.
Massachusetts: *Boston Atlas.* Boston Pub. Lib.
Boston Post. Boston Pub. Lib.
Puritan Recorder (Boston). L. of C.
Minnesota: *Minneapolis Journal.* L. of C.
Mississippi: *Natchez Courier.* L. of C.
New Hampshire: *Patriot* (Concord). N. H. State Hist. Soc.
State Capital Reporter (Concord). N. H. State Hist. Soc.
Statesman (Concord). N. H. State Hist. Soc.
New Jersey: *Morristown True Democratic Banner.* N. J. Hist. Soc.
Newark Daily Advertiser. N. J. Hist. Soc.
Newark Morning Eagle. Newark, N. J., Pub. Lib.
Trenton State Gazette. L. of C.
New York: *Albany Argus.* N. Y. Pub. Lib.
New York Express. Marcy MSS.
New York Herald. N. Y. Pub. Lib.
New York Times. N. Y. Pub. Lib.
New York Tribune. N. Y. Pub. Lib.
North Carolina: *Standard* (Raleigh). Pierce Scrap Book.
Ohio: *Cincinnati Gazette.* N. Y. Pub. Lib.
Pennsylvania: *Pennsylvanian* (Philadelphia). L. of C.
Philadelphia Public Ledger. N. Y. Pub. Lib.
Tennessee: *Memphis Daily Eagle and Enquirer.* L. of C.
Nashville Union. L. of C.
Virginia: *Richmond Enquirer.* L. of C.

II. NEWSPAPER CLIPPINGS:

Bowdoin Class Scrap Book, Bowdoin College Library.
Pierce Scrap Book, New Hampshire Historical Society Library.

III. MAGAZINES:

American Historical Review.
Georgia Historical Quarterly.
Indiana Magazine of History.
Pennsylvania Magazine of History.
Tennessee Historical Magazine.
United States Democratic Review.

D. PAMPHLETS

I. CAMPAIGN OF 1852

1. *Democratic*

Abolitionists' Attack.
The Crisis: Shall Sewardism rule?
Evening Post Documents, Nos. 1-10.
Frank Pierce and his Abolition Allies.
Galphin Case: The Dangers of Electing an Incompetent Man President.
General Scott's Correspondence with Secretary Marcy.
Letter of General James Shields.
Lives of Pierce and King (English and German editions).
Memoir of General Scott from records contemporaneous with events.
Old Soldier's Letter to General Scott.
Papers for the People, Nos. i-xvii.
Political Letters and Writings of General Scott Reviewed, Discussed and Compared.
Record the best refutation of Whig Slander.
Southern Opinion of Scott and Pierce.
Speeches:
Buchanan at Greensburg, Pa., Oct. 7, 1852.
Gilbert Dean in Congress, Aug. 23, 1852.
John A. Dix at Newburgh, N. Y., July 26, 1852.
Senator Douglas at Richmond, Va., July 9, 1852.
Chas. J. Faulkner in Congress, Aug. 2, 1852.
M. P. Gentry in Congress, June 14, 1852.
Benj. F. Hallett at Reading, Pa., Sept. 4, 1852.
Robert Toombs in Congress, July 3, 1852.
Vindication of Pierce's Military Career by his Companions in Arms.
Virginia and Kentucky Resolutions.
Whig Charge of Religious Intolerance against the New Hampshire Democracy and General Franklin Pierce.
Whig Testimony against the election of General Scott.

2. *Whig*

Brief Chapter on the Life of Gen. F. Pierce from the *National Era* of June 17, 1852.

The Contrast.

Frank Pierce and his Abolition Allies.

History of the Wrongs inflicted on Winfield Scott by the supporters of Franklin Pierce.

The Presidency: Winfield Scott and Franklin Pierce: Their Qualifications and Fitness for the high office.

II. MISCELLANEOUS

New York Hards and Softs: Which is the true Democracy? New York, 1856.

Proceedings of a Union Meeting held at Castle Garden, October 30, 1850, New York, 1850.

Proceedings of the Democratic National Convention Held at Baltimore, June 1-5, 1852 for the nomination of Candidates for President and Vice-President of the United States, Washington, 1852. Printed by Robert Armstrong.

Ibid., Reported and published by Wm. Hincks and F. H. Smith, Washington, 1852, Buell and Blanchard, Printers.

Softs, The True Democracy of the State of New York, N. Y., 1856.

Speeches:

Benjamin Bailey, to the Democratic Convention at Carmel, N. Y., Oct. 8, 1853.

Benjamin Barstow at Boston, Sept. 22, 1853.

James E. Cooley at Syracuse, Nov. 1, 1853.

E. General Works, Biographies and Reminiscences

(REFERENCES ARE HERE GIVEN TO ONLY THOSE WORKS FROM WHICH CITATIONS ARE MADE)

Alexander, De Alva S., *Political History of the State of New York*, New York, 1906.

Bancroft, Frederick, *Life of Seward*, New York and London, 1900.

Barnes, Thurlow W., *Memoir of Thurlow Weed*, vol. ii, Boston, 1884.

Bigelow, John, *Retrospections of an Active Life*, New York, 1909.

Boutwell, George S., *Reminiscences of Sixty Years in Public Affairs*, New York, 1902.

Caldwell, Joshua W., *Sketches of the Bench and Bar of Tennessee*, Knoxville, 1898.

Clay, Mrs. C. C., Jr., *A Belle of the Fifties*, New York, 1905.

Clifford, Philip G., *Nathan Clifford, Democrat*, New York, 1922.

Cole, Arthur C., *Centennial History of Illinois*, vol. iii, Springfield, 1919.

Corning, Charles R., *Amos Tuck*, Exeter, N. H., 1902.

Davis, Jefferson, *Rise and Fall of the Confederate Government*, New York, 1881.

Detroit Post and Tribune, *Life of Zachariah Chandler*, Detroit, 1880.

Dickinson, John R., *Speeches and Correspondence of Daniel S. Dickinson*, New York, 1867.

Dix, Morgan, *Memoir of John A. Dix*, New York, 1883.

Dodd, William E., *Jefferson Davis*, Philadelphia, 1907.

DuBose, John W., *Life and Times of William L. Yancey*, Birmingham, Ala., 1892.

Field, Maunsell B., *Memories of Many Men and Some Women*, New York, 1874.

Foote, Henry S., *Casket of Reminiscences*, Washington, 1874.

Fox, Dixon Ryan, *The Decline of the Aristocracy in the Politics of New York*, New York, 1919.

George, John H., *Paul Rolfe George*, Concord, N. H., 1875.

Gillet, Ransom H., *Life and Times of Silas Wright*, Albany, 1874.

Godwin, Parke, *Biography of William Cullen Bryant*, New York, 1883.

Grinnell, Josiah B., *Men and Events of Forty Years*, Boston, 1892.

Hamlin, Charles E., *Life and Times of Hannibal Hamlin*, Cambridge, 1899.

Hammond, Jabez, D., *History of Political Parties in New York*, Buffalo, 1850.

——, *Life and Times of Silas Wright*, Syracuse, 1848.

Harden, Edward J., *George W. Troup*, Savannah, 1859.

Hart, Albert B., *Salmon P. Chase*, Boston, 1899.

Hawthorne, Nathaniel, *Life of Pierce*, Boston, 1852.

Hodgson, Joseph, *Cradle of the Confederacy*, Mobile, 1876.

Hunter, Martha T., *Robert M. T. Hunter*, Washington, 1903.

Irelan, John R., *History of the Life, Administration and Times of Franklin Pierce*, Chicago, 1888.

Jenkins, John S., *Life of Silas Wright*, Auburn, N. Y., 1849.

——, *Lives of the Governors of the State of New York*, Auburn, N. Y., 1851.

Johnson, Allen, *Stephen A. Douglas*, New York, 1908.

Lawrence, William R., *Diary and Correspondence of Amos Lawrence*, Boston, 1855.

Linn, William A., *Horace Greeley*, New York, 1903.

McClure, Alexander K., *Old Time Notes of Pennsylvania*, Philadelphia, 1905.

——, *Our Presidents and How We Make Them*, New York, 1902.

——, *Recollections of Half a Century*, Salem, Mass., 1902.

McCormac, Eugene I., *James K. Polk*, Berkeley, Cal., 1922.

McLaughlin, Andrew C., *Lewis Cass*, Boston and New York, 1891.

McMaster, John B., *History of the People of the United States*, vol. viii, New York, 1913.

Mann, Mary T., *Life of Horace Mann*, Boston, 1891.
Moore, A. Y., *Schuyler Colfax*, Philadelphia, 1868.
Mueller, Henry R., *Whig Party in Pennsylvania*, New York, 1922.
Myers, Gustavus, *History of Tammany Hall*, New York, 1917.
Ogg, Frederick A., *Daniel Webster*, Philadelphia, 1914.
Parker, Edward G., *Reminiscences of Rufus Choate*, New York, 1860.
Parish, John C., *George W. Jones*, Iowa City, 1912.
Phillips, Ulrich B., *Robert Toombs*, New York, 1913.
Poore, Ben. Perley, *Perley's Reminiscences*, Philadelphia, 1886.
Pryor, Mrs. Roger A., *Reminiscences of Peace and War*, New York, 1905.
Quaife, Milo M., *Doctrine of Non-Intervention with Slavery in the Territories*, Chicago, 1910.
Rhodes, James F., *History of the United States from the Compromise of 1850*, New York, 1893.
Sargent, Nathan, *Public Men and Events*, Philadelphia, 1875.
Shepard, Edward M., *Martin Van Buren*, Boston and New York, 1888.
Stanton, Henry B., *Random Recollections*, New York, 1886 (2nd Ed.).
New York, 1887 (3rd Ed.).
Tyler, Lyon G., *Letters and Times of the Tylers*, vol. ii, Richmond, 1885.
Webster, Sidney, *Franklin Pierce and his Administration*, New York, 1892.
White, M. J., *Secession Movement in the United States, 1847-51*, Univ. of Wis., 1920.
Whitford, Noble E., *History of the Canal System of the State of New York*, Albany, 1906.
Wilson, Henry, *Rise and Fall of the Slave Power*, Boston, 1874.
Wise, John S., *Recollections of Thirteen Presidents*, New York, 1906.

F. Official and Miscellaneous

Appleton's Cyclopedia of American Biography, New York, 1887.
Biographical Congressional Directory, 61st Cong., 2nd Sess., Sen. Doc. 56 (5655).
Biographical Review of Broome County, N. Y., Boston, 1894.
Congressional Globe.
Messages of the Presidents of the United States, James D. Richardson, compiler, Washington, 1908.
Messages from the Governors of New York, Charles Z. Lincoln, ed., Albany, 1909.
Register of Officers and Agents, Civil, Military and Naval in the service of the United States, 1853, 1855.
Senate Report No. 1, 33rd Cong. special session (688).
Tribune Almanac, 1850-1854.

INDEX

C